What Your Colleagues Are Saying . . .

Drs. Margo Gottlieb and Gisela Ernst-Slavit's original series has always been my go-to resource for understanding academic language and its application to curriculum, instruction, and assessment. The reconceptualization of academic language in this new edition brings educators to the most contemporary, research-informed, and evidence-based understanding of academic languaging as an active process that honors multilingualism and invites students to use their full linguistic repertoires across various contexts. The chapter-by-chapter guidance across the core content areas prompts readers to critically examine how students' rich cultural and linguistic heritages and experiences are authentically embedded in all learning opportunities while also suggesting actionable steps to support multilingual learners' self-expression and agency. A must-read for all educators!

—**Andrea Honigsfeld**, Professor and Author Consultant at Molloy University, New York

As educators, we want to embrace students' languages, cultures, lived experiences, interests, perspectives, and multiliteracies. How can we do this and simultaneously support them to master academic language across the content areas? Scholars Ernst-Slavit and Gottlieb's latest contribution brilliantly shows us how to engage all language learners, put their language assets and cultural perspectives front and center, and support them as empowered autonomous learners.

—**Debbie Zacarian**, Founder Director of Zacarian & Associates and Author

In this timely and vital new edition, Ernst-Slavit and Gottlieb reconfigure academic language for an era defined by artificial intelligence, heightened student stress, and the embrace of asset-based approaches, such as translanguaging pedagogy. The book is packed with essential updates for today's classrooms, including rich strategies for digital literacy and multimodal learning; creative approaches to movement, visual arts, and hands-on learning; practical ways to build student voice and agency; and clear connections between social-emotional learning and academic success. Few scholars have impacted multilingual education as profoundly as Ernst-Slavit and Gottlieb. The authors provide both the research foundation teachers need to understand why these approaches work and the practical tools to implement them successfully. Through carefully scaffolded instruction and meaningful engagement with content, multilingual learners can thrive with rigorous academic work from their first day in the classroom.

—**Andrea B. Hellman**, Professor of TESOL-Linguistics at Missouri State University

Academic Languaging: Engaging Multilingual Students in Content Area Learning arrives at a pivotal moment for K–12 education, offering educators a timely and transformative approach for supporting multilingual learners. With the notion of "academic language" evolving to acknowledge the dynamic concept of "languag*ing*," this book redefines how we view and approach language in content classrooms. Academic languaging moves beyond the constraints of traditional school language, embracing students' diverse linguistic and cultural assets as integral to learning. Authors Ernst-Slavit and Gottlieb provide a practical and insightful guide for teachers, administrators, and language specialists, emphasizing the importance of creating learning environments that honor students' backgrounds and encourage agency. The book's structured strategies and content-specific chapters offer actionable methods for embedding academic language through multimodal, culturally relevant practices. As multilingualism becomes the norm, *Academic Languag*ing stands as an essential resource, advocating for education that empowers students to leverage their whole linguistic repertoire. It's a must-read for any educator committed to transforming their classroom into a space of active, meaningful learning for all students.

—**Amelia Larson**, Chief Academic Officer at Summit K12

Congratulations to Drs. Ernst-Slavit and Gottlieb and their new book replete with essential academic content and pragmatic applications for educators of multilingual learners to use in their everyday work. This book moves the field of multilingual education forward by addressing both the complexities of the construct "academic language" and its prior limitations and definitions, and building into the dynamic concept of "academic languag*ing*," an action-oriented approach to schooling that underscores the interactive nature of how language is used in multiple formats and modalities. Readers will find the Stop and Think features, imagery, model texts, and tables essential as they engage in their own exploration of language and languaging. I cannot wait to use this book with my students and to share this work with colleagues.

—**Maria Coady**, Distinguished Professor in Educational Equity at North Carolina State University

This insightful book invites all educators, monolingual or multilingual—particularly future and in-service teachers, coaches, administrators, and teacher educators—to embrace all the languages and cultural experiences multilingual students bring to school as they support their development of "academic languaging." The examples provide practical ideas for educators on "what" it is and "how" to create languaging opportunities for multilingual learners to make meaning of and access content area knowledge using their complete language systems and cultural perspectives. The authors also include thought-provoking questions embedded throughout the chapters to help readers interact with new ideas and construct meaning grounded in their contexts and experiences. This is a must-read for all educators who want to embrace a social justice stance and create a more flexible and empowering environment for multilingual students.

—**Sandra Mercuri**, Sandra Mercuri Educational Consultants

This book engages teachers in a deep examination of the notion of academic language, not as a fixed or static concept but as a reflection of the dynamic "languag*ing*" practices that are enacted within multilingual schools and communities. It provides rich tools and resources for a variety of classroom contexts, grade levels, and content areas, with concrete examples to help teachers adapt and modify suggested strategies for their own particular settings. Most importantly, it offers an approach to language teaching and learning that honors multilingual learners' identities and sense of agency, placing them at the center of schooling.

—**Maria Dantas-Whitney**, Professor of ESOL and Bilingual Education at Western Oregon University

In this much-needed collection for teachers and teacher educators interested in language and content integration for multilingual learners, Ernst-Slavit and Gottlieb offer ways to support and incorporate multimodalities and multiple means of expression into instruction to optimize multilingual learners' content learning. Model texts demonstrating how language features function within specific content areas serve as tools to support multilingual learners in their oral language and literacy development. Like everything that Gottlieb and Ernst-Slavit do, this is another wonderful and practical contribution to the TESOL field!

—**Luciana de Oliveira**, Associate Dean for Academic Affairs and Graduate Studies at Virginia Commonwealth University

What an exciting way to approach languaging in the content areas! Gisela's and Margo's book lays the groundwork for looking at language, literacy, and core content through the actions of multilingual learners and their teachers. They show how multilingualism is at the heart of multilingual learners' identities and how multimodalities can open doors for increasing their access to content and showing evidence for learning. Through model texts, they illustrate how to make dimensions of language come to life to promote student engagement. They showcase academic languaging for building teacher and peer relationships, and for applying technology to advance learning in math, science, social studies, and language arts. This book is a must for ESL/ELD and dual language teachers, programs, and school administrators.

—**Margarita Calderón**, Professor Emerita at Johns Hopkins University

Academic Languag*ing*

First Edition

We dedicate this book to Graham, Max, Arthur, and Hunter and the next generation of students who will draw strength from academic languaging in building agency as they face growing linguistic diversification and technological advancements in this increasingly multilingual multicultural world.

Academic Languag*ing*

Engaging Multilingual Students in Content Area Learning

First Edition

Gisela Ernst-Slavit

Margo Gottlieb

Foreword by Jeff Zwiers

CORWIN

FOR INFORMATION

Corwin
A SAGE Company
2455 Teller Road
Thousand Oaks, California 91320
(800) 233-9936
www.corwin.com

SAGE Publications Ltd.
1 Oliver's Yard
55 City Road
London EC1Y 1SP
United Kingdom

SAGE Publications India Pvt. Ltd.
Unit No 323-333, Third Floor, F-Block
International Trade Tower Nehru Place
New Delhi 110 019
India

SAGE Publications Asia-Pacific Pte. Ltd.
18 Cross Street #10-10/11/12
China Square Central
Singapore 048423

Vice President and Editorial Director: Monica Eckman
Acquisitions Editor: Megan Bedell
Content Development Manager: Lucas Schleicher
Senior Editorial Assistant: Natalie Delpino
Production Editor: Nicole Burns-Ascue
Copy Editor: Melinda Masson
Typesetter: C&M Digitals (P) Ltd.
Proofreader: Rae-Ann Goodwin
Indexer: Integra
Graphic Designer: Scott Van Atta
Marketing Manager: Melissa Duclos

Printed in the United States of America

ISBN: 9781071956076

This book is printed on acid-free paper.

26 27 28 29 30 10 9 8 7 6 5 4 3 2 1

Contents

Visit the companion website at **https://companion.corwin.com/courses/Academic-Languaging** for downloadable resources.

List of Figures, Tables, and Companion Website Contents

Chapter 1

Chapter 2

Chapter 3

Chapter 4

Chapter 5

Chapter 6

Chapter 7

Companion Website Contents

Please visit https://companion.corwin.com/courses/Academic-Languaging to download the following resources:

Foreword

In the ever-evolving landscape of education, equipping multilingual learners with the skills necessary for academic and life success has never been more important. As our classrooms become increasingly diverse, there is a growing need to reimagine our lingering ways of understanding and teaching what has traditionally been called academic language.

A clear and useful definition of academic language has eluded us for decades. Sure, we have used definitions such as a set of terms, grammar rules, and discourse moves that help students engage in academic tasks in school. And for many years we have taught language as a set of linguistic terms and skills to learn, much like the long lists of standards in other disciplines. And yet, teaching academic language as a list of terms, rules, and skills, in a nutshell, has not worked well enough.

What we have needed is a comprehensive yet practical guide for moving from teaching academic language as a static collection of things and skills to empowering students to use language for academic and professional purposes. We need to shift from static to dynamic, from rigid to fluid, from piling up to building up, and from learning academic language to "academic languaging." What we have needed is in this book.

Why change our framework for thinking about academic language development? Because our students are deep and dynamic; their linguistic and cultural resources are rich and varied. Our classrooms are filled with learners who bring unique experiences and languages, and so our approach must change. Yes, our approach must change—we must reimagine the contexts and purposes for which students use language in school. We must, as the authors of this book argue, view language development as a social and collaborative process, deeply intertwined with the ways students interact with the world.

Historically, educators have taught academic language formulaically, focusing on academic vocabulary lists, grammar activities, and sentence frames, stems, and starters. Such methods tend to overlook the broader, more holistic ways in which students use language to think, express themselves, and engage with content. The approach presented in this book acknowledges where we have come from, but takes us to the next level—toward teaching practices that value students' existing linguistic repertoires, encourage their active engagement with language, and build bridges between home and school cultures. In doing so, this approach empowers students, particularly multilingual learners, to use language creatively and critically across disciplines.

Effective use of academic language holds immense power in the realms of education and professional communication. It serves as a key to understanding complex concepts and facilitating the exchange of knowledge in a precise, effective manner. Unlike everyday conversational language, academic language is characterized by a more structured, formal, and specific nature, designed to communicate ideas clearly and unambiguously. When students and educators use academic language, they are not merely sharing information—they are engaging in a process of collaborative meaning-making, wherein ideas are constructed, refined, and elevated.

One of the fundamental strengths of academic language is its ability to articulate complex ideas succinctly. In subjects like science, mathematics, or social studies, the vocabulary, syntax, and text structures associated with academic discourse help convey intricate theories and relationships that tend not to be as clearly explained using more casual variations of language. For example, the use of precise and abstract terms such as *hypothesis*, *theorem*, or *economic disparity* allows for a shared understanding among those familiar with the subject, ensuring that the message is received as intended. This specificity minimizes ambiguity and allows for more effective discussions, arguments, and explorations of academic content.

Academic language also empowers its users to participate in scholarly conversations, both in and out of the classroom. Students become better equipped to argue effectively, analyze critically, and synthesize information across disciplines. This capability not only enhances their academic performance but also prepares them for professional environments where precise and complex communication is essential.

Students who improve in their uses of academic language(s) develop the confidence and agency to engage meaningfully with peers, educators, and experts, making their voices heard in discussions that shape knowledge and understanding. This confidence reinforces and accelerates students' uses of language to construct and communicate more complex ideas.

Finally, the ability to communicate using academic language is a matter of equity. In a world where educational and professional opportunities can vary widely, providing students with the tools to understand and employ different registers of language equips them to succeed in academic and professional spheres. It offers every learner the chance to access challenging content and express their unique ideas clearly. When multilingual learners, for example, are taught to communicate using academic language, they are empowered to read, write, and participate in discussions that might otherwise feel overwhelming. Academic language becomes not just a means of communication but a vehicle for inclusion, opportunity, and academic advancement.

How do students achieve the proficiency, gain the accesses, and build the confidences described in the previous paragraphs? By engaging in academic languaging.

Academic languaging is an action-centered approach to using language that emphasizes the dynamic and engaged participation of multilingual learners in constructing and communicating academic ideas. It is grounded in sociocultural perspectives that see language use as purposeful and practical. From this perspective, students are viewed as active contributing members of their community, whose voices, experiences, and cultural backgrounds enrich the learning environment. This understanding empowers students with agency and autonomy, allowing them to take ownership of their learning and confidently express their ideas.

Academic languaging in the classroom encourages students to engage in academic tasks that are meaningful and pique their interest, enabling them to be motivated and invested in their learning process. An action-based mindset is central to this approach, where language is seen as doing. This means that language learning involves the whole person—the mind, the body, emotions, and all the senses. Students are encouraged to use language collaboratively, co-constructing a range of meanings and products such as written texts, multimedia presentations, and research projects that reflect their understanding, deep thinking, and creativity.

In this approach, educators embrace the contributions of students' families and communities, recognizing their rich cultural and linguistic backgrounds as valuable building blocks for the big ideas they are constructing. By integrating these lived experiences into the classroom, students can see their identities reflected and valued, which fosters a deeper sense of belonging and confidence. Academic languaging thus becomes a way of empowering students to participate fully and effectively in academic and community life, using language as a tool for meaningful action and expression.

Chapter 1 lays the groundwork by challenging traditional limited definitions of academic language. The authors introduce the concept of academic languaging as an active, flexible process that adapts to the context and needs of the learner. By reframing academic language as something situational and purposeful, this chapter provides a fresh lens through which we can better understand and support the evolving linguistic capabilities of our students.

In Chapter 2 the focus shifts to practical strategies that serve as foundational anchors in classrooms. These teaching and learning anchors not only guide educators in planning and instruction but also ensure that multilingual learners are engaged and active participants in their educational journey. From scaffolding techniques to culturally responsive teaching practices, this chapter emphasizes the need for educators to create supportive environments where students' linguistic and cultural assets are recognized and valued.

Chapter 3 explores how to foster a deep appreciation of literature and writing while supporting students' language development. It provides techniques for teaching reading comprehension, literary analysis, and writing in ways that make complex texts more accessible to multilingual learners. By emphasizing the graceful interplay between academic language and content, the chapter demonstrates how teachers can help students build their linguistic skills while engaging meaningfully with the language arts curriculum.

Chapter 4 addresses the specific challenges that multilingual learners face in mathematics classrooms. Understanding mathematical concepts requires a strong grasp of academic vocabulary and discourse. This chapter offers strategies for breaking down language barriers in mathematics instruction, making abstract concepts clearer, and encouraging students to articulate their reasoning. By cultivating language development in mathematics lessons, teachers create inclusive classrooms where all students have the opportunity to excel.

In Chapter 5 the authors emphasize the importance of connecting historical, cultural, and social content to students' lived experiences. This chapter provides methods for helping multilingual learners make sense of historical narratives, analyze primary sources, and participate in critical discussions. By situating academic language within real-world contexts, educators make social studies content relevant and accessible, empowering students to become informed and engaged citizens.

Chapter 6 helps educators leverage the powerful intersection of language and science education. Science is a discipline rich with specialized vocabulary and complex processes, which can be daunting for multilingual learners. This chapter offers strategies for making scientific language come alive for students, using language-rich strategies such as visuals, hands-on experiments, and collaborative learning opportunities. By promoting inquiry-based learning and emphasizing the language of scientific discourse, educators can ignite students' curiosity while supporting their language development.

Finally, Chapter 7 brings together the key concepts and strategies discussed throughout the book. It encourages educators to adopt a dynamic, growth-oriented approach to teaching multilingual learners, one that is responsive to students' needs and informed by ongoing reflection and professional development. This chapter serves as a call to action, inviting educators to continue learning, adapting, and advocating for the needs of multilingual students in an ever-changing educational landscape. And in many cases, it is a call for a major overhaul of the existing static, sterile, and unempowering curriculums and instructional practices that are not valuing many multilingual students during the precious little time they spend with us in school.

This book is a testament to the power of language and the role it plays in shaping educational outcomes. It is a reminder that language is not just a tool for communication but a vital component of learning and identity. The strategies and insights provided here are grounded in extensive research yet are deeply practical, offering a road map for educators who are passionate about making a difference in the lives of all students.

Whatever your past or current connection is to the development of academic language proficiency, this book will inspire and equip you to create classrooms where multilingual learners can thrive. It will challenge you to rethink traditional approaches to language development and embrace a more holistic, dynamic model that recognizes and celebrates the linguistic diversity of our students.

—Jeff Zwiers, EdD

Preface

Why This Book Now, and For Whom Is It Intended?

Since the 1980s, the notion of academic language has been prominent in the K–12 educational landscape. However, it has taken on divergent interpretations, especially in discussions involving the language development of multilingual learners. In large part, academic language has tended to be perceived as and associated with the following:

- Language of textbooks
- Language of grade-level materials
- Language of literacy
- Language of content area assessment
- Language of school success
- Language of power

Academic language has also been linked to the idea that in elementary and secondary classrooms each content area has precise technical language, including specialized vocabulary, phrases, and discourses. Case in point—when you refer to metamorphosis, multiple regression analysis, or protagonists in fairy tales, there is an unequivocable connection with the specific subjects of science, mathematics (statistics), and language arts, respectively. However, as we elaborate, that is just one facet of this complex construct.

It is time to recognize that students' worlds extend beyond school and to accept learning as an expression of students' entire lived experiences. Multilingual learners' homes and communities also influence their language choices, and these contexts are inclusive of academic language. Said another way, we must abandon the elitism associated with school language as the sole purveyor of complex ideas and grammar and open conceptual space for leveraging multilingual learners' home language varieties (MacSwan, 2020).

Over a decade ago, our Academic Language in Diverse Classrooms book series (Gottlieb & Ernst-Slavit, 2013a, 2013b, 2014) highlighted the role of academic language in curricula, instruction, and assessment. Developed in the context of the newly released Common Core State Standards, the series offered evidence-based practical examples of how teachers could support academic language development across grade levels, content areas, and diverse learner groups. Now, 12 years later, in reexamining academic language, we have chosen to expand and represent it not as a static concept but as an agentive ongoing process by multilingual learners who employ their full linguistic repertoires. Hence, we take on the active form of languaging. This reconceptualized approach empowers students to take ownership of their learning and engage in language practices that are meaningful to their unique identities and strengths.

It is now the mid-2020s. The construct of academic language in relation to instruction for multilingual learners has broadened and become more sophisticated. The once almost exclusive monoglossic stance that adheres to monolingualism (English) as the only viable route to learning in the U.S. context has slowly been eroding. As an educational community, we have come to embrace the assets of our students along with their multilingual multicultural resources. We have moved to valuing the knowledge of multiple languages (a heteroglossic stance) and acknowledging bi-/multilingualism as the norm (Gottlieb & Honigsfeld, 2025; Seltzer & de los Ríos, 2021). In doing so, we accept academic language as not being exclusively associated with English; all other languages and language varieties enhance our understanding of the language patterns of our multilingual learners. Additionally, the credence of translanguaging, or the natural dynamic flow and interchange of languages, as a bona fide communication mode has added to our notion of academic languaging.

The increasing recognition of the benefits of dual language educational programs as an effective model for educating multilingual learners has contributed to its growing popularity worldwide. While this trend continues in the United States, the participation of multilingual learners varies based on state, district, and school policies. Instructional models range along a continuum from English-only instruction, whose intent is to accelerate English language development, to dual language programs, where the primary goal is to foster and maintain biliteracy and bilingualism. Regardless of the instructional model, language development is essential to, and to be integrated into, the education of multilingual learners.

Throughout the book, we offer ways to support and incorporate multimodalities—or multiple means of expression, such as kinesthetics, graphics, and visual representation in addition to oral and written text—into instruction to optimize multilingual learners' accessibility to content. For example, we view art as a medium for students to express their language and cultural heritage as well as being integral to science, technology, engineering, and mathematics (STEAM). With today's increasing heterogeneity of multilingual learners, we encourage the integration of the arts and also suggest the interweaving of social and emotional learning within language, literacy, and content area instruction (Calderón & Montenegro, 2022).

Audiences

Given all these potential shifts in thinking, the overarching purpose for writing this book is quite straightforward—to add clarity, primarily for teachers, future teachers, coaches, administrators, and teacher educators, as to what comprises language learning through an academic languaging lens as seen through the eyes of the content areas. Our attention is on classroom teachers, content area specialists, and language specialists, often working in collaboration, who are responsible for instructing or coteaching language arts, mathematics, science, and social studies in K–12 settings. We also recognize the important role of counselors, social workers, bilingual family liaisons, and even psychologists and social workers in the education and support of multilingual learners and how their specializations can add to the linguistic and cultural richness of schooling. They, too, can contribute to the central tenet of academic languaging—that is, encouraging students to make decisions and become agents of their own learning.

Our invitation for adopting academic languaging is open to all educators, from monolingual, to bilingual, to multilingual; the only requirement is that you come with a multilingual multicultural strengths-based mindset. With academic languaging, there is acceptance of all varieties of language; there is not one register with greater recognition or more correctness, nor is there one culture that is valued over another. What's most important is that you advocate for all your multilingual learners (and their families) and defend their right to maintain their languages, cultures, and identities as they develop English and become drivers of their own learning.

We encourage teachers to collaborate in grade-level or department teams, offer topics of interest for their professional learning communities, or form communities of practice to share resources and find inspiration in creating and connecting ideas. Together, educators can engage in deep discussion and come to a common understanding of how multilingual learners and their families can enrich every classroom and school. From a strengths-based perspective, the schoolwide community can then formulate and adopt policies that highlight the beauty and benefit of centering academic languaging as a core instructional practice.

So, what might you do to consolidate and highlight a student's linguistic, cultural, and experiential learning at home with that at school? How might you introduce and sustain academic languaging so that in gaining agency students also take action? How might you convince your colleagues that multilingual learners can take the initiative to engage in deep learning and share it with others?

Here are some suggested strategies to set the tone for academic languaging illustrated throughout the book:

- Frame learning within sociocultural contexts familiar to the students.
- Ensure linguistic and cultural relevance in every lesson and unit of learning.
- Encourage student-to-student interaction, including translanguaging, as an everyday classroom activity.
- Incorporate multimodalities (e.g., videos, multimedia, kinesthetics, graphics, artifacts) seamlessly into instruction and assessment to optimize student access to content.
- Invite students to make increasingly more complex language choices.
- Facilitate ways for students to express their perspectives.
- Instill curiosity and motivate students to delve into inquiry.
- Co-construct with students evidence for learning that is personally meaningful.
- Set clear high expectations and achievable goals with all students.

How This Book Is Organized

Chapters 1, 2, and 7 lay the groundwork for and summarize our approach to academic languaging, drawing on both theoretical insights and practical applications. Between these bookends are Chapters 3 through 6, each one addressing a different content area and following a structured format that exemplifies how academic languaging can be integrated into content learning using evidence-based strategies.

Chapter 1 provides an overview of how the concept of academic language has evolved over time and present a rationale for shifting from "academic language" to "academic languaging." We then explore the dimensions of academic languaging, including discourse, sentences, words/phrases, and symbols. The chapter concludes with a discussion of model texts as an essential instructional tool for dissecting language within content.

Chapter 2 focuses on 10 anchors that provide a framework to guide our work with multilingual learners. These anchors ultimately treat academic languaging as critical, representing a continuous process that draws on multilingual learners' lived experiences, their linguistic and cultural identities, and their interactions at home and school.

Chapter 3 centers on language and literacy development, marking the first of four chapters dedicated to enacting academic languaging in content area classrooms. After an overview of three interconnected language-related fields—language development, language arts, and structured literacy—the chapter discusses how multilingual learners can be advantaged in developing biliteracy and multiliteracies.

Chapter 4 examines current perspectives on teaching and learning mathematics for multilingual learners and highlights the role of academic languaging in mathematics classrooms. It reviews the eight Standards for Mathematical Practice and their applicability to multilingual learners, suggests teaching strategies for language-responsive mathematics instruction, and offers recommendations for fostering meaningful interaction among students. Following a discussion of the dimensions of academic languaging for mathematics, the chapter analyzes two model texts: a story problem and a science, technology, engineering, and mathematics (STEM) assignment that illustrate how everyday mathematics tasks can be confounded by linguistic and cultural nuances.

Chapter 5 addresses the challenges posed by the disciplines that comprise social studies for multilingual learners, as well as the diverse perspectives and personal histories these "citizens of the world" bring to the classroom. A central theme of this chapter is the importance of understanding your students and making social studies instruction relevant and meaningfully connected to their families and lives.

Chapter 6 presents academic languaging as a tool for students to take the initiative to build knowledge and take action to solve complex scientific and engineering problems, fostering personal confidence and agency. We illustrate how authenticity, in combination with linguistic and cultural relevance in a practice-oriented classroom, creates a supportive and motivating environment for students to pursue language and science learning.

Chapter 7 revisits academic languaging as a vehicle for students to make choices and take meaningful action, emphasizing their gaining of personal confidence and agency in the process. We close by focusing on three critical areas with potential impact on multilingual learners and their future: translanguaging, dual language education, and student agency.

Features

Several features stand out in this book. First, we highlight **Model Texts** as tools to support multilingual learners in their oral language and literacy development. These texts—whether excerpts, assignments, or story problems—demonstrate how language features function within specific content areas. In analyzing these examples, teachers can identify linguistic patterns along with potential cultural and/or linguistic challenges students might face.

Chapter 1 presents and analyzes three model texts while Chapters 3, 4, 5, and 6 offer two model texts each followed by teaching strategies connecting language and content to help students engage in learning. Additionally, Chapter 1 and the four content area chapters (i.e., Chapters 3, 4, 5, and 6) offer descriptions and examples of the dimensions of academic language—discourse, sentences, words/phrases, and symbols. As will become clear, academic languaging is not a collection of discrete items or features for students to memorize but a process in which students actively participate as they develop into competent language users and successful content area learners. Thus, academic languaging encompasses cultural knowledge, including "ways of being in the world, ways of acting, thinking, interacting, valuing, believing, speaking, and sometimes writing and reading, connected to particular identities and social roles" (Gee, 1992, p. 73).

In addition, each chapter offers activities or questions that invite readers to reflect on the material (**Stop and Think**). There is also a **Look Closer** box that suggests additional resources, links, and references.

Finally, each chapter concludes with a **Chapter Summary**, followed by a section titled **Extensions**, which includes two subsections: **For Reflection** and **For Action**. These subsections aim to foster deeper thinking (reflection) and encourage readers to apply the material independently or collaboratively with peers (action). Finally, the **Resources** section offers a list of additional references or links related to chapter topics.

Academic Languaging is poised to become an essential resource for K–12 educators working with multilingual learners, demonstrating how to embed language into key content areas—language arts, mathematics, science, and social studies—in actionable ways. We argue that all teachers should recognize and affirm academic languaging as an active process shaped by multilingual learners' lived experiences and social interactions, not just their engagement with texts and materials. As the population of multilingual learners continues to grow, this book is an indispensable addition to every educator's library, supporting students in becoming active agents of their own learning in an increasingly digital world.

Acknowledgments

We are deeply grateful to teachers, students, and their families for welcoming us into their classrooms and communities and sharing their expertise and experiences. Their dedication, resilience, and commitment to multilingual students are at the core of our thinking on academic languaging.

We extend our heartfelt thanks to our editor, Megan Bedell, for her support throughout this project and to our content development manager, Lucas Schleicher, for his thoughtful timely feedback, helpful suggestions, and meticulous attention to detail. We are also grateful to our senior project editor, Nicole Burns-Ascue, for her guidance and steady support throughout the journey of this book's production and to Melinda Masson, copy editor, whose sharp eye and commitment to precision brought clarity to our work. We also wish to express our appreciation to Natalie Delpino, senior editorial assistant and Rae-Ann Goodwin, proofreader, for their invaluable assistance in preparing the manuscript for publication. Lastly, our thanks to Melissa Duclos, senior marketing manager, for her vision and suggestions for reaching diverse audiences.

A special thanks goes to Arthur Slavit for creating key illustrations and icons featured in the book, to Steven J. Morrison for his photographs, to Melissa Sifuentes Phillips for her beautiful bilingual welcome poster in Chapter 1, and to artist Sandra Q. Miller for her bright handmade quilt in Chapter 2. Additionally, we thank Dr. David Slavit for his feedback on several aspects of the mathematics chapter and to Giovanna Frederick and Ida Crocamo-Farley for allowing us to share photos of their classrooms.

About the Authors

Dr. Gisela Ernst-Slavit (PhD, University of Florida) is a professor emerita at Washington State University with an active program of research that focuses on how students and teachers use languaging to construct knowledge and to create and maintain a community of learners where members' languages and cultures are acknowledged and validated. Gisela is a native from Peru who grew up languaging in Spanish, German, and English. She is the author, coauthor, or coeditor of 12 books and over 100 articles and chapters, and she frequently speaks at regional, national, and international conferences on multilingual learner education, with a particular focus on teacher preparation for multilingual youth. Gisela has been a visiting professor at the Universidad Autónoma de Madrid, has served as president of the Washington Association for the Education of Speakers of Other Languages, and has held leadership roles in several professional organizations, including the American Educational Research Association, the Council of Anthropology and Education, and TESOL International Association.

Dr. Margo Gottlieb (PhD, University of Illinois Chicago) has been a bilingual teacher, coordinator, facilitator, consultant, and mentor across K–20 settings. Having worked with universities, organizations, governments, states, school districts, networks, and schools across the United States and internationally, Margo has co-constructed linguistic and culturally sustainable curriculum and reconceptualized classroom assessment, policy, and practice. As cofounder and lead developer of WIDA at the University of Wisconsin–Madison in 2003, Margo helped design and contributed to all the editions of WIDA's English and Spanish language development standards frameworks and their derivative products. She has been appointed to national and state advisory boards, served as a Fulbright Senior Scholar, was honored by TESOL International Association for her significant contribution to the field, and was recently inducted into the inaugural class of the Multilingual Education Hall of Fame, receiving a Multilingual Education Medal of Honor by Summit K12–NABE. Having authored, coauthored, or coedited over 100 publications, including 22 books, Margo's third edition of *Assessing Multilingual Learners: Bridges to Empowerment* (2024a) and *Collaborative Assessment for Multilingual Learners and Teachers: Pathways to Partnerships* (with A. Honigsfeld, 2025) are the latest additions to her Corwin compendium.

1 Moving From Academic Language to Academic Languag*ing*

Anyone who has visited Planet Word, a Smithsonian museum in Washington, DC, will have witnessed language in action, demonstrated in interactive boards with individuals from around the world describing differences between their languages and English, audio coupled with video vividly illustrating through Technicolor the borrowing of English words from multiple language families, and a hypothetical library doubled in size through mirrors—all made possible through innovative technology. These exhibits remind us of the power of language, such as the display in Figure 1.1, and its constant evolution through translingualism, the crisscrossing and continuous interaction among languages as they come in contact with each other and interconnect.

Figure 1.1 The Power of Words

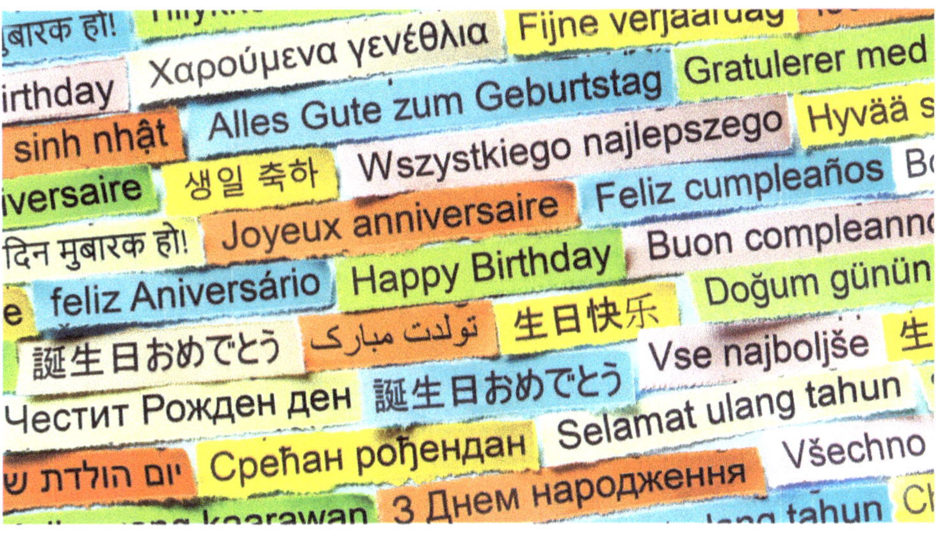

Source: iStock.com/ivosar

Academic languaging, although associated with ongoing technological advancement, is much more—it is a human activity all about the negotiation of language(s) for specific purposes that is crafted for particular audiences and uses. In essence, in this book we concentrate on the interaction among K–12 students, viewing the construct through the lens of multilingual learners. This interest group has been most impacted by and historically criticized for their absence of expression of academic language in English, and we wish to rectify this misunderstanding. And so we initiate our discussion of academic languaging with Figure 1.2, sharing the warmth of a welcoming classroom filled with multilingual voices.

Figure 1.2 A Bilingual Welcoming Poster in an Elementary Classroom

Source: Melissa Sifuentes Phillips

Multilingual learners, a broad heterogeneous, ever-increasing, and expansive group of students, have the distinction of having been or currently being exposed to multiple languages at home, in the community, and/or at school, thus having access and opportunity to communicate in two or more languages (Hornberger, 1990). A subset of multilingual learners whose English language proficiency precludes them from full participation in classrooms where English is the medium of instruction are often labeled English learners. Per federal legislation, these students—many of whom were born and have been raised in the United States, and some of whom have been dually identified as students with exceptionalities—are eligible for participation in a range of language support services. Other student groups include newcomers to the U.S. educational system, students with interrupted formal schooling, and long-term English learners—all of whom qualify and participate in language programs. We also have to acknowledge multilingual learners who have been identified as gifted and talented and receive highly capable services.

In large part, multilingual learners retain their multiple languages and cultures although some have been reclassified from designated language programs per their state's regulations. Additionally, there are heritage language learners, including members of Indigenous communities, with oral language proficiency or cultural connections to multiple languages whose overall English language proficiency has met or exceeded state criteria for eligibility. Indeed, multilingual learners are an eclectic heterogeneous mix of students!

All students have the power of language that needs to be nurtured and released; we consider that action academic languaging. Throughout the first two chapters we offer various conceptualizations of academic language and how they might become more student centric and converted to reflect the more personalized term *academic languaging*. Most important, though, is what academic languaging means to you and its implications for your multilingual learners. To what extent are you accepting of your students' personal assets and those from their home environment as part of your definition?

Here is the first of several icons sprinkled throughout the chapters. **Stop and Think** is specifically designed with the idea of reflection in mind. So, take some time to pause and ponder the information at hand and its implications for you, your colleagues, and your multilingual learners.

Stop and Think

What Is the Meaning of Academic Languaging to You and Your Colleagues?

Jot down your conceptualization of academic language and, if you choose, the theorists who have contributed to your thinking. Now, make note of how you might define academic languaging.

After each chapter, you might wish to revisit your notes and add how you are being influenced by our writing and moving toward a more academic languaging stance.

Why Our Change in Thinking? Where We Came From and Where We're Going

As we proposed more than a decade ago and reiterate here, the teaching and learning of academic language requires *more* than linguistic knowledge—it also involves cultural knowledge about "ways of being in the world, ways of acting, thinking, interacting, valuing, believing, speaking, and sometimes writing and reading, connected to particular identities and social roles" (Gee, 1992, p. 73). Ultimately, one important goal for learning academic language is to afford and promote thinking and communicating about issues in more abstract, technical, and deeper ways. "Having teachers and school leaders recognize and incorporate the linguistic and cultural influences of home and community into school enables students to unite their experiential and academic worlds to build their academic language use" (Gottlieb & Ernst-Slavit, 2014, p. 27).

Since then, we have taken a more dynamic action-oriented stance of language that implies language use that relays a specific message, has a specific purpose, and is intended for a specific audience to effect change, thus the term *languaging*. In essence, we tend to think like linguistic anthropologists who see and use language as social action. Action-based teaching centers on promoting student agency and its relation to the development of self and identity (van Lier, 2007) to foster academic languaging.

In an action-oriented approach, language learning is a social practice that considers students as active participants in the (co)construction of knowledge where a variety of social and cultural factors influence teaching and learning. It involves students learning pragmatics (situational language use) to understand the context in which language learning occurs as part of their classroom routine. For example, students need to know when they can ask a question about a classroom presentation, under what circumstances they can use information from artificial intelligence (AI), or when can they speak without raising their hands. This stance of languaging, combining sociocultural and actionable perspectives as the bases for communication, supports language learning as a social practice where talk and interaction are central to human development and learning.

For us, academic languaging implies a more prominent role of students as contributing members of their classroom community—taking the reins, gaining agency, and exerting autonomy as they become confident and competent users of language. Taking an action-based perspective, multilingual learners help in determining, engaging, and reflecting on meaningful activities, such as research, projects, and presentations that pique their interest. Language development is fostered through student interaction in planning, exploring, discussing, and co-constructing a range of products. In this orientation, language learning is more than a cognitive process; it involves the mind, the body, emotions, and all the senses. Viewing language learning within an action-based mindset places the forms (structures) of language in the background while foregrounding language as doing.

In adopting academic languaging as a way of thinking and doing, we no longer envision language dichotomously (as social *or* academic); nor do we confine learning to school, but rather we embrace the contributions of students', families', and communities' "funds of knowledge" (González et al., 2005). Along with valuing students' languages, cultures, traditions, and experiences, we acknowledge how both educators and family members help shape the identities of multilingual learners. In essence, we privilege the resources and assets that constitute multilingual learners' self-definition, self-expression, and self-understanding—that is, their "funds of identity" that are actively used in self-definition (Esteban-Guitart & Moll, 2014). Features associated with the identities of multilingual learners are highlighted in Figure 1.3.

Figure 1.3 Features Contributing to Multilingual Learners' Identities

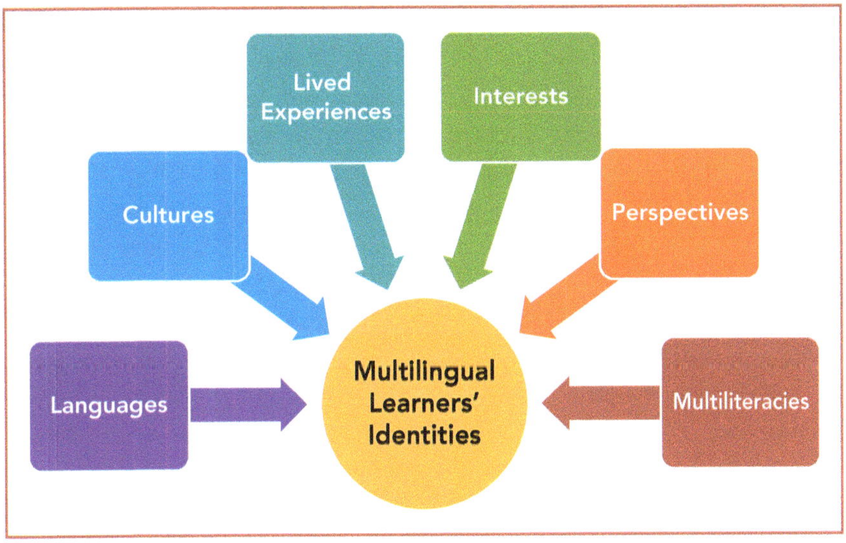

Languaging for multilingual learners is also an empowerment issue across content area learning that can be upheld by inviting students to interact in the language(s) of their choice. We have specifically chosen the term *languaging* for activities that portray language use when communicating with others for distinct purposes. Dynamic languaging—"the process of making meaning and shaping knowledge and experience through language" (Swain, 2006, p. 98)—occurs at home, in school, and around the community. Similarly, Diane Larsen-Freeman (2003) challenges the focus on grammar and rules of grammar as a dynamic process, something she calls grammaring. For multilingual learners, meaning-making can entail the imperfect use of language, dialectal variations, and different varieties of language.

Ultimately, switching from notions of academic language to academic languaging may just be a morphological tweak; however, its implications are huge, allowing educators to notice what multilingual learners can do in more empowering ways (Proctor, 2020). We agree with Sembiante and Tran (2021) who see academic languaging as the "agentive verbal action taken by language users who wield their full linguistic repertoires in functional ways to support the dynamic communicative and literary contexts of schooling" (p. 102).

Several researchers have challenged the notion of academic language over the years, claiming that academic registers are perceived as being more complex, specialized, and sophisticated than nonacademic registers, ultimately privileging white middle-class teaching practices as the default linguistic standard against which multilingual learners are evaluated (Flores & Rosa, 2015). In principle, this raciolinguistic ideology (emanating from the intersections of race, language, and social class) challenges the ever-present white middle-class dominance in schools as schools are increasingly becoming more minoritized with financially impoverished student populations. According to Flores (2020), this racialized ideology frames low-income students as being linguistically deficient and in need of remediation due to their failure to master academic language. In lieu of using "academic language," "language architecture" is suggested as a means of analyzing the literacy demands of state academic content standards, thus enabling students to be language architects capable of manipulating language for specific purposes (Flores, 2020).

Another suggested replacement for "academic language" is the "language of ideas." This reframing of academic language focuses on students' language use when engaging in school-based content area work. It accounts for the linguistic resources that students bring to academic tasks, including their (1) conversational or social language, (2) accomplishments related to academic tasks, and (3) awareness and strategic use of a range of registers for different purposes and audiences (Bunch, 2014; Bunch & Martin, 2021).

There has not been universal acceptance of what constitutes academic language, nor do we expect that there will be agreement on academic languaging. So that you can formulate your own opinion on the discussion at hand, we have inserted an icon of a magnifying glass to signal a set of resources that offers additional references on the topic. The following list is our first one on varying views of academic language over the years.

Look Closer

Contributors to Academic Language

There is a long history in language education that revolves around academic language and how it has evolved into academic languaging. Here are some of the major theorists and researchers who have contributed to the construct, attributed, in large part, to the groundbreaking work of Jim Cummins in the early 1980s.

Bailey, A. L., & Heritage, M. (2008). *Formative assessment for literacy, grades K–6: Building reading and academic language skills across the curriculum*. Corwin.

Bunch, C. B., & Martin, D. (2021). From "academic language" to the "language of ideas": A disciplinary perspective on using language in K–12 settings. *Language and Education*, *35*(1), 1–18.

Cummins, J. (1981). Four misconceptions about language proficiency in bilingual education. *NABE Journal*, *5*(3), 31–45.

Cummins, J. (2008). BICS and CALP: Empirical and theoretical status of the distinction. In B. Street & N. H. Hornberger (Eds.), *Encyclopedia of language and education: Vol. 2. Literacy* (2nd ed., pp. 71–83). Springer Science + Business Media.

Gee, J. P. (1990). *Social linguistics and literacies: Ideology in discourses*. Falmer Press.

Gibbons, P. (2009). *English learners, academic literacy, and thinking: Learning in the challenge zone*. Heinemann.

Gottlieb, M., & Castro, M. (2017). *Language power: Key uses for accessing content*. Corwin.

Gottlieb, M., & Ernst-Slavit, G. (2014). *Academic language in diverse classrooms: Definitions and contexts*. Corwin.

Scarcella, R. (2003). *Academic English: A conceptual framework* (Technical Report No. 1). University of California Linguistic Minority Research Institute.

Schleppegrell, M. J. (2004). *The language of schooling: A functional linguistics perspective*. Erlbaum.

Snow, C. E., & Uccelli, P. (2009). The challenge of academic language. In D. R. Olson & N. Torrance (Eds.), *The Cambridge handbook of literacy* (pp. 112–133). Cambridge University Press.

Zwiers, J. (2008). *Building academic language: Essential practices for content classrooms*. Jossey-Bass.

Why Shift to Academic Languag*ing*, and What Does It Entail?

As we, a global village, are becoming increasingly affected by advancements in technology—in particular, AI—our named languages are becoming more and more in flux. The shift from *language* to *languaging* involves a subtle yet powerful distinction between views of language as a static object versus languaging as an ongoing process and action. The construct of languaging has its roots in several related and overlapping fields of study including linguistics, applied linguistics (e.g., Swain, 2006), sociolinguistics (e.g., Bloome et al., 2022), and linguistic anthropology (Becker, 1991). The term suggests that "there is no such thing as language, only continual languaging, an activity of human beings in the world" (Becker, 1991). In other words, speaking and writing are themselves language production activities that mediate remembering, attending, and other aspects of higher mental functioning. When we talk or write, our attention is focused on certain objects or ideas and not others; we create artifacts that we can refer back to, challenge, and change—processes that help us to remember and learn.

Based on the preceding conceptualization of languaging, we treat it as an agentive, verbal, or written action taken by language users who employ their full linguistic resources in functional ways to support the dynamic communicative and literary-related contexts of schooling (Proctor et al., 2020; Sembiante & Tian, 2021). This focus serves a threefold purpose. First, and as discussed earlier, a languaging perspective positions students, teachers, and community members and their language practices as inseparable, constantly shaping and reshaping language. Second, the shift from *language* as a noun to *languaging* as a verb moves our understanding of the construct away from prescriptive, fixed, and exclusive notions that have traditionally pervaded in the field to ones that are flexible and dynamic. Finally, this view of academic languaging offers a timely response to recent criticism of academic language that is seen as

- A set of static linguistic forms to be learned (e.g., Flores & Rosa, 2015)
- One that prioritizes white standard linguistic practices (e.g., Paris, 2012)
- More complex and of higher status than nonacademic registers (MacSwan, 2020)
- A tool for segregation and exclusion (e.g., Jensen et al., 2021)

In sum, the shift from a conception of language as a tacit noun to an active verb supports our premise that all educators should view academic languaging as an ongoing process that draws from and centers the lived experiences of multilingual learners and their interactions with others and different text forms.

You will notice how Figure 1.4 represents multilingual learners' interaction with the world. School, home, and community influences underscore the grounding of multilingual learners' identity formation, agency, and empowerment. The brilliance of the stars, representing the content areas of language arts, mathematics, social studies and science, is filtered through academic languaging, enabling multilingual learners to humanize their learning experiences through multiple languages, literacies, and perspectives.

Figure 1.4 The Larger Context of Academic Languaging

Source: Arthur Slavit

A Classroom Example

At the end of her sixth-grade social studies class, Mrs. Baskin announces that tomorrow class will start with a discussion of a brief article published recently in the local newspaper titled "City Mayor Pushes the Envelope and Bans Plastic Bags" while showing a copy of the article on the screen. As the students leave the classroom, Bouzid stares at the screen, a puzzled expression on his face (see Figure 1.5).

CHAPTER 1

Figure 1.5 A Social Studies Article

Source: Arthur Slavit

Stop and Think

What Would You Do?

Bouzid is one of seven multilingual students in Mrs. Baskin's classroom. Before you proceed, take a moment to reflect on how you might introduce this newspaper article to your students and explain the idiomatic expression.

As Figure 1.5 suggests, students proficient in English in this class understood the meaning of the newspaper headline and probably had a sense of what the article is about. On the other hand, for multilingual learners like Bouzid, the headline might not make sense due to the idiomatic expression "pushing the envelope." This idiomatic expression, and others like it, can be puzzling, generating misunderstanding in comprehension because its meaning is different than the sum of the meaning of its single words.

For students growing up in English-speaking homes, such idiomatic expressions form part of their language repertoire and may not need clarification. However, for multilingual learners, who often translate concepts literally, this kind of "opaque language" (Ernst-Slavit & Mason, 2011) can cloud their understanding. This example reminds us of Bartolomé's (1998) assertion that "even well-intentioned teachers often fail to overtly teach the academic discourses necessary for school success" (p. 3).

Important to highlight is that colloquial and idiomatic expressions are used regularly in oral language discussions and in written contexts (e.g., podcasts, blogs, cartoons, or newspaper headlines). For multilingual learners, colloquialisms and idiomatic expressions are one other aspect of academic languaging to incorporate into their linguistic repertoire.

What Are the Dimensions of Academic Language?

Academic language is the basis for academic languaging. Historically, academic language has been couched within three hierarchical dimensions from discourse, the overall organization of chunks of language (oral or written text); to sentences, one or more words that denote a statement, question, command, or exclamation; to words/phrases, the smallest units of meaningful communication (e.g., A. Bailey & Butler, 2003; Gottlieb & Ernst-Slavit, 2014; Scarcella, 2003). Sociocultural context, specifying the situation and interaction in which academic language is operationalized, has also been recognized as a critical element in language standards frameworks (WIDA, 2004, 2012, 2020, 2023).

As shown in Table 1.1, academic languaging is grounded in the dimensions of other language frameworks (with the addition of symbols—a multimodal feature); however, it captures an underlying motivation and purpose for language use that makes learning actionable—that is, through student-led

Table 1.1 Inquiry-Based Learning Framing the Four Dimensions of Academic Language/Languaging

Discourse	• Genres • Organization of text • Coherence of ideas
Sentences	• Questioning • Statements • Simple, compound, complex structures
Words/Phrases	• Prepositional phrases • Multiple meanings • Colloquial expressions
Symbols	• Greek letters • Numerals • Map icons

Adapted from Gottlieb & Ernst-Slavit, 2014, p. 6

inquiry. Student-led inquiry revolves around student-generated authentic questions about a topic, an issue, or a phenomenon and their genuine pursuit of the answers. In essence, teachers facilitate an experience that unfolds in such a way that student learning is stimulated through discovery and problem-solving.

As you may have noticed, we have added a fourth dimension—symbols, as they are used widely for communicative purposes in and out of academic settings. We further describe each dimension of academic languaging as follows.

Discourse Dimension

Discourse refers to the broader bodies of language, their organization, coherence, and cohesion. It also refers to different communication modes as in spoken, written, and visual. Within discourse, there are genres, which are specific categories for what we read, write, speak, watch, and listen. In terms of literary genres, for example, fiction, nonfiction, and poetry are three broad categories. In addition, within each category there are a variety of different types of works. Examples of nonfiction material in science include a manual to use the 3D printer, a biographical sketch of Marie Curie, and a podcast by astrophysicist Neil deGrasse Tyson. Likewise, a variety of discourse forms are used in language arts classrooms that range from the more conventional printed materials such as essays, journal entries, and acrostic poems to current multimodal types of genres such as podcasts, digital collages, and slideshows. For students to access content area material and to show understanding of that material, they will need to understand and use the structures, conventions, and complexities required by each discourse form. Table 1.2 presents examples of a variety of genre-based discourses typically associated with the content areas.

Table 1.2 Examples of Genre-Based Discourse by Content Area

CONTENT AREA	EXAMPLES OF GENRE-BASED DISCOURSE
Language Arts	Oral histories, autobiographies, editorials, audiobooks
Mathematics	Graphs, story problems, proofs, diagrams
Science	Research reports, tabular representations, digital applications, large data sets
Social Studies	Speeches, political cartoons, maps, historical diaries, reenactments
Art and Music	Scripts, music scores, 2D and 3D portfolios, lyric analyses
Health and Wellness	Health compendia, exercise training logs, module packets

The range of discourse options that can be used in today's classrooms is enormous (see Table 1.3 for examples of discourses throughout the content areas). Important to highlight is the heterogeneity of the students sitting in today's classrooms; while some multilingual students might be more familiar with linear and printed texts, others maybe be whizzes at interacting with a variety of multimedia and multilanguage materials.

Table 1.3 Examples of Genre-Based Discourse Across Formats

PRINT-BASED	DIGITAL	VISUAL/ MULTIMEDIA	SPOKEN
Ballads	AI searches	Charts	Asking questions
Book reports	Apple Books	Claymations	Audio recordings
Essays	Apps	Drawings	Brief recitations
Expository texts	Digital storytelling	Films	Debates
Fables/fairy tales	Emails	Graphics	Dialogues
Informational texts	Gaming	Graphic organizers	Giving directions
Myths	Podcasts	Photo collages/ murals	Monologues
Novels	QR codes	Podcasts	Reciting poetry
Opinion pieces	Rewording tools	PowerPoints	(Re)telling stories
Poems	Texts	Prezi presentations	Role plays
Song lyrics	Visual read-alouds	Sketches	Speeches
Tall tales	Web pages	Videos	
Theses	Wikis	Vocabulary pictures	
		YouTube videos	

Adapted from Gottlieb & Ernst-Slavit, 2014 (ELA 6–8)

Stop and Think

What Is Discourse?

The term *discourse*, like many other words in English, has multiple meanings. Traditionally, *discourse* refers to dialogue or conversation between two parties. However, Gee (2011) introduces a broader concept, which he calls "Discourse with a big 'D'" (p. 34). This refers to socially accepted ways of using language that involve "thinking, valuing, acting, and interacting in the 'right' places, at the 'right' times, with the 'right' objects" (p. 34). Being proficient in academic languaging means knowing what to say, when to say it, and how to say and apply it within various oral and written disciplinary contexts.

Sentences Dimension

The sentence dimension includes grammatical structures, language forms, and conventions that characterize languaging in inquiry-based situations. Students encounter these patterns primarily in the different types of texts they read, the talk in and out of classrooms, school-based tasks, and assessments. For all students, including multilingual students, learning how to use grammatical structures simultaneously facilitates both language development and content area learning.

The challenge is that many features in English are not intuitive. In fact, like all languages, English is also arbitrary, and some basic structures are illogical or dissimilar to the home languages of our students and thus difficult to understand and learn—even when taught in context. Think about the following examples:

> **Phrasal verbs.** Most proficient English speakers do not need to think about how two or more words are strung together as a verb that may have multiple meanings. Read through the following examples:
>
> | | |
> |---|---|
> | *break down* | *get through* |
> | *come around* | *run out* |
> | *get across* | *turn down* |
>
> **Future tense.** In English there are several different ways for expressing future-related meanings. This range of forms of expressing the future nature of an occurrence may be extremely frustrating for multilingual learners, particularly for those who speak languages that do not use verb tenses at all (e.g., several varieties of Chinese, Thai, Vietnamese, and Yucatec Maya). To illustrate this, here are six different constructions in English that express an action that will take place in the future:
>
> > *I'll study this afternoon.*
> >
> > *I'm going (planning) to study this afternoon.*
> >
> > *I'm studying this afternoon.*
> >
> > *I'll be studying this afternoon.*
> >
> > *I will have been studying this afternoon.*
> >
> > *I was going to study this afternoon.*

Clearly, learning English can be very confusing! Multilingual learners will encounter additional irregularities—for example, learning that the word *syllabus* is singular, not plural. They will also have to learn that many words can have two opposite meanings (e.g., *clip* means both "to cut apart" and "to attach together"), that the meanings of words can change depending on which syllable is stressed (e.g., as in *address*: *ADDress* as the particulars of a place and *addRESS* as a talk or lecture), and that the words *hundred, thousand, million*, and *billion* are singular after plural numbers (e.g., winning *three million* dollars).

In addition to irregular count nouns, prepositions, and interrogatives, students will encounter complex structures (e.g., parallel clauses, passive voice, and complex noun sentences). While there are numerous grammatical structures that cross content areas and disciplines, some are used more often in particular disciplines. Table 1.4 provides selected grammatical structures and pertinent examples used in specific content areas.

Table 1.4 Examples of Grammatical Features by Content Area

CONTENT AREA	FEATURE	EXAMPLES
Language Arts	Simile	*Cool as a cucumber, white as a ghost*
	Compare and contrast	*In the same way, both, similarly, unlike, on the other hand, however*
Mathematics	Logical connectors	*But, and, if, then, if and only if*
	Compare (multiplication)	*Times as many, times as much, times more, times as large*
Science	Passive voice	*The cells were infected by the virus.* *The experiment was conducted by the researchers.*
	Complex noun phrases	*Waste product excretion mechanisms* *Carbon dioxide removal methods*
Social Studies	Sequencing	*First, second, last, finally* *Soon, meanwhile, subsequently, in the end*
	Historical present	*It is a dark and rainy day in 1939.* *Today, Lewis and Clark decided to approach the voyage in a different manner.*

Words/Phrases Dimension

Academic vocabulary includes words and phrases that cut across content areas or that can be specific to particular disciplines. General words and phrases include *in spite of, summary*, and *introduction*, whereas content-specific words and phrases in mathematics might include *multiplication, cardinal numbers*, and *square root*. Many general academic words have been identified through analysis of academic texts. For instance, Averil Coxhead (2000) developed an academic word list (AWL) to help set vocabulary goals for language courses, guide independent study, and inform curriculum designers in selecting texts and creating learning activities. Based on a corpus of 3.5 million words from academic texts, Coxhead identified 570 word families that college students are likely to encounter, such as the word *analyze* and its related forms (e.g., *analytic, analytical, analytically, analysis*). Although the list is aimed at postsecondary education, many words align with word lists that are now available in grade-level curricula.

Your multilingual learners may already know a range of disciplinary language since most of the language of science and technology has Greek and Latin roots that serve as a bridge between the Romance languages and English. Students who speak Spanish, French, Italian, Portuguese, or Romanian (i.e., Romance languages derived from Latin) can leverage their existing linguistic knowledge and make connections to the English language. Table 1.5 includes cognates (i.e., words that are written similarly and have a similar meaning) in five different languages. Notice how similar their spelling is (although beware that their pronunciation might be very different).

Table 1.5 Cognates in Five Different Languages

ENGLISH	ESPAÑOL	PORTUGUÊS	ITALIANO	FRANÇAISE
Active carbon	Carbón activo	Carbono ativo	Carbone attivo	Carbone actif
Instant	Instante	Instant	Istantaneo	Instantané
Legal	Legal	Legal	Legale	Légale
Mental	Mental	Mental	Mentale	Mentale
Metamorphosis	Metamorfosis	Metamorfose	Metamorfosi	Métamorphose
Polymer	Polímero	Polímero	Polimero	Polymère
Version	Versión	Versão	Versione	Version

For all students, particularly multilingual learners, providing opportunities to explore Greek and Latin root-word construction in context can be a meaningful way of engaging in translinguistic transfer to learn new content area vocabulary. Figure 1.6 is an example of the kind of work students can do with their tablets or laptops as they inquire about the many words that can be derived from the Latin root *press*.

Figure 1.6 Circle-Spoke Diagram for the Latin Root *Press*

online resources This resource is available for download at https://companion.corwin.com/courses/Academic-Languaging.

Important to remember is that children acquire large vocabularies when they engage in meaningful interactions about topics that are of interest to them (Snow, 2017). Focusing solely on vocabulary—such as by teaching 5 or 10 words per week—is ineffective because vocabulary is only valuable insofar as it reflects a student's broader conceptual understanding.

> A child's vocabulary is not important except to the extent that it signals something about conceptual or knowledge development. Indeed, the excellent academic outcomes of second-language learners with strong first language skills strongly support the notion that "knowing the words" is less important than knowing the concepts the words label. (Snow, 2017, p. 5)

Stated differently, the strong academic performance of multilingual learners with a solid foundation in their home language underscores that understanding and applying the concepts behind words is more crucial than merely knowing the words themselves.

Symbols Dimension

A symbol is something that represents something else. Similar to words and language structures, symbols can help people comprehend the world. However, if unknown, a symbol can hinder communication and understanding. A symbol can represent a noun (e.g., a tree on a map), an action (e.g., printing on a computer), or a concept (Uncle Sam). Just as we rely on symbols when driving in the city, symbols, such as the examples listed in Figure 1.7, are vital for navigating the K–12 school curriculum.

Figure 1.7 Examples of Symbols Across Content Areas

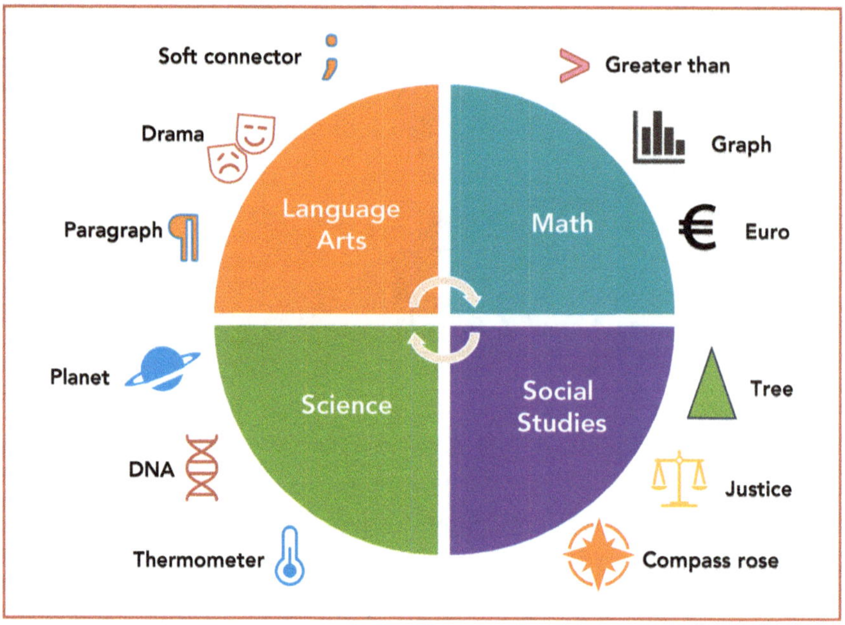

Symbols and Digital Media

Students today are digital natives, and most are prepared to navigate the constantly changing nature of technology and its related digital skills. However, because we know that multilingual learners in our schools are a heterogeneous population, we cannot assume that a student who is developing English will also be learning digital literacy. In fact, some students may rely on their smartphones or tablets for all sorts of communicative needs, entertainment, inquiry, and school work.

In digital communication, symbols in English have been adopted across the globe for social media, emails, and text messages. Likewise, emojis—those popular icons that convey thoughts and emotions in any language and across languages—are originally from Japan. Some symbols are used to communicate complete messages (e.g., thumbs-up emoji), emotions (e.g., smiley face), and tone (e.g., *haha* or IMAO—In My Arrogant Opinion). In addition, hashtags (#) and symbols (@) have become useful tools on social media platforms. Hashtags allow users to identify posts under a specific topic. For example, New Mexico has established some set hashtags for emergency communication such as #NMFire and #NMStorm. While some educators and families might feel that this new way of digital communication may reduce opportunities for students to use and practice "proper" English, current research (e.g., Crystal, 2008; McSweeney, 2017) indicates that using social media in English may, in fact, support English literacy development as a whole.

Look Closer

Technology and Multilingual Learners

For viewing:

British Council Serbia. (2013, November 29). *David Crystal—The effect of new technologies on English* [Video]. YouTube. https://www.youtube.com/watch?v=qVqcoB798Is&ab_channel=BritishCouncilSerbia

Gassalasca4. (2013, May 11). *David Crystal on texting (S1E2 of It's only a theory)* [Video]. YouTube. https://www.youtube.com/watch?v=h79V_qUp91M&ab_channel=Gassalasca4

For reading:

Altavilla, J. (2020). How technology affects instruction for English learners. *Kappan, 102*(1), 18–23.

Dalton, B. (2020). Bringing together multimodal composition and maker education in K–8 classrooms. *Language Arts, 97*(3), 159–171.

Egbert, J., & Panday-Shukla, P. (2024). *Task engagement across disciplines: Research and practical strategies to increase student achievement*. Taylor and Francis.

McSweeney, M. A. (2017). I text English to everyone: Links between second-language texting and academic proficiency. *Languages, 27*. https://doi.org/10.3390/languages2030007

Model Texts as an Instructional Staple

In this opening chapter, we introduce three model texts, while the content area chapters each feature two model texts. These texts are intended to inspire teachers and students alike to take action. They are pieces of culturally relevant literature or informational text that can at times be expressed in multimodal ways, such as with an app, a PowerPoint, or a podcast, so that students can read/listen to and reread/relisten to them for specific purposes. Applicable across content areas, some of the model texts in this book have been inspired by AI, others are the imaginations of the authors, and still others are excerpts from informational or narrative texts.

Traditionally, model texts provide an example of how a target text might look (Derewianka & Jones, 2023). They are designed to showcase the features and expectations of text we hope students will eventually produce. In addition, we include different kinds of model text, one that may come from a grade-level textbook or classroom materials (e.g., a story problem, an assignment, or a paragraph from a textbook). In those instances, the goal is for educators to deconstruct the text and analyze its different linguistic and cultural aspects for clarification or additional support.

Model texts serve as a catalyst for teachers to regularly analyze the texts and materials they use in classrooms and to identify the language and content challenges for students, especially multilingual learners. The goal is for teachers to become aware of how language is used in the materials we are asking students to read and in the activities we are asking students to do. The following is a brief vignette from a Grade 2 classroom that illustrates this point.

> Early in the school year, Mr. Martin and his second graders read a brief story about children doing their homework that appeared in the students' language arts textbook. After finishing the story, Mr. Martin assigned a task where students were asked to draw a picture of their favorite spot at home for doing homework and write one or two sentences explaining why they liked that space. At a first glance, both the reading and the accompanying assignment seemed harmless. However, Mr. Martin later discovered that the task had proved to be challenging for several students, including three who were experiencing homelessness, one who spent three hours after school at the public library, and a multilingual student from Afghanistan whose family had recently relocated and was living in a small room adjacent to a local church.

In this case, Mr. Martin would have benefited from knowing about the lives and circumstances of his students. And although this may not always be feasible, a careful review of the reading and the ensuing task might have helped Mr. Martin identify potential troublesome areas—both linguistic and sociocultural.

You will notice that model texts can also illustrate a means of bridging content, language, and literacy either initiated by students or inspiring students to take action. Thus, they illustrate how academic languaging can come to life through open-ended questioning or responding to controversy in writing or orally. In this book, we have carefully created or selected model texts based on the following features:

- Selecting topics of interest to students that spur action
- Ensuring that students can relate to the text in positive ways
- Enabling students to identify the purpose of the text
- Illustrating how writers/speakers express themselves
- Encouraging students to take risks as authors
- Examining grade-level textbooks and materials
- Analyzing tasks and classroom assessment

There are many classroom applications for model texts, such as the following:

- Serving as a model or prototype for oral language or literacy development
- Connecting to students' languages, cultures, perspectives, and experiences
- Determining author's purpose (e.g., visualization, making inferences, expressing opinions or points of view) and offering feedback
- Introducing a new genre to students
- Exemplifying specified language structures in context
- Combining oral and written modes in meaningful ways
- Representing an array of genres, such as music, poetry, blogs, and recipes

Most model texts reflect specific genres, different types or categories of literary or artistic work, and that their analysis begins with the discourse dimension. The following model text, a story problem, is typically used in mathematics curricula and assessment across the United States, starting in kindergarten. As you read the brief story problem, reflect on how the text is constructed, how certain language features are used, and what are the potential linguistic and cultural aspects that may confuse students, particularly multilingual learners.

Model Text 1: A Story Problem

Mrs. Hilt reads 13 books on every day that starts with the letters T and S. How many books does she read in one week?

(K5 Learning, www.k5learning.com)

Although this Grade 2 word problem is about using addition, like most story problems, it is language dependent. One overall challenge in word problem-solving is getting students to understand that the written story on the page can be translated into a mathematics story and then into an equation. As the analysis will illustrate, this very short story problem can trouble many students' understanding.

Discourse

This is a story problem, a typical type of genre (a discourse pattern) used in mathematics throughout K–12 education that is heavily represented in standardized-test items in mathematics.

Sentences

The sentence structure, especially the conditional clause "on every day that starts with the letters *T* and *S*," is complex. Second graders need to grasp how the days of the week relate to the number of books read. In addition, understanding "How many books does she read in one week?" involves interpreting the time frame (one week) and linking it to the information provided in the first sentence.

Words/Phrases

For students to solve the problem they need to (1) understand the phrase "Every day that starts with the letters *T* and *S*," (2) know the names of the days of the week, and (3) identify the first letter of the days of the week. While most second graders may know the days of the week, that might not be the case for multilingual learners who may be unfamiliar with their English names. In addition, understanding the phrase "How many books . . ." is critical for recognizing that the problem asks for a quantity of books and that students must add to reach a total.

Symbols

In the short story problem, three symbols are used: 13, *T*, and *S*. While students will likely recognize the number 13, they must also understand that the letters *T* and *S* are abbreviations for four different days of the week—Tuesday, Thursday, Saturday, and Sunday.

Sociocultural Aspects

Multilingual learners may not be familiar with the convention of a seven-day week starting on Sunday, since a few cultures count the days of the week differently (e.g., Burma). A second issue here is the amount of books Mrs. Hilt reads per day. For many, including Grade 2 students, reading 13 books per day may be unrealistic. Then again, would listening to books on tape or books in languages other than English count?

Model Text 2: Social Media Etiquette

The following model text could be considered an advice column or a blog that is designed to inform middle school students, who most likely are familiar with texting and/or emailing. We suggest that you invite students to analyze and comment as well as elaborate this excerpt, extending the text by adding their personal experiences and sharing their comments with classmates. Their reactions, captured in a journal or self-reflection tool, can become the basis for academic languaging.

Do you spend a lot of time on social media every day? Using social media can be fun, but you also should be careful. Don't let people you don't know trick you! If someone you don't know contacts you via social media, you should be on alert. If necessary, report the information to a family member or your teacher.

Here are some ideas for what you should do and not do for texting, emailing, or using popular apps on social media. See if you agree with this advice for what you should and should not do.

- Do be careful before clicking links or downloading attachments from unknown sources.
- Do be aware of ads or pop-ups that sound too good to be true.
- Do be respectful and polite in what you say.

- *Don't share personal information like your address or phone number with anyone you don't know.*
- *Don't cyberbully or use hurtful language—think how you would feel if you received the message.*
- *Don't use the language you use with friends with your teachers.*

You should always take the time to reread what you write. In that way, you have a second chance to make sure that information is what you want to send. Remember, your online behavior is your responsibility!

There are various ways to deconstruct model texts. Generally, our approach is to dissect the text according to the four dimensions of language starting with the largest chunk of language—discourse, followed by sentences, words/phrases, and, if present, symbols—always keeping in mind the overall theme and context. For example, after reading or reacting to this model text on social media, students may decide to

- produce a classroom or schoolwide policy or guidelines on social media etiquette;
- create a slogan or campaign about social media and display it throughout the community;
- design a mini video for the school website; or
- collect evidence of dos and don'ts from social media posts and offer feedback to classmates.

At other times, such as in Chapter 6, we analyze the text by asking a series of questions to stimulate discussion. These questions can also spark deep thinking and appeal to you and your students to take action in their classrooms, schools, or communities.

As academic language is the basis for academic languaging, we reiterate what we have said: "Discourse is the overarching dimension or umbrella which helps shape the types of sentence structures that, in turn, dictate the most appropriate words and phrases" (Gottlieb & Ernst-Slavit, 2014, p. 6). In other words, the discourse dimension provides the context for learning, so we begin there. Briefly, here is how the model text on social media etiquette might be deconstructed.

Discourse

Relating advice for engaging in social media in this model text is direct and concise with a consistently clear organization. Active voice adds to the cohesion of the text and the message it relays. The register of this piece is rather informal, appealing to students and giving credible guidance to them.

Sentences

The opening question is a stimulus for reading the remaining text, which assumes that the answer is "Of course!" It is followed by a series of bulleted sentences that form a list, reinforcing the message of what to do and not to do. It is not an argument as a position is not taken; rather, this model text elaborates both the positive and negative aspects of using social media. Note the use of imperatives or commands at the beginning of sentences.

Words/Phrases

Several phrases are interesting: The collective noun *social media*, for example, is used in conjunction with the singular verb *is*. In addition, *second chance* is used to mean "another try"; although you may never be given a "first chance," you may give something a "first try." As a phrase, "dos and don'ts" is a collocation; one would never say "don'ts and dos." "Pop-ups" have a specific meaning on smartphones or computer screens, where ads have become so prevalent; "clicking links" and "downloading" also specify actions one takes with a computer.

In this opening chapter we present three model texts. The third model text is an example of another current hot topic that middle and high schoolers (and their teachers) are grappling with—how to deal with AI.

Model Text 3: Is Artificial Intelligence Biased Against Multilingual Students?

Artificial intelligence (AI) has become part of life. It has advantages and disadvantages for students, including multilingual multicultural learners. First read the disadvantages and then the advantages to decide the position you might take.

Beware, AI can be biased against some students, so you should always approach its use with care. AI systems can unknowingly be prejudiced that can lead to misperceptions and misguided conclusions. The following argument points out the potential harm of this emerging technology.

1. If the data used to train AI models are not understood, then AI will learn and reproduce those biases. For example, if the information indicates that students from certain backgrounds are at a deficit or disadvantage, AI might mistakenly make similar predictions.

2. *If multilingual leaners are not proportionally represented in AI systems, there will be an imbalance or misrepresentation of information. This will lead to inaccurately portraying the students' experiences and perspectives. Not including the complete picture can lead to misinterpretations about different languages and cultures.*

3. *If schools overemphasize the value of AI, it will lead to a loss of confidence in human judgment. The overreliance on what AI produces can lead to inappropriate conclusions about students. This mistake could cause inappropriate high-stakes decisions, such as placing students in special services.*

On the other hand, AI can potentially be an empowering tool for students. Rather than being viewed as potentially biased, the following argument shows how these new technologies can be beneficial for multilingual learners.

1. *AI can power tutorial programs adaptive to individual learning preferences and paces. They can detect and adjust the amount of student engagement.*

2. *AI can promote interaction between students or between students and teachers, thus serving as a source of feedback for instruction and assessment.*

3. *AI can help empower multilingual communities through language translation (although with caution). Thus AI may enhance students' and families' access to information and communication.*

As a student, you and your teachers should be cautious of the pros (advantages) and cons (disadvantages) of using AI. It is going to be part of your life, and you should be aware of its potential, both beneficial and harmful. The sooner you understand its power, the better!

Academic language describes complex concepts, thinking processes, and abstract ideas and relationships that can only be captured through discourse. Here is where we begin our analysis of the model text, followed by sentences and words/phrases.

Discourse

As AI is such a new field of inquiry for students (and teachers), students can self-appoint themselves as ethnographers or data collectors to gain a better sense of AI uses among their classmates and in the community. The discourse of this model text is organized around argumentation; there are claims and counterclaims for each position, each with reasons and evidence.

Sentences

At the sentence level, we see three pros and three cons to AI. Students might create a point-counterpoint for each statement. Conditional sentences that all begin with "If" express potential harm from AI while those points that state its potential benefits all begin with "AI can."

Words/Phrases

Students may not be well versed in "artificial intelligence" and how it might compare with "intelligence." In arguing, the phrase "on the other hand" triggers a transition to a contradiction as does "rather than." Also, you might consider having a discussion with your students about "bias"—what it means to them and examples from home and community. Finally, generating examples of "high-stakes decisions" should be a lively topic for students to discuss.

We close this chapter with a table, one that is illustrative of how you might envision linguistic and cultural sustainability across curriculum, instruction, and classroom assessment as a requisite for multilingual learners' engagement in academic languaging. Applying Table 1.6, you might think of ways to center multilingual learners and infuse academic languaging into curricular or interdisciplinary projects with your grade-level or department teams, always including student voice in the process.

Table 1.6 Ideas for Designing Linguistic and Culturally Sustaining Curriculum, Instruction, and Assessment With Embedded Academic Languaging

CENTERING MULTILINGUAL LEARNERS BY HAVING STUDENTS . . .	EXTENSION TO ACADEMIC LANGUAGING: WHAT ACTIONS CAN MULTILINGUAL LEARNERS TAKE?
1. Create individual portraits of their linguistic, cultural, and experiential histories, conceptual understandings, literacies, language use, and multimodal preferences	
2. Brainstorm or modify themes and essential questions with teachers based on student, family, and community resources	
3. Co-construct integrated learning goals with teachers that weave content, language, and multimodalities along with criteria for success	

(Continued)

(Continued)

CENTERING MULTILINGUAL LEARNERS BY HAVING STUDENTS . . .	EXTENSION TO ACADEMIC LANGUAGING: WHAT ACTIONS CAN MULTILINGUAL LEARNERS TAKE?
4. Design end-of-unit products, projects, and/or performances with student and family connections	
5. Choose their language(s) for interaction and expression along with multimodal representation	
6. Self- and peer assess by analyzing, interpreting, and reporting evidence for learning against a project's criteria for success	
7. Give concrete timely feedback along the way to classmates and respond to that of teachers and peers	

Adapted from Gottlieb (2024, p. 175)

This resource is available for download at https://companion.corwin.com/courses/Academic-Languaging.

Stop and Think

Linguistically and Culturally Relevant Materials for Multilingual Learners

To some extent, the instructional models in which multilingual learners participate influence the approaches, content, and languages of curricular materials. No matter the instructional design and content area, multilingual learners should have access to materials and resources in their multiple languages that reflect their cultures and interests. To what extent do you feel your instructional materials represent your multilingual learners? To what extent do your instructional materials for multilingual learners interweave content and language? What other resources or modalities might improve students' accessibility? One organization dedicated to improving the quality of instructional materials for multilingual learners in English and other languages is the English Learners Success Forum (see www.elsuccessforum.org/about).

Chapter Summary

In this first chapter, we lay the groundwork for converting notions of academic language to academic languaging through actions of multilingual learners and their teachers. Basically, we center multilingual learners' ways of acting, thinking, interacting, valuing, and believing that they gain at home, at school, and in the community. Through analysis of model texts, we illustrate how to make the dimensions of language come to life to promote student engagement. We encourage students to employ their linguistic prowess and contribute their cultural perspectives to gain agency and autonomy. In essence, we envision academic languaging as a humanizing activity where multilingual learners develop relationships with peers and teachers, apply technology to advance learning, and use language and multimodalities to build their identities and make their marks in the world.

Extensions

For Reflection

1. In this introductory chapter, we wish to dispel the myth that academic language is confined to content area literacy and learning in school as it is just as present in students' homes and communities. As an extension, we focus on academic languaging, where students are encouraged to take action based on their beliefs and convictions verified through inquiry and exploration. In reflecting, we ask, "How have your views of academic language shifted, especially for multilingual learners, based on claims, reasoning, and evidence you have witnessed? How might you define academic languaging as a viable means of pursuing student learning?"
2. Reflect on your own academic languaging throughout the day, including time spent in your home and community. How might you describe the totality of your academic languaging and the actions you have taken? How does your everyday life shape the way you use language beyond the school setting?

For Action

1. Since academic languaging is tied to taking action, this last segment of the chapter is an opportunity to extend your thinking and that of others who work with multilingual

learners. How might you move away from a historically dichotomous concept, often presented as academic language versus social language, to introduce one based on language inquiry? How might you introduce academic languaging to your professional learning community and others in your school building or district? How might you include other educators, such as counselors, specials, coaches, or paraprofessionals, in the discussion? How might you also be more accepting of multilingual learners and families as members of and contributors to educational decision making?

2. You might consider engaging in collaborative action research to evaluate your potential change in practice as you embark upon enacting more inquiry-based strategies with your students. In this chapter, we have shown how information and communication technologies have sparked transformation and innovation through AI, how multimodalities have opened doors for students by increasing their access to content and showing evidence for learning, and how multilingualism is at the heart of multilingual learners' identities. Additionally, we have laid out a set of strategies that contextualize academic languaging for classroom use. You might wish to select one or two ideas, formulate some questions, investigate their usability for you and your students, and reflect on their potential impact.

Resources

In revisiting academic language to help formulate academic languaging, the following resources might prove helpful in representing and contrasting varying views and frameworks. You might wish to revisit these broad concepts throughout the book as the basis for discussion and to ground your thinking.

- **CALP vs. BICS** (cognitive academic language proficiency [CALP]) vs. social language (basic interpersonal communication skills [BICS]):

Cummins, J. (1981). Four misconceptions about language proficiency in bilingual education. *NABE Journal*, *5*(3), 31–45.

Cummins, J. (2008). BICS and CALP: Empirical and theoretical status of the distinction. In B. Street & N. H. Hornberger (Eds.), *Encyclopedia of language and education: Vol. 2. Literacy* (2nd ed., pp. 71–83). Springer Science.

- **Systemic functional linguistics**—language as a social meaning-making system:

Gibbons, P. (2009). *English learners, academic literacy, and thinking: Learning in the challenge zone*. Heinemann.

Halliday, M. A. K., & Martin, J. R. (1993). *Writing science: Literacy and discursive power*. University of Pittsburgh Press.

Schleppegrell, M. J. (2004). *The language of schooling: A functional linguistics perspective*. Erlbaum.

- **Sociocultural perspectives**—language as a social interactive activity:

Gee, J. P. (2004). *Situated language and learning: A critique of traditional schooling*. Routledge.

Heath, S. B. (1983). *Ways with words: Language, life and work in communities and classrooms*. Cambridge University Press.

- **Language as social action:**

García, O., & Kleifgen, J. A. (2019). Translanguaging and literacies. *Reading Research Quarterly*, *55*(4), 553–571.

García, O., & Sylvan, C. E. (2011). Pedagogies and practices in multilingual classrooms. *The Modern Language Journal*, *95*(3), 385–400.

Walqui, A., & van Lier, L. (2010). *Scaffolding the academic success of adolescent English language learners: A pedagogy of promise*. WestEd.

2 Anchors for Teaching Multilingual Learners

Introduction

"I'm not sure what the problem is. These kids can't speak well in English or Spanish. Rather than teaching them both languages, we should just focus on English."

—Middle school teacher

The opening quotation, from a middle school teacher, exemplifies a narrow, monolithic view of what it means to speak a language. When students' language proficiency is assessed with standardized tests that focus on adherence to rigid, discrete systems rather than authentic communication, the results often reflect low proficiency across all languages. This creates significant educational challenges for bilingual students who, despite their multilingual abilities, are deemed not proficient in any language.

A contrasting perspective comes from Isabella, a bilingual second-grade teacher in a dual Spanish–English classroom (as cited in Pratt & Ernst-Slavit, 2019, pp. 361, 364):

> In a [dual language] program, the kids are very in tune with [Spanish], that's all they speak. They have been speaking it since kindergarten. There is more confidence in them, they don't fear what they say, they are not afraid to say it. . . .
> I know that immersion is the best avenue for all kids, it is going to benefit all kids but more so [kids learning English]. . . .
> When you empower them and they know their voice, they know their worth.

This teacher's compelling rationale for teaching content in Spanish was to empower students to recognize their voices and sense of self-worth.

The importance of adopting asset-based perspectives—acknowledging students' linguistic and cultural repertoires and connecting with their lived experiences—cannot be overstated. The teacher's affirmation of students' use of Spanish reflects an understanding that education should not only draw from students' home languages and cultural experiences but also maintain and nurture them.

In this classroom, students engaged in flexible language practices, creating a bilingual, biliterate, and bicultural community. Languaging involved students drawing from their full linguistic repertoire across varying levels of proficiency (Pratt & Ernst-Slavit, 2019) as they engaged in academic work.

A focus on languaging that integrates students' unique linguistic trajectories with culturally and linguistically sustaining instruction has the potential to bridge content learning and language development. By doing so, students gain meaningful access to the curriculum, optimizing their opportunities for academic success.

Our work in this volume builds upon 10 key anchors that both guide and provide a framework for engaging with multilingual learners. These anchors, explored in detail throughout this chapter, shape our understanding of academic languaging as an ongoing process rooted in the lived experiences of multilingual learners and their interactions with others and various text forms. The 10 anchors are listed as follows:

1. Valuing and maintaining students' multiple languages and cultures
2. Learning from our students
3. Connecting to students' lives and experiences
4. Becoming aware of the language we use
5. Making language visible to students
6. Using linguistically and culturally sustaining practices
7. Carving opportunities for translanguaging
8. Developing linguistic and cultural consciousness through metalinguistic and metacultural awareness
9. Strengthening language development within content learning
10. Applying academic languaging as a transformative priority

1. Valuing and Maintaining Students' Multiple Languages and Cultures

A very important anchor that is the North Star for the rest is recognizing, capturing, and embedding the strengths of multilingual learners into teaching and learning. Other principles of language development to adhere to include the following:

- Multilingual learners come to school with resources and assets.
- Multilingual learners understand that language use is variable, fluid, and dynamic.
- Multilingual learners develop language through meaningful interaction (e.g., Weiss & Sandstead, 2020; WIDA, 2023).
- Multilingual learners use and develop language to interpret and present different perspectives, engage in relationship building, and affirm their identities.
- Multilingual learners use language to access information, ideas, and concepts from a variety of multimodal sources.
- Multilingual learners use their full linguistic resources, including translanguaging practices, to enhance their language development and deepen their learning.
- Multilingual learners develop metacognitive, metalinguistic, and metacultural awareness as they become effective language users (e.g., Gottlieb, 2021a; WIDA, 2019).

Academic languaging, as an extension of each of these principles, accelerates the process of language development by enabling students to take initiatives based on their choices and meaningfully engage in grade-level activities with their peers.

2. Learning From Our Students

Although many school districts and state agencies have developed various surveys, protocols, and intake forms to gather basic information about multilingual learners (e.g., home language surveys, state language and literacy screeners), this information may not always be available when needed or sufficient to fully understand the strengths and needs of these students.

Getting to know your students should begin on the first day—or even earlier, if possible, by meeting them (and their families) before the academic year starts—and should continue throughout the year. Understanding multilingual students' educational trajectories and current experiences can significantly impact their academic success.

Table 2.1 outlines key information that teachers can gather, along with words of caution to ensure sensitivity when requesting information from students and their families. Some may feel uncomfortable or intimidated by certain questions. It is essential to reassure families that the purpose of gathering this information is to provide the best possible educational opportunities for the student. Information in Table 2.1 can be collected through home visits, autobiographical activities (e.g., a math autobiography as described in Chapter 4), surveys, or meetings with students, guardians, and school staff, such as a bilingual liaison, a translator, or an English language learning specialist. Additionally, in the **Look Closer** box, there is a list of resources for learning about your students.

Table 2.1 Types of Student Information and Words of Caution

TYPE OF STUDENT INFORMATION	WORDS OF CAUTION
Student's name Learn the correct spelling and pronunciation of students' names; do not Anglicize or change names (e.g., calling your Laotian student "Dee" instead of "Deesabun"), unless a student chooses a different name.	In most Spanish-speaking countries students use two last names (e.g., Marina Astorga Retamozo), so inquire if the family and records use one or both last names.
Birth country and other places of residence Learn about students' country of birth and, for some students (e.g., refugees), their recent place of residence.	Avoid assumptions about students' nationality, immigration status, cultural affiliation, and religion.
Family history Who lives with your student? Are siblings also in the school? Does the student have responsibilities such as caring for younger siblings or relatives? Does the student have a job? Is there someone in the home who speaks English and can act as the main point of contact?	Avoid asking direct questions about these topics to students. Preferably, ask the guardians or school liaison. Keep in mind that some students may not live with their parents or their siblings.
Home language(s) You can find some information in the home language survey (required when registering a new student). In addition, you may want to inquire about (a) what languages are spoken at home, in the community, and with whom; and (b) at what age the student started speaking the home language.	Be careful not to prioritize English. The importance of the home language cannot be overestimated. A student's identity and early learning is rooted in that language.
Prior schooling Inquire about students' experiences in schools in the United States and abroad and if there were interruptions in their schooling. Ask about the students' favorite content areas and activities and schooling in their country of origin, if applicable.	Multilingual students come from very diverse backgrounds and may have different norms and expectations regarding education, communication, and interaction with school personnel.

(Continued)

(Continued)

TYPE OF STUDENT INFORMATION	WORDS OF CAUTION
English language proficiency Students' enrollment file should have this information in each of the main language domains (i.e., listening, speaking, reading, and writing). If information is unavailable, talk with your school/district English as a second language (ESL) or bilingual specialist.	Notice that students can be at different levels of language proficiency in each language domain.
Literacy Knowing students' literacy development in the home language is crucial. Identify (a) what literacy practices are found in the home and community (e.g., family members take turns in reading the Qur'an); and (b) what possible challenges might affect reading in English (e.g., a different alphabet).	Beware that most students' content area knowledge and literacy is often assessed in English, not in the home language; thus, you are obtaining insufficient information on which to make important decisions.
Talents and interests Learning about students' talents and interests is pivotal in making instruction relevant and meaningful. Via questionnaires, interviews with students and their families, home visits, and observation, teachers can learn much about what students like and already know.	Beware of your unconscious biases or assumptions about multilingual students' abilities or interests based on stereotypes or limited knowledge of their languages and cultures.
Stressors Some students may have experienced trauma, war, interrupted schooling, or stressful journeys. Other students may feel unsafe due to current immigration policies. Work with the family, language specialist, or family liaison to find out about these issues.	Students and their families may not feel comfortable discussing their schooling experiences with teachers or other school staff due to a lack of trust or fear of being judged. In those cases, do not insist and go to another topic.

Look Closer

Learning About Your Students

¡Colorín colorado! (colorincolorado.org) has an array of resources regarding thoughtful ways of learning about your students, including home visits. In addition, check the following resources:

Evans, M. P. (2013). Educating preservice teachers for family, school, and community engagement. *Teaching Education, 24*(2), 123–133.

Johnson, E. J. (2014). From the classroom to the living room: Eroding academic inequities through home visits. *Journal of School Leadership, 24*(2), 357–385.

Mancenido, Z., & Pello, R. (2020). What do we know about how to effectively prepare teachers to engage with families? *School Community Journal, 30*(2), 9–38.

Newcomer, S. N. (2017). Investigating the power of authentically caring teacher-student relationships for Latinx students. *Journal of Latinos and Education, 17*(2), 179–193. https://doi.org/10.1080/15348431.2017.1310104

Newcomer, S. N., & Ernst-Slavit, G. (in press). ¡Juntos logramos más!: Apoyando a futuros docentes a promover la participación familiar y comunitaria. In E. J. Johnson & L. A. Murillo (Eds.), *Alianzas familiares en la educación multilingüe / Family alliances in multilingual education*. Information Age.

Newcomer, S. N., Ernst-Slavit, G., Morrison, S. J., Morrison, J. A., Lightner, L. K., Ardasheva, Y., & Carbonneau, K. J. (in press). "An important piece of the puzzle": Preparing future teachers for family and community engagement. *Teaching Education*.

3. Connecting to Students' Lives and Experiences

Utilizing asset-based perspectives—building on students' individual, familial, and community strengths and interests—helps students answer the question "So what?" or "Why is this important?" Academic connections are also essential, focusing on what students already know, what they want and need to learn, and their prior schooling experiences.

Our work draws from two frameworks: *funds of knowledge* (Moll et al., 1992) and *community cultural wealth* (Yosso, 2005). Both frameworks emphasize recognizing and leveraging the resources found in linguistically, culturally, and ethnically diverse communities.

The funds of knowledge (FoK) framework focuses on individuals' historically accumulated skills, experiences, and bodies of knowledge (González et al., 2005; Vélez-Ibáñez & Greenberg, 1992) as valuable resources for learning. These "funds" encompass a broad range of strategies, skills, and knowledge that families use to support their well-being.

For example, during a home visit to Oksana's house, her teacher, Ms. Somera, discovered the various funds of knowledge that Oksana, a quiet fifth grader, possesses. Oksana takes on numerous household responsibilities, such as cooking, baking, cleaning, and helping her younger siblings with their schoolwork. At home, she primarily speaks Ukrainian, translating school communications for her parents, assisting them with paying bills, and even translating during medical appointments, including those concerning her mother's health.

Ms. Somera also learned that Oksana has developed strong technological skills from helping her younger siblings use school-issued tablets and laptops. She was instrumental in setting up a new computer at home and often consults with the school's tech specialist for guidance. Oksana's mother (with the help of a translator) shared that, in addition to technology, Oksana enjoys science and frequently reads about and conducts experiments. When helping her mother bake large batches of *vatrushka* (sweet buns) and traditional black bread to sell at a local bakery, Oksana converts ingredient measurements between metric and U.S. customary units, treating it as an investigation. During the visit, the family also discussed their connection to conflict-affected areas and how the war was impacting them, prompting Ms. Somera to explore appropriate district support. Inspired by what she learned, Ms. Somera created a plan to build on Oksana's strengths (see Table 2.2).

Table 2.2 Oksana's Funds of Knowledge Inventory

HOME AND COMMUNITY PRACTICES	FUNDS OF KNOWLEDGE	CLASSROOM APPLICATIONS
Oksana regularly translates between English and Ukrainian.	Language and Being Bilingual	Encourage dual language work and access to materials written in Ukrainian to foster language and literacy development in both languages.
Oksana is an experienced babysitter and school tutor for her siblings.	Childcare and Tutoring	Enlist Oksana as a tutor for the recently initiated cross-age peer tutoring art program.
Oksana helps her mother convert measurements from the metric system.	Economics	This skill is perfect for a math unit on conversions and fractions.
Oksana has accumulated tons of experience supporting her siblings and family with their iPads and computers.	Technology	Since Oksana is not afraid of technology, we can encourage her to use multimedia and gamification in her projects.
Oksana helps her mother bake goods to sell at the neighborhood bakery.	Cooking	Since Oksana treats baking as a science investigation, we can use her leadership during our nutrition unit.

Similarly, the community cultural wealth (CCW) framework aligns with many of the same principles as FoK. CCW highlights the various forms of wealth present within communities of color, which are often viewed through a deficit lens focused on what these communities lack rather than what they possess (Yosso, 2005). This framework helps explain the systemic disparities that result in lower academic outcomes for students of color compared to their white peers (Yosso, 2005).

CCW, grounded in critical race theory, challenges racism in American society (Solórzano, 1997) by rejecting dominant ideologies and white privilege, instead affirming the lived experiences of people of color. As Yosso (2005) explains, "community cultural wealth is an array of knowledge, skills, abilities, and contacts possessed and utilized by Communities of Color to survive" (p. 77). The six forms of CCW are summarized in Table 2.3.

Table 2.3 Forms of Community Cultural Wealth

CAPITAL	DEFINITION
Aspirational Capital	The ability to hold on to hope when confronted by structured inequality and without apparent means to make those dreams a reality
Linguistic Capital	The intellectual and social prowess needed to communicate in more than one language or style
Familial Capital	The cultural knowledge rooted in awareness of, respect for, and connection to one's family, community, and cultural heritage
Social Capital	The networks of people and community members that help people navigate through social institutions
Navigational Capital	The ability to traverse social institutions, especially those that historically have tended to exclude people of color
Resistant Capital	The awareness of the structures of oppression and privilege and the ability to challenge, resist, and oppose those structures of inequality and oppression

Adapted from Yosso, 2005.

Ultimately, when teachers take the time to learn about the knowledge, skills, abilities, and networks of their students and communities, they can build these forms of capital into curriculum, instruction, and classroom assessment. This array of strategies empowers minoritized students with the strength and tools to persevere and succeed in school.

Look Closer

Funds of Knowledge and Community Cultural Wealth

For more information about the funds of knowledge and community cultural wealth frameworks and their application in educational contexts, see the following resources:

Ernst-Slavit, G., Newcomer, S. N., Morrison, S. J., Lightner, L. K., Morrison, J. A., Ardasheva, Y., & Carbonneau, K. J. (2022). Latina paraeducators' stories of resistance, resilience, and adaptation in an alternative route to teaching program. *Journal of Career Development, 49*(5), 1021–1038. https://doi.org/10.1177/08948453211005000

Johnson, E., & Johnson, A. (2016). Enhancing academic investment through home-school connections and building on ELL students' scholastic funds of knowledge. *Journal of Language and Literacy Education, 12*(1), 103–121.

McDonald, A. (2018, February 18). *How to use funds of knowledge in your classroom and create better connections.* No Time for Flash Cards. https://www.notimeforflashcards.com/2018/02/funds-of-knowledge.html

Moll, L. C., Amanti, C., Neff, D. & Gonzalez, N. (1992). Funds of knowledge for teaching: Using a qualitative approach to connect homes and classrooms. *Theory Into Practice, 31*(2), 132–141. https://doi.org/10.1080/00405849209543534

Yosso, T. J. (2005). Whose culture has capital? A critical race theory discussion of community cultural wealth. *Race, Ethnicity, and Education, 8*(1), 69–91. https://doi.org/10.1080/1361332052000341006

4. Becoming Aware of the Language We Use

Classroom discussions, in particular teacher talk, influence and shape the values, beliefs, and understandings of students. According to Harvard Professor Courtney Cazden (1988), "we have to consider how the words spoken in classrooms affect the outcomes of education: how observable classroom discourse affects the unobservable thought processes of each of the participants, and thereby the nature of what all students learn" (p. 99).

The language awareness movement has its roots in the United Kingdom beginning in the early 1980s (Andrews, 2007; Granville, 2003; Janks, 2000). Basically, language awareness refers to the development of an enhanced consciousness of and sensitivity to the forms and functions of language (Carter, 2003).

Being aware of the language we use in our teaching involves (1) acknowledging the implicit and explicit ideologies and power structures inherent in language, (2) understanding that the use of such language, even unintentionally, can and does legitimate and reproduce social inequalities, and (3) striving to become agents of long-term change in society (Clark et al., 1990). Teachers who demonstrate cultural and linguistic awareness are not only aware of the ideologies that shape language but are also aware of and exercise great care in their own use of language (Clark et al., 1990). Consider the words of Lake (1990), a member of the Cherokee and Seneca tribes, to the teacher of his son, Wind-Wolf:

> What you say and what you do in the classroom, what you teach and how you teach it, and what you don't say and don't teach will have a significant effect on the potential success or failure of my child. (p. 53)

"An Indian Father's Plea" by Robert Lake (1990), also known as Medicine Grizzlybear, is a powerful letter written to a teacher by a Native American father advocating for his son Wind-Wolf's education and cultural identity. It provides insight into the challenges faced by Indigenous students in predominantly Western educational settings, which may be similar to some of the challenges multilingual students face. The letter can be found at https://nisnresourcehub.org/wp-content/uploads/2021/01/An-Indian-Fathers-Plea-1.pdf.

Look Closer

"Observing" Classroom Talk

Educators can learn a great deal by "observing" and evaluating their own language use. For example, by audio or video recording themselves, classroom teachers can assess the types of questions they ask and how often they ask them. Do they provide enough wait time? (One to two seconds is insufficient.) Teachers can also determine how they model the language they want students to learn and determine what opportunities they provide for students to participate orally in class. For more information on tracking classroom talk, refer to the following resources:

Ernst-Slavit, G., & Pratt, K. L. (2017). Teacher questions: Learning the discourse of science in a linguistically diverse elementary classroom. *Linguistics and Education*, *40*, 1–10. https://doi.org/10.1016/j.linged.2017.05.005

Ernst-Slavit, G., & Wenger, K. J. (2016). Surrounded by water: Talking to learn in today's classrooms. *Kappa Delta Pi Record*, *52*(1), 28–34. https://doi.org/10.1080/00228958.2016.1123042

Kelly, L. B., Ogden, M. K., & Moses, L. (2019). Collaborative conversations: Speaking and listening in the primary grades. *Young Children*, *74*(1), 30–36. https://www.naeyc.org/resources/pubs/yc/mar2019/speaking-listening-primary-grades

Mason, M. R., & Ernst-Slavit, G. (2010). Representations of Native Americans in elementary school social studies: A critical look at instructional language. *Multicultural Education*, *18*, 10–17. https://files.eric.ed.gov/fulltext/EJ916841.pdf

Walqui, A., & Heritage, M. (2018). Meaningful classroom talk: Supporting English learners' oral language development. *The American Educator*, *42*, 18. https://www.aft.org/ae/fall2018/walqui_heritage

5. Making Language Visible to Students

Expert language users (e.g., teachers, instructors, and advanced students) view language as a transparent medium for communication. In contrast, inexperienced language users (e.g., less advanced students and language learners) struggle not only with the abstract content they need to learn but also with acquiring a language they often find obscure. The language used by teachers in content area classrooms and found in

K–12 materials, assignments, and assessments is often characterized by specific grammatical structures, language forms, vocabulary, and conventions unique to each discipline that should be accentuated as part of language learning.

"Mainstream teachers must learn to look at rather than through language used in the classroom in order to understand the linguistic demands of their content areas and, in response, carefully structure learning tasks according to [multilingual learners'] needs."

—Pauline Gibbons (2002, p. 158)

Additionally, multilingual learners may face challenges when teachers use "tricky" language, such as idiomatic expressions (e.g., "learn this by heart" or "the assignment is a walk in the park"), culturally specific terms (i.e., Americana) referring to U.S. history and folklore (e.g., *stars and stripes* or *Old Glory*), homonyms (e.g., *accept* vs. *except* or *blue* vs. *blew*), slang (e.g., *legit* or *bro*), and text abbreviations (e.g., *BTW* or *idk*). Teachers should take time to allow students to interact with each other and play with language.

To further illustrate this, consider Figure 2.1, "Quilt With a House," by American quilter Sandra Q. Miller. The quilt depicts a house with a yard beneath a blue sky with scattered clouds. If observers are asked who lives in this house, most may not know the answer. Some might search for clues and describe the quilt's elements—such as the blue roof, yellow path, six trees, birdbath, white picket fence, and yellow floral border—but still remain uncertain. However, a quilter would likely answer, "A grandmother lives in this house," recognizing the border's flower pattern as Grandmother's Flower Garden.

This example highlights the importance of recognizing specific features to unlock meaning. Just as identifying the Grandmother's Flower Garden pattern provides insight into the quilt's narrative, making linguistic features visible helps students understand how these features contribute to broader comprehension. For instance, students learn that an interrogation mark signals a question. Similarly, they can learn that phrases like "Once upon a time" or "A long, long time ago" signal that the text will present a story with characters, setting, and plot; in other words, students will gain insight into different literary genres.

Figure 2.1 Quilt With a House

Source: Quilt made by Sandra Q. Miller. Used with permission.

Stop and Think

"Once Upon a Time" in Other Languages

Did you know that variations of the phrase "Once upon a time" (2025; see also InDifferentLanguages.com, 2025) have appeared in different languages since the 14th century? For instance, Charles Perrault used "Il était une fois" in **French**, while Hans Christian Andersen's stories were translated to include "Der var engang"

("There was once") from **Danish**. Similarly, the Brothers Grimm used "Es war einmal" in **German**, meaning "Once there was." This storytelling convention extends to many other languages: in **Spanish**, "Había una vez" ("There was once"); in **Polish**, "Za siódmą górą, za siódmym lasem" ("Beyond seven mountains, beyond seven forests"); in **Filipino**, "Noong unang panahon" ("At the beginning of time"); in **Quechua**, "Huk kutis kaq kasqa" ("There was once"); in **Swahili**, "Hapo zamani za kale" ("A long time ago"); in **Persian**, "Ruzi uzgāri" ("Someday, sometime"); in **Finnish**, "Olipa kerran" ("Once there was"); in **Hindi**, "Kisī zamāne meṃ" ("In one era"); in **Chinese**, "Hěnjiǔ hěnjiǔ yǐqián" ("A very very long time ago"); and in **Gujarati**, "Vaṣô pahelã" ("A long back"). This universal opening formula evokes timelessness and introduces audiences to the narrative world of folktales and fables.

Educators must ensure students have access to disciplinary content while explicitly teaching the academic writing, reading strategies, oral practices, and multimodal activities essential for multilingual learners to engage with academic languaging. As highlighted in Chapter 1, a key strategy for making language visible is through the use of model texts. Model texts allow teachers to anticipate potential linguistic or sociocultural challenges and demonstrate how particular language features operate within a given context.

6. Using Linguistically and Culturally Sustaining Practices

We draw on the concept of culturally sustaining pedagogy, or CSP (Paris & Alim, 2014), which aims to "perpetuate and foster . . . linguistic, literate, and cultural pluralism as part of the democratic project of schooling and as a necessary response to demographic and social change" (p. 88). According to Mizell (2020), language pedagogy that offers explicit linguistic tools "promotes and apprentices youth and [educators] to become reflective, critical, and thoughtful architects and remixers of languages and literacies" (p. 87). This approach provides access not only to schooling but also to an evolving society.

In essence, CSP reimagines multicultural education by combining identity exploration and affirmation with youth agency (Paris & Alim, 2017). It requires more than teaching practices that are merely responsive or relevant to students' cultural and linguistic experiences. Instead, educators must support students in "sustaining the cultural and linguistic competence of their communities while simultaneously offering access to dominant cultural competence" (Paris & Alim, 2017, p. 4).

Table 2.4 illustrates this shift from deficit-based views of students' languages and cultures to asset-based approaches that honor and build upon the strengths of students, their families, and their communities.

Table 2.4 From Deficit- to Asset-Based Approaches

APPROACH	GOAL	VIEW OF HOME AND COMMUNITY CULTURE
Deficit	To eradicate home and community practices representing multiple languages and cultures and replace them with "superior" monoglossic practices	Bankrupt of value
Difference	To link "dominant" practices without regard for maintaining home and community practices	Equal to, but different from, practices of value for teaching and learning
Asset-based	To provide opportunities and access to dominant practices along with sustaining home and community practices	Resources to honor, explore, and build upon

Adapted from Paris, 2012, pp. 93–97.

CSP encourages students not only to draw from their cultural and linguistic experiences from home in school but also to maintain and nurture them. As educators, we must ask critical questions: *What do students already know? What are their strengths? What strengths do their families and communities possess? How can we connect to the strengths of our students and families?*

7. Carving Opportunities for Translanguaging

Developing bilingualism and biliteracy is an enriching process for multilingual learners who can interact in multiple languages with each other and dive deeply into learning. Let's remember that the root of translanguaging is languaging, the action on the part of multilingual learners of making sense of the world around them (Castro, 2020). In essence, translanguaging refers to the "complex languaging practices of bilinguals in actual communicative settings" (García, 2009, p. 45).

As the natural fluid and dynamic use of multiple languages, translanguaging is an authentic expression of bilingualism and biliteracy that is becoming more of an accepted instructional routine and communication mode for multilingual learners and their teachers across content areas. Three examples of translanguaing practices from different countries are presented in Figure 2.2.

Figure 2.2 Examples of Translanguaging From Different Countries and Contexts

San Diego, CA

Innsbruck, Austria

Oaxaca, México

Source: Photos by Margo Gottlieb

Furthermore, García and Kleifgen (2019) describe the connection of translanguaging to literacy as unbounded, fluid across languages, and empowering or agentive for participating multilingual learners. Translanguaging can play a critical role in shifting teachers' understanding of students' multiple languages and their linguistic capital. In gaining a multilingual perspective, translanguaging normalizes multilingual learners' linguistic resources and ultimately impacts how teachers design instruction (Ascenzi-Moreno, 2024).

In the following two vignettes from work by Pratt and Ernst-Slavit (2019, p. 366), Isabella, whom we met earlier in the chapter, leads a small group of bilingual students in guided reading conducted in English. Although English is the language of instruction, Isabella strategically uses Spanish to affirm students' responses and manage the conversation.

Vignette 1

Teacher	What do you see there, what are these called?
Liliana	Feathers
Mario	Plumas
Teacher	Very nice, yes, plumas

Vignette 2

Teacher	Can someone tell me what the genre is? Sergio, ¿qué estás haciendo?
José	Estamos leyendo
Teacher	Oh, okay. Sit over there, honey. Yes dear, Liliana?
Liliana	Realistic fiction

In these vignettes, both teacher and students fluidly shift between English and Spanish while focusing on literacy in English. This bilingual interaction allows students to think across multiple languages simultaneously, using their home language as a tool for acquiring academic content. These examples illustrate the languaging practices of bilingual learners, who purposefully and adaptively construct meaning by engaging their full linguistic repertoires (García, 2009).

The next **Stop and Think** box asks you to contemplate your views on translanguaging—that is, whether it augments or detracts from teaching—and the different instructional models for multilingual learners. You may want to visit Table 2.6 in the Resources section at the end of this chapter to review the variety of instructional models and their features.

Stop and Think

Translanguaging: A Disruption or Enhancement for Multilingual Learners?

With a strong research base, the use of translanguaging, particularly in language and literacy classrooms, has shown to have positive effects for both teachers and students (Seltzer & de los Ríos, 2021). Bilingual and multilingual learners with their extensive language resources will naturally think in multiple languages, even mentally analyze and converse in their languages, no matter the language of instruction. Therefore, it is beneficial for educators and researchers to honor and invite "the silenced translanguaging" (the cognitive stimulation) and accept it as a valid mode of communication that is inherently part of multilingual learners' everyday language practices (García & Kleifgen, 2019).

However, not all educators are convinced of the benefits of translanguaging. Some believe that the strict separation of languages is required to promote language learning; others are of the conviction that translanguaging is a crutch or a compensatory strategy for students that is detrimental to their achievement (see Gottlieb, 2021b, for more information about these views). Thinking about one's control over translanguaging as a form of academic languaging, which position do you and your colleagues take, and how might you defend it? How might you convert your stance into a language policy or co-construct a policy with multilingual learners?

Given the growing acceptance and robust evidence of languaging across named languages, or translanguaging practices of multilingual learners, teachers and administrators need to determine their compatibility with dual language program models, especially if organized around specified percentages of language allocation (e.g., 80/10 or 50/50). Equally if not more important is extending a school's languaging policy to a classroom's translanguaging policy for multilingual learners. Some student-initiated literacy activities shared among multilingual learners in the same partner language that can be enhanced through translanguaging include the following:

- Asking and answering questions
- Joining in conversation with classmates
- Exchanging information or ideas with classmates
- Researching topics and taking notes
- Producing oral or written drafts

- Giving feedback to classmates
- Expressing emotionality to bilingual others
- Engaging in self- and peer assessment

An example of the natural flow of translanguaging by a bilingual storyteller is illustrated in the model text on Chicano Park in Chapter 3.

8. Developing Linguistic and Cultural Consciousness Through Metalinguistic and Metacultural Awareness

Academic languaging is never to be treated in isolation; rather, it is to be interwoven into the fabric of classroom life. As students become more aware of and exert their identities, they become critically conscious of the important role of language and culture in shaping who they are and how they exert their agency. Table 2.5 is a learner-centered rating scale intended for teachers to gauge the contributions of their multilingual learners to the linguistic and cultural sustainability of the classroom. Giving multilingual learners choices that tap their full linguistic and cultural repertoires leads to students who are confident self-sufficient learners.

Table 2.5 Linguistic and Cultural Accessibility for Multilingual Learners: A Rating Scale

Use this rating scale to ascertain the presence of linguistic and cultural sustainability across the curriculum according to your multilingual learners. You may also think of how this checklist can spur topics for students' social and emotional learning. Above all, you may wish to ask your older multilingual learners or have them respond to the questions read aloud.

DO LEARNERS HAVE OPPORTUNITIES TO . . .	YES	AT TIMES	NOT YET
Utilize digital texts and resources in multiple languages to validate or extend their thinking and perspectives?			
Connect their lived experiences and histories with text and other modes?			
Explore and critique stereotypes often held by the Anglocentric culture?			
Utilize images and narratives of multilingual identities and cultures from marginalized communities?			

DO LEARNERS HAVE OPPORTUNITIES TO . . .	YES	AT TIMES	NOT YET
Consider how different groups might respond when producing texts for a variety of audiences?			
Show pride in their languages and heritage?			
Heal from personal assaults or the damages from microagressions made on marginalized communities that are apparent in the curriculum?			

This resource is available for download at https://companion.corwin.com/courses/Academic-Languaging.

Metalinguistic and metacultural awareness is a unique quality of multilingual learners that combines to shape their identities and thus potentially impact their vision as language experts in academic languaging (Gottlieb, 2023). Having students become metalinguistically aware by consciously reflecting on and comparing expressions, feelings evoked, syntax (the structure), vocabulary (such as cognates), and even phonemes (the sounds of a language) across languages strengthens and deepens their knowledge of both languages. This knowledge can be brought to the analysis of model texts. In addition, with the gaining of acceptance of translanguaging among multilingual learners as part of the instructional routine, connections between languages are becoming part of pedagogy (García et al., 2017).

Stop and Think

Metalinguistic Awareness

The term *meta* comes from ancient Greek, meaning "beyond." In language learning, *meta* can be understood as moving beyond communication and meaning to focus on the underlying structures of language instead. For example, when a three-year-old says, "Yesterday I goed to the store," she intuitively has added *ed* to a word to refer to something she has done in the past. However, when her dad repeats back, "Oh, yesterday you went to the store," the child begins to learn the English grammar rule. This child is using metalinguistic awareness skills in both instances: to add the *ed*, which makes some words past tense, and to realize that in the case of the verb *to go* the past tense is different. Thus, metalinguistic awareness is the ability to recognize and analyze the underlying structure of language. It involves understanding rules and focusing on different elements of a sentence or word, such as its form or meaning.

Metacultural awareness is a companion to metalinguistic awareness. It refers to the ability to reflect on and understand cultural norms, values, and practices beyond one's own, thus enabling students (and others) to navigate and function competently in different cultural settings. Metacultural awareness also involves one's personal introspections of their cultural roots to uncover preconceptions and prejudices that might color their perspectives. Probing students' metalinguistic and metacultural awareness brings language and culture explicitly into the classroom. Most importantly, being sensitive to our cultural nature helps bring awareness to our own cultural identities and the acceptance of cultural differences.

9. Strengthening Language Development Within Content Learning

Simply stated, teachers must connect content and language in curriculum, instruction, and assessment for multilingual learners to optimize their access to and engage in learning. This interaction must be strategic and intentional, such as highlighted in the Big Ideas of WIDA's (2020, 2023) English and Spanish language development standards frameworks. The integration of content and language facilitates the enactment of academic languaging, enabling multilingual learners to gradually take control over their language use in content area classrooms.

An alternate strategy where language and content are juxtaposed in instructional and assessment planning are content and language objectives/learning targets, also a practice by teachers of multilingual learners. Understanding students' strengths and needs aids in designing content and language objectives that are relevant to their lives. Once content objectives for a lesson are identified, the next step is to ask, "What do my students need to do with language to accomplish the task and demonstrate their understanding?"

Said another way, content objectives identify *what* students should achieve by the end of the lesson, while language objectives specify *how* students will demonstrate their learning. The following are examples of content and language objectives for different subject areas, presented in a variety of formats. Examples of integrated learning targets that seamlessly combine content and language within a sociocultural context follow. You are welcome to use the format of your choice, as long as you are conscious of the close ties of content and language for teaching and learning.

Example 1: Science

CONTENT OBJECTIVE	LANGUAGE OBJECTIVE
Distinguish among igneous, sedimentary, and metamorphic rocks.	Speaking: Explain how igneous, sedimentary, and metamorphic rocks differ to a partner using compare and contrast language. Writing: Describe igneous, sedimentary, and metamorphic rocks and include a drawing of each type of rock.

INTEGRATED LEARNING TARGET
I can analyze the characteristics of the sample rocks I have collected and, with a partner, compare their similarities and differences using photos and explanations from online guides.

Example 2: Social Studies

CONTENT OBJECTIVE	LANGUAGE OBJECTIVE
I can create a timeline of my life.	Speaking: I can tell the events on my timeline to my classmates using sequential words: *first*, *next*, *last year*, *in the past*, and so on.

INTEGRATED LEARNING TARGET
Using my timeline, I can exchange information with a classmate (graphically, orally, or in writing), using sequential words to describe its events in chronological order.

Example 3: Language Arts

CONTENT OBJECTIVE	LANGUAGE OBJECTIVE
Students will be able to draft a conclusion paragraph for their expository essay.	Students use transitional phrases (e.g., *as a result*) in writing at the end of their essay.

INTEGRATED LEARNING TARGET
I can use one or multiple languages to express the final thoughts of my essay (orally or in writing) using transitional phrases to relate a family tradition.

Example 4: Mathematics

CONTENT OBJECTIVES	DIFFERENTIATED LANGUAGE OBJECTIVES	
Students will be able to solve word problems involving unit rates. Students will be able to justify their decisions based on unit rates in real-life scenarios (e.g., choosing which car to buy based on gas mileage in miles per gallon).	Language Objective: Levels 1–3	Compare choices based on real-life rate calculations using a graphic organizer and sentence starters (e.g., ________ is greater than ________).
	Language Objective: Levels 4–5	Critique choices based on others' mathematical reasoning from sample solutions to real-life rate problems.

INTEGRATED LEARNING TARGET
I can defend how I solve mathematical problems about cars related to my family's experiences either here or in their home countries (e.g., liters vs. gallons or kilometers vs. miles) using real-life scenarios and multimodal supports (e.g., calculators and graphic organizers).

Important to underscore in these examples is the need to set realistic expectations consonant with the students' cultures and experiences that encourage engagement yet challenge students in the learning process. Additionally, for multilingual learners, it is important to overlay principles of language development to better understand the interplay between the content areas and the language *for* the content areas (WIDA, 2020). Principles should be derived from a broad base—current research and theory about language learning, human development, and pedagogy—and highlight key concepts of students who are learning in one or multiple languages.

10. Applying Academic Languaging as a Transformative Priority

If *we* don't challenge the status quo regarding the improvement of educational opportunities for multilingual learners through equitable practices and policies, who will? And as educators, how might we accomplish this lofty goal through advocacy and assistance in shaping positive linguistic and cultural identities of our students? How might we, through deep knowledge of each of our students, facilitate multilingual learners' use and development of language to enhance and enrich their lives?

In this last but most important anchor, we wish to reiterate that academic languaging is equated with ensuring that our students gain confidence and agency, think for themselves, and put their thoughts into favorable actions at home, at school, and in their communities. By promoting student choice and voice, where curriculum, instruction, and classroom assessment are linguistic and culturally sustainable, we commit to linguistic fairness—cultivating and preserving learning environments where all languages and cultures are invited, represented, and respected. With academic languaging as a transformative imperative, let's apply Richard Ruiz's 1984 three-pronged policy plan to our educational system so that we move away from the paradigm of language as a *problem* to language as a *right* and *resource* and, in doing so, shift our mindset to center the assets of our multilingual learners.

Chapter Summary

In this chapter, we have explored 10 foundational anchors that provide both guidance and a framework for supporting multilingual learners. These anchors embody our understanding of academic languaging as an ongoing process grounded in the lived experiences of multilingual learners that is shaped by their interactions with others and diverse forms of oral and written text.

Returning to Isabella, the bilingual teacher mentioned earlier in the chapter, she exemplified many of these foundational principles in practice. For instance, she deliberately avoided correcting her students' attempts in English or Spanish, recalling her own experience of being labeled as using "improper" language in both (Pratt & Ernst-Slavit, 2019). Instead, she maintained high academic expectations while creating opportunities for students to leverage all their cultural and linguistic assets in literacy, biliteracy, and content area learning. This, of course, is no small task. The challenge lies in affirming students' languages and cultures while putting these anchors firmly into practice—a task we hope you will take on in your own work.

Extensions

For Reflection

1. After reading Robert Lake's (1990) letter to his son's teachers, please reflect on the following questions:
   a. What assumptions do you think you hold about your students' backgrounds, and how might these assumptions impact your teaching?
   b. What support or resources do you need from your school or community to make your teaching more culturally sustaining?
2. Table 2.6, A Continuum of Instructional Models Illustrating the Progressive Use of Multiple Languages (see Resources section), includes five instructional models for multilingual learners currently implemented across the nation. Reflect on the program models available in your district and region. Do you think any of those programs would better meet the needs of your multilingual learners compared to the ones they are currently in? Why or why not?

For Action

1. In relation to learning about your students and connecting with your students' families and communities:
   a. What specific steps can you take to learn more about the cultural contexts of your students and their families and to integrate this knowledge into your lessons and units? List all the specific actions you will take next week, next month, and throughout the school year.
   b. What can you do to build stronger, more culturally respectful relationships with the families of your students? List the specific actions you will take next week, next month, and throughout the school year.
2. In the section on linguistically and culturally sustaining practices (Anchor 6), we draw on the words of Paris and Alim (2017) to encourage educators to support students in maintaining the cultural and linguistic competencies of their communities, while also providing them access to dominant cultural knowledge. In this spirit, we offer the following reflective questions for educators to consider:

a. How can you ensure that students' cultural and linguistic identities are reflected in your classroom environment, materials, and activities?
b. In what ways do you incorporate students' home languages and cultural knowledge into your lessons? Can you provide an example?
c. What role does student agency play in your lessons, and how do you encourage students to see their identities as assets in their learning?
d. How do you balance teaching dominant cultural norms with affirming and sustaining students' cultural practices?
e. Can you describe a time when you adjusted your teaching practices based on feedback from students or their families?

Resources

Instructional models for multilingual learners vary in their types and amount of language support. The languages of instruction fall along a continuum from the sole use of English on the left-hand side to sustained maintenance of students' other language along with English on the right (Howard & Simpson, 2023). Table 2.6 identifies a range of typical instructional models (understanding that there are varying labels) and their language(s) of instruction for multilingual learners.

Table 2.6 A Continuum of Instructional Models Illustrating the Progressive Use and Development of Multiple Languages

INSTRUCTIONAL MODEL	STRUCTURED ENGLISH IMMERSION	ENGLISH LANGUAGE DEVELOPMENT	SHELTERED ENGLISH (OF CONTENT)	TRANSITIONAL BILINGUAL EDUCATION	DEVELOPMENTAL AND DUAL LANGUAGE EDUCATION
Language(s) of Instruction	English only	Predominantly English with some metalinguistic awareness across languages	Predominantly English across the content areas with occasional use of other languages	English and an additional language that is gradually subtracted	English with development and maintenance of an additional language

Adapted from Gottlieb (2022, p. 14).

3 Academic Languag*ing* for Language Arts

MULTILINGUAL LEARNERS IN THE LANGUAGE ARTS CLASSROOM SHOULD

- Develop a sense of their own story and identity from the perspective of their language and cultural resources
- Have access to multilingual multicultural authors and literature from around the globe
- Strive to become bilingual and biliterate in English and another language
- Translanguage to enhance their oral and written communication

MULTILINGUAL LEARNERS IN THE LANGUAGE ARTS CLASSROOM SHOULD

- Collaboratively engage with classmates to become metalinguistically and metaculturally aware
- Be exposed to rich informational text and grade-level literature they can relate to

SPOTLIGHT ON LANGUAGE ARTS CONTENT

- Multilingual learners with strong literacy in one language can readily transfer that knowledge to develop literacy in another language.
- The goal of language arts is not for multilingual learners to use the perfect standard language of "native" speakers; students' imperfect language should be acceptable.
- Language arts instruction for multilingual learners should complement and reinforce instruction for their language development.
- Language arts curriculum does not/should not have to be confined to English for multilingual learners to learn about the world around them.

SPOTLIGHT ON LANGUAGE AND CULTURE

- Knowledge of etymology (the origin and evolution of words) and metalinguistic awareness (focusing, reflecting, comparing, and evaluating language) facilitate cross-linguistic transfer.
- Teachers and students alike should uncover ways in which literature is culturally bound and, at times, biased.
- Students learn best when they can see their languages and cultures represented, respected, and supported in stories and literary text.
- Each language is unique in its structure and how it portrays the culture of the people who speak it.
- Language helps shape one's identities and cultures that can be expressed through autobiography, biography, memoirs, and narrative genres.
- Language, culture, and literature are interwoven; literature should be a rich resource to develop empathy and understanding of multiple cultures.

Introduction

Language and literacy development is generally deemed the cornerstone of schooling. Yet, the linguistic resources of multilingual learners, such as their versatility in multiple languages and their knowledge of cultural traditions, are often not valued or tapped. Academic languaging in the language arts classroom supports multilingual learners in helping to shape their positive identities and see relevance in learning through linguistic and culturally sustainable practices.

Language Development, Language Arts, and Structured Literacy

Academic languaging in the language arts classroom is complicated as it presents itself in different, yet related, contexts. Whether the language of instruction is English and/or another language, such as the presence of two languages in dual language settings, multilingual learners are simultaneously learning language, literacy, and content. As the *content* of language arts is delivered through and integrated with the *language* and *literacy* for language arts, it is often difficult to decipher one from another, especially when students are nearing reclassification from English language support.

In our book, we distinguish among three connected, yet distinct, language-related fields that pertain to multilingual learners in school. **Language development** is a process where multilingual learners continuously grow in their language proficiency as they become effective communicators. **Language arts** is a content area for all students, a subject taught in school with coverage of foundations of language, communication, and critical thinking. **Structured literacy** or the Science of Reading, in large part, is a model that focuses on five specific areas of reading for students in early elementary school. Table 3.1 describes the characteristics of these three language-related fields.

Table 3.1 Comparison Among Features of Language Development, Language Arts, and Structured Literacy

LANGUAGE DEVELOPMENT	LANGUAGE ARTS	STRUCTURED LITERACY (THE SCIENCE OF READING)
Students' language use for specific purposes, topics, audiences, and contexts	Students' exposure to grade-level language, literacy, and communication skills	Students' mastery of foundational language skills
Students' effectiveness in interpreting and expressing language across dimensions of discourse, sentences, and words/phrases	Students' comprehension of literary and informational text and its application to oracy and writing	Students' knowledge of phonological components of language: phonemic awareness, phonics, fluency, vocabulary, and comprehension

LANGUAGE DEVELOPMENT	LANGUAGE ARTS	STRUCTURED LITERACY (THE SCIENCE OF READING)
Students' growth in their linguistic repertoire tied to content area oracy and literacy	Students' growth in grade-level language, informational text, and literature	Students' growth in discrete language skills that lead to reading comprehension
Students' interaction with a range of communication modes (interpretive, interactive, expressive)	Students' understanding and application of the basic features of language	Students' decoding of language in decontextualized ways
Students screened for English language proficiency and eligibility for language support	Students screened for grade-level literacy	Students screened for dyslexia

Language proficiency levels that show growth in language development over time are not correlated with grade levels. There is variability in language proficiency levels among multilingual learners in every grade.

This chapter presents current trends in language and literacy, the heart of the content area of language arts. After distinguishing among language arts and language proficiency, we examine four literacy orientations, from structured literacy to multiliteracies, and relate their associated standards. Next, we reorient teaching and learning language arts through linguistic and cultural sustainability with emphasis on the importance and contribution of open discussion among students. Using model texts, we analyze two narrative pieces, one informational and the other fictionalized, according to four dimensions of language—discourse, sentences, words/phrases, and symbols—and note how through the lens of academic languaging they can be converted to more actionable, student-centered exemplars. Finally, we offer strategies for teachers based on the strengths of multilingual learners in the language arts classroom.

Literacy for Multilingual Learners

"Literacy (or better stated, literacies) is not a single or monolithic entity. Rather it is a set of multi-faceted social practices that are shaped by contexts, participants, and technologies" (National Council of Teachers of English [NCTE], 2011, p. 1). In other words, literacy has moved beyond the printed page to encompass multimodalities that help students make meaning and teachers facilitate student engagement (Lent, 2016). Literacies help mold the educational experience for all students, yet there seems to be an ephemeral quality, with pedagogies vacillating from mastery of discrete skills to holistic interpretation of meaning.

We assert that literacy or literacies for multilingual learners is at the hub of language arts and language development while simultaneously integral to content learning (Lattimer, 2014). It encompasses both independent and combined language domains (listening, speaking, reading, and writing), often coupled with multimodalities (e.g., viewing, illustrating, translanguaging, and other forms of representation), to optimize student access to and meaning of oral and written text. Additionally, sociocultural research, with its range of literacies across schools and communities, represents academic language as a specialized form of literacy across disciplines (Hull & Moje, 2012).

Literacy trends over the past 50 years, in general, have wavered from presenting learning as a contextualized and authentic set of interactive practices to a decontextualized and decodable set of cognitive processes and strategies. With the introduction of each new literacy trend or perspective has come a paradigm shift, and with each shift, views of literacy have become increasingly polarized. Today (the mid-2020s), although the Science of Reading or structured literacy has been legislated in most states, there are still remnants of other literacy movements that are more socialized, multimodal, and technology driven. Figure 3.1 gives a thumbnail sketch of literacy perspectives over the last half century.

Figure 3.1 Prominent Literacy Perspectives Over the Decades

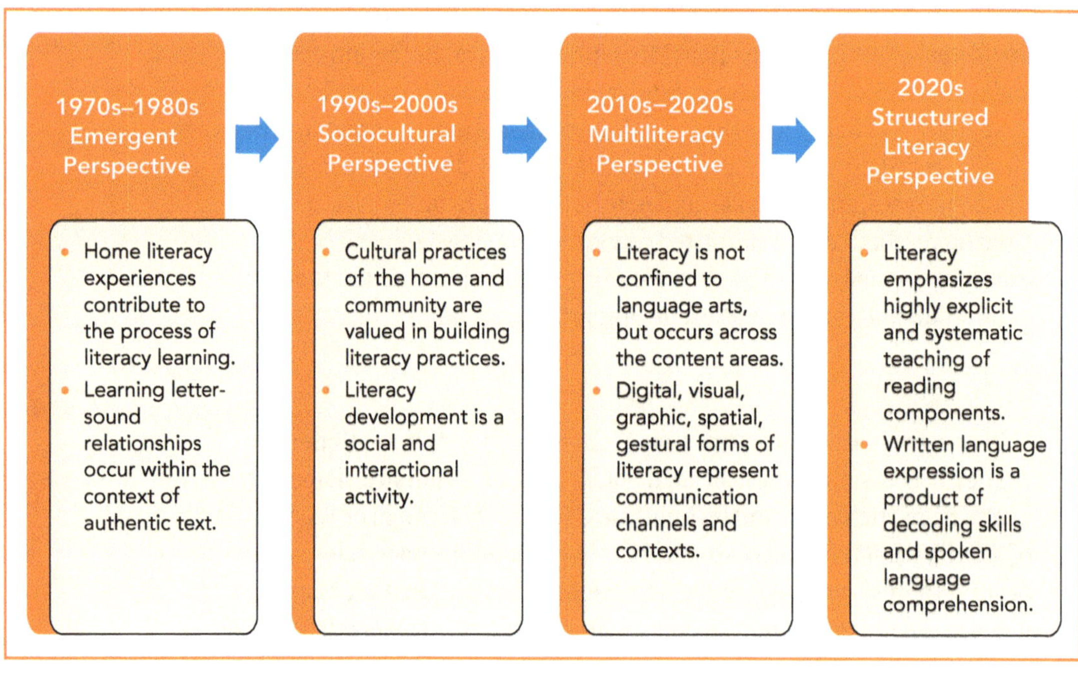

In the United States literacy has generally been envisioned as monolingual and monolithic with English as the de facto language of school and instruction. With the growth of dual language education, however, bi-/multilingualism has slowly been gaining ground. Literacy practices also fall within a range of a frame of reference or context. The intersection of these two continua (multilingualism and contextualization) forms four quadrants that are descriptive of today's language arts classrooms. They are summarized as follows and depicted in Figure 3.2.

Figure 3.2 Configurations of Early Literacy for Multilingual Learners

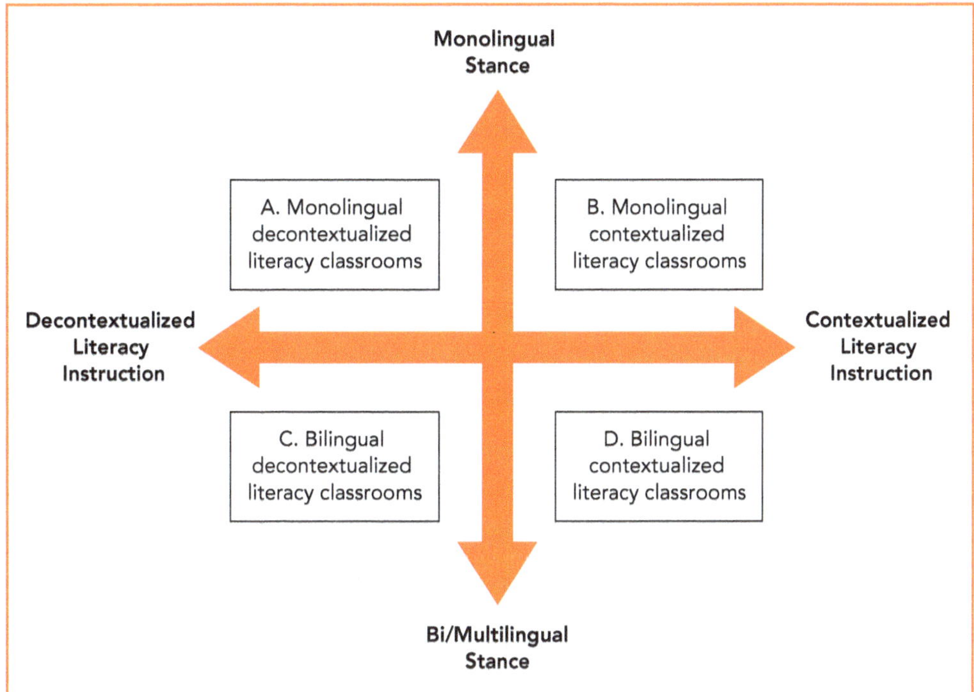

Quadrant A: Literacy instruction where letters and sounds are presented in isolation in English

Quadrant B: Literacy instruction where letters and sounds are presented within oral stories or storybooks and connected to students' school-related experiences in English

Quadrant C: Literacy instruction where letters and sounds are presented in isolation in English and the students' additional language

Quadrant D: Literacy instruction where letters and sounds are presented within storybooks and oral stories connected to the students' school, home, and community experiences in English and the students' additional language

Stop and Think

How Would You Describe Your Language Arts Classroom?

With your grade-level team or professional learning community, analyze the features of your language arts instruction according to its degree of contextualization and use/access of languages in addition to English. In which quadrant does it fall? Are you satisfied with its placement, or would you prefer for it to move to another quadrant? Why or why not?

To elaborate, the four quadrants represent distinct orientations of literacy for multilingual learners. These views (A–D) are seen as a nested model (see Figure 3.3) and described more in detail in the next section.

A and C. Structured literacy or the Science of Reading, foundational for the early stages of literacy in one or two languages

B. Literacy development for multilingual learners in English, accounting for their unique multilingual and multicultural assets

D. Biliteracy development for multilingual learners enhanced by both their languages and cultures

To quell the eternal reading debate, we suggest adopting a nested model (Figure 3.3) that acknowledges and builds on the major theoretical orientations currently shaping literacy instruction (Gottlieb, 2023; Gottlieb, 2025). Instead of presenting literacy as a dichotomy (as in the reading wars), here we envision literacy as additive in nature with an expansive breadth and depth. With structured literacy as foundational, additional layers serve to strengthen bi-/literacy development, culminating with technological advancements of multiliteracies.

Structured Literacy or the Science of Reading for Multilingual Learners

The Science of Reading is a body of evidence drawn from research from cognitive psychology, neuroscience, and educational intervention or special education. Defined as being systematic, discrete, and explicit, the Science of Reading is often implemented in Tier 1 literacy interventions within a multitiered system of support (MTSS), a model originating in the field of special education. Its five pillars or foundational skills—phonemic awareness, phonics, fluency, vocabulary, and comprehension—are coupled with structured practice for oral language and writing.

Figure 3.3 From Structured Literacy to Multiliteracies: An Additive Model of Literacy Orientations for Multilingual Learners

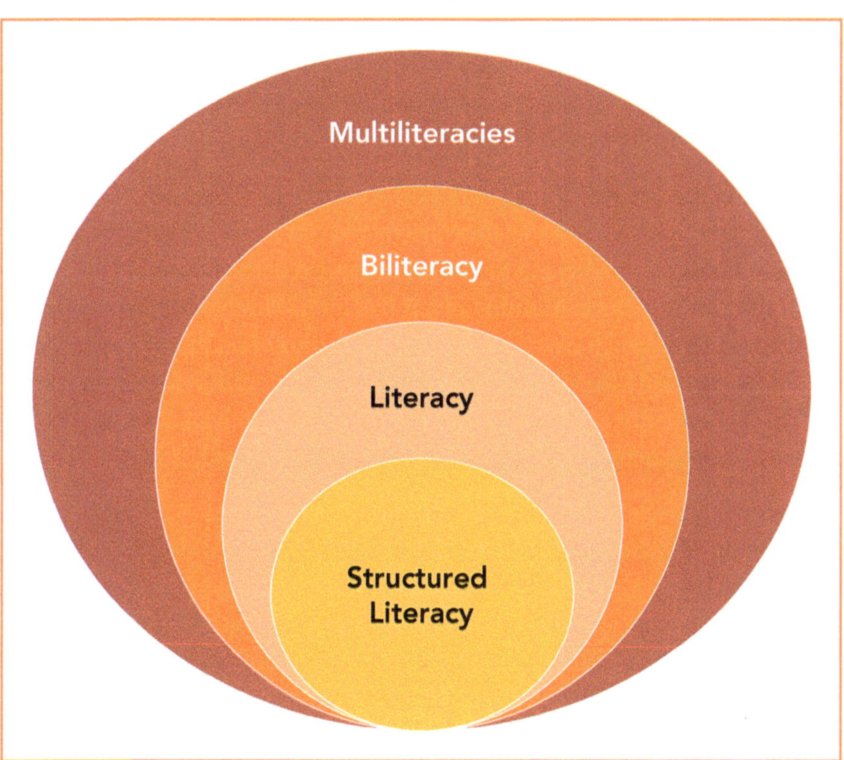

Source: Gottlieb (2023)

Structured literacy (International Dyslexia Association, 2019), sometimes referred to as the "simple view of reading" (Gough & Tunmer, 1986), is an approach to be subsumed under, rather than be a surrogate of, the content area of language arts. With its grounding in dyslexia and brain science, it is commonly depicted as Decoding (D) × Language Comprehension (LC) = Reading. Scarborough's (2001) reading rope is a metaphorical model of two sets of subskills often equated with the Science of Reading. Here, word recognition and language comprehension become increasingly intertwined and integrated as students become skilled readers. The simple view of reading and the rope model are often applied in identifying the elements of the reading development process in young learners through Grade 3 (Stewart, 2019).

Literacy

By definition, literacy requires the orchestration of multiple complex cognitive, social, affective, and linguistic tasks; understanding literacy therefore requires the application of multiple scientific fields (Gabriel, 2021). Literacy encompasses four language domains, whether independent—listening, speaking, reading, and writing—or integrated—interpretative (listening, reading, viewing) and expressive (speaking, writing, representing). No matter how one conceptualizes literacy, there is agreement that literacy is the backbone of academic languaging across the content areas to describe what students do with language.

While some equate literacy with skill attainment, others see literacy as a set of practices that are socially constructed and locally negotiated. In this view, literacy is connected to the larger context of the home, school, community, and society. Additionally, it has increasingly become more student centered and focused on the understanding of relationships between the learners and those who contribute to their identities (Norton, 2013). This student-driven focus is evident in the active view of reading with its emphasis on active self-regulation (Duke & Cartwright, 2021).

Referring back to Figure 3.2, although in quadrant B English is the medium of instruction, it does not preclude bilingualism being treated as a resource for English language and literacy development. That is, even in settings where multilingual learners are developing literacy only in English, schools and classrooms can still promote positive dispositions toward multilingualism (Palmer & Martínez, 2016). That means that all teachers can strive to offer multilingual learners linguistically and culturally relevant materials and resources, whether they are bilingual or not (Gottlieb, 2021a, 2021b).

From Literacy to Biliteracy for Multilingual Learners

Bi-/multilingualism and biliteracy, the development of two languages, are supported by robust evidence from educational policy, research, theory, and practice. First, strong policy upholds the statement that "bi-/multilingualism is not a deviation from the norm, (but rather) is itself the norm, and classrooms must be organized with students' dynamic, fluid language practices at the center of all learning" (Seltzer & de los Ríos, 2021, p. 2). In addition to policy, research confirms bilingualism as an asset, as it contributes to learning to read when language-specific skills can transfer across languages (see Bialystok, 2002; Cenoz & Gorter, 2011; among others). Numerous studies also point to bilinguals who have developed metalinguistic awareness through biliteracy outperforming their peers in one or both of their languages (Roehr-Brackin, 2018). Third, theory, such as the continua of biliteracy, an evidence-based ecological framework, speaks to the attributes of bilingualism in multilingual settings (Hornberger, 1990, 2003). Lastly, the hypergrowth of dual language education programs across the United States coupled with technology attests to the growing acceptance and effectiveness of two languages as media of instruction for all students (The New London Group, 1996).

Despite support for biliteracy, when examining the literature in teacher preparation programs inclusive of multilingual students, we discover much is grounded in monolingual views of language development that emphasize linguistic structure (quadrant A in Figure 3.2). Recently, however, there has been a gradual shift to a different perspective on language—one that normalizes bilingualism and that frames language as a social and cultural practice (quadrant D), a form of action that emerges within social and cultural contexts (Palmer & Martínez, 2016).

Biliteracy involves multilingual learners accessing and using their full language resources to optimize learning (García, 2009). Multimodal literacy, making meaning through visual, audio, and spatial systems, often through technologies (demonstrated through digital literacy), is an important part of biliteracy (Schwinge, 2016). Academic languaging, where multilingual learners engage in two or more languages to contribute to their worldview, is an outgrowth of biliteracy development.

In large part, the definition of a bilingual as being two monolinguals in one or a combination of two linguistic systems—indeed, a monolingual view or orientation—has been discarded. Rather, bilingualism is shaped by a person's unique configuration of languages that constitute an integrated whole (Grosjean, 1989). Biliteracy represents the simultaneous development of reading, oral language, and writing in two languages across a range of purposes and contexts; in essence, it is the interaction among content, literacy, and language (Calderón et al., 2019).

Biliteracy is multifaceted and involves an array of stakeholders. Often it is conceptualized, operationalized, and supported by administrators at the school and/or district level through specific instructional models such as dual language immersion or developmental bilingual programs. Biliteracy can also be promoted through curriculum design where teachers can engage students in multiculturally themed units, linking them to different cultures through content. Biliteracy is honoring students' own cultures and languages and encouraging student-to-student interaction in their multiple languages to solve issues, engage in discussion, and provide unique perspectives. Lastly, biliteracy can be part of, encouraged by, and accomplished through family engagement with family members sharing stories, histories, and traditions embedded within their "funds of knowledge" (González et al., 2005).

"How we understand language and bilingualism matters because language arts teachers are uniquely situated as powerful social actors within linguistically diverse classroom contexts."

—Deborah K. Palmer and R. A. Martínez (2016, p. 384)

From Biliteracy to Multiliteracies

Enriching students' literacy experiences in multimodal technologically enhanced environments supports *multiliteracies*, the term coined by The New London Group in 1996. The National Council of Teachers of English (NCTE, 2019) describes 21st century literacies as "multiple, dynamic, and malleable" and highlights the ability to "design and share information" and "create multimedia texts." Offering these increased prospects for multilingual learners to access their linguistic and cultural resources opens greater options and pathways to achieve their learning aspirations.

Multiliteracies are adaptable to contexts, participants, and technologies. Said another way, literacies, in addition to traditional literacy applications such as reading a novel or writing an essay, encompass widespread communication modes. Have you recently engaged in texting or emailing friends and colleagues, searching and responding to information online, creating multimodal presentations, or participating in virtual meetings with shared documents? If your answer is in the affirmative, then you are part of the multiliteracies movement!

"(Multi)literacies recognize that our ideas of reading and writing are continually evolving in response to new contexts, new purposes, and new media. Developing competence in this world of literacies requires more than phonemic awareness, the ability to decode and comprehend; it requires recognizing, adapting, and responding to new purposes, audiences, and forms—a definition that fits the demands of the twenty-first-century workplace, community, and civic life."

—Heather Lattimer (2014, p. 3)

Multiliteracies enrich biliteracy by offering numerous ways to interpret communication channels to meet students' personal and global interests and needs. Multiliteracies are two-pronged in nature. One dimension of multiliteracies is consideration for the social context in which learning occurs. It encompasses incorporating differences in students' languages, cultures, gender, and life experiences into instruction and assessment to ensure linguistic and cultural sustainability.

The second dimension of multiliteracies embraces the fast-paced growth of technology in our information age and its associated communications media. Here meaning is increasingly multimodal, where written and linguistic modes seamlessly interface with oral, visual, audio, gestural, tactile, and spatial patterns of meaning (see examples in the section "Using Model Texts in the Language Arts Classroom"). Thus, in expanding biliteracy to multiliteracies we are inclusive of the social and cultural contexts of learning and increase accessibility through its variety of modes, including artificial intelligence (AI), thus optimizing teaching and learning for multilingual learners.

Stop and Think

What Is the Role of AI for Multilingual Learners and Their Teachers?

Do you think that AI—integral to multiliteracies—is a multimodal support or a crutch for multilingual learners? It can be supportive in giving students agency so they gain confidence and autonomy in pursuing learning in one or more languages and understand how their own linguistic resources can enrich their learning experience. Thus, on one level, AI can reinforce students' bilingualism along with their metalinguistic and metacultural awareness. On the other hand, multilingual learners can become too dependent on AI, such as in providing ideas to copy onto different assignments or translating large chunks of text, especially for English language arts.

AI as a tool for teachers opens the floodgates to suggest comprehensible input for multilingual learners, not only through text but with other modes, such as PowerPoints, photos, and diagrams. Teachers can gear students in learning new content, producing model texts, and discovering interesting accessible texts. With the ever-growing applications of AI, perhaps it would be advantageous to create a policy with your multilingual learners as to what is appropriate or acceptable use for your classroom or school.

Current Perspectives on Teaching and Learning Language Arts for Multilingual Learners

We have seen how characteristics of multilingual learners and their instructional programs affect the treatment of literacy (refer to Figure 3.2). Notice that throughout the chapter we do not confine our discussion to English language arts, but rather address the study of language arts in general, and its application to other languages as well. To further accentuate the growing attention to multilingual learners in the language arts classroom, we explore three topics:

1. Implementing Language Arts Through the Lens of Multilingual Learners
2. Infusing Linguistic and Cultural Sustainability Into the Language Arts Curriculum
3. Facilitating Meaningful Discussion in the Language Arts Classroom

Implementing Language Arts Through the Lens of Multilingual Learners

Academic languaging is all about acquiring and applying disciplinary literacy, "understanding the ways knowledge is constructed in each content area and how literacy supports that knowledge in discipline-specific ways" (Lent, 2016, p. 10). In other words, academic literacies extend beyond decoding and comprehension to encompass complex concepts, control of new language, precise and concise expression of complicated ideas, and problem-solving that evokes thinking (Gibbons, 2009). At the same time, the content area of language arts is often parsed into the individual language domains of listening, speaking, reading, and writing. Understanding that multilingual learners bring a wealth of linguistic and cultural resources to the classroom, Table 3.2 offers some strategies across language domains to stimulate students' deep thinking.

Table 3.2 Student Engagement in Literacy: Reading, Writing, Listening/Speaking, and Thinking in the Language Arts Classroom

WHEN MULTILINGUAL LEARNERS READ, THEY	WHEN MULTILINGUAL LEARNERS WRITE, THEY
• Figure out how literal and figurative language works within and across languages • Discover how underlying messages represent connected themes • Interpret text through their multilingual multicultural lens • Attend to multimodal ways of expression to reinforce meaning	• Engage in a process that includes planning, drafting, acting on feedback, revising, and editing • Use model texts as exemplars to aid in refining their craft • Pay attention to discourse (organization, detail, elaboration, and voice) in conjunction with sentences and vocabulary • Rely on concrete feedback along with self-reflection

(Continued)

(Continued)

WHEN MULTILINGUAL LEARNERS LISTEN AND SPEAK, THEY	WHEN MULTILINGUAL LEARNERS THINK, THEY
• Communicate information and ideas to others in their language(s) of choice • Exchange information on a variety of topics from a variety of perspectives • Engage in discussion with peers • Ask and answer a variety of questions • Give talks, speeches, or multimedia presentations	• Reflect on and compare multiple sources of information (in their preferred languages) • Question the author and their position • Contemplate/analyze information, consider research findings, or scrutinize others' ideas • Make connections between ideas and themes • Perceive/challenge potential bias in oral and written text

Adapted from Lent (2016).

"Academic literacy development for multilingual learners involves making meaning across languages, modes of communication, text genres, and literacy practices used in home and school contexts."

—WIDA (2024)

One of the first steps in implementing a language arts curriculum is for you to ascertain the background knowledge of your students. For multilingual learners, the natural place to begin is making family and community connections—people, places, traditions, and cultural insights with which students are familiar. Not only does having multilingual learners relate what they already know about a topic boost their confidence in learning, but it fosters a sense of belonging and offers a familiar context for new learning to occur.

Students can also gain initial familiarity with a topic through multimodalities. Often teachers rely on visuals, graphic organizers, hands-on materials, and even field experiences before launching into text. Multilingual learners can be invited to use their home languages as an entrée into a new topic. Gamification, apps, and other technologies are additional strategies for engaging multilingual learners at the start of a unit or for scaffolding their learning throughout. Your classroom can become a vibrant space, one that fosters respect and inclusivity, where multilingual learners can thrive and develop their language skills in English and their home languages.

Look Closer

Literacy-Related Resources

To support literacy development for multilingual learners, you might wish to refer to the following:

Collier, V. P., & Thomas, W. P. (2019). *The role of bilingualism in improving literacy achievement.* International Literacy Association. https://www.literacyworldwide.org/docs/default-source/where-we-stand/ila-role-bilingualism-improving-literacy-achievement.pdf

Council of the Great City Schools. (2023). *A framework for foundational literacy skills instruction for English Learners: Instructional practice and materials considerations.* https://www.cgcs.org/cms/lib/DC00001581/Centricity/domain/35/publication%20docs/CGCS_Foundational%20Literacy%20Skills_Pub_v11.pdf

National Academies of Sciences, Engineering, and Medicine (2017). *Promoting the educational successes of children and youth learning English: Promising futures. Consensus Study Report.* National Academies Press. https://nap.nationalacademies.org/read/24677/chapter/2

Pearson, P. D., Palincsar, A. S., Biancarosa, G., & Berman, A. I. (Eds.). (2020). *Reaping the rewards of the Reading for Understanding Initiative.* National Academy of Education.

Infusing Linguistic and Cultural Sustainability Into the Language Arts Curriculum

When communication is linguistically and culturally sustaining, learners (and teachers) are inspired to draw on a range of racial, cultural, and linguistic modalities integral to their learning space. Teaching practices grounded in this framework create opportunities for learners to inquire about how language and power converge in print or digital texts to represent an array of biases, often against marginalized communities. In the language arts classroom, in particular, learners need guidance in recognizing and responding to discourse patterns that are rooted in the oppression of nondominant groups.

"Culturally responsive teaching sees cultural differences as assets; creating caring learning communities where culturally different individuals and heritages are valued; using cultural knowledge of ethnically diverse cultures, families, and communities to guide curriculum development, classroom climates, instructional strategies, and relationships with students; [and] challenging racial and cultural stereotypes, prejudices, racism, and other forms of being change agents for social justice and academic equity."

—Geneva Gay (2010, p. 31)

Linguistic and cultural sensitivity can only evolve into sustainability if educators, families, and the community at large take an assets-based approach to teaching, learning, and life. Although this discussion is being addressed within the context of language arts, it has applicability across every content area and classroom in a school.

In moving from learners and classrooms to systems, Table 3.3 serves as a thumbnail evaluation of your school's or district's linguistic and cultural sustainability. You might wish to use the following criteria: 1 = *traces*, 2 = *intermittent signs*, 3 = *noticeable presence*, and 4 = *fully integrated*—to describe your school's or district's status. Then discuss your responses with administrators and colleagues or request forming a task force to recommend action steps.

Table 3.3 How Does Your School or District Rate in Terms of Its Linguistic and Cultural Sustainability?

LINGUISTIC AND CULTURAL SUSTAINABILITY OF MY SCHOOL OR DISTRICT	1	2	3	4
Multilingualism and multiculturalism are integral to the school's or district's mission, vision, and values.				
Multilingualism and multiculturalism permeate the environment, from signage to murals to conversations in the halls.				
High expectations are set for all students, and multilingual learners can reach their learning goals by accessing one or more languages.				
Students' and families' languages and cultures are always valued.				

(Continued)

(Continued)

LINGUISTIC AND CULTURAL SUSTAINABILITY OF MY SCHOOL OR DISTRICT	1	2	3	4
The linguistic and cultural resources of the community and family members' "funds of knowledge" are an extension of the school or district.				
Curriculum, instruction, and assessment invite multiple cultures and perspectives.				
The assets and experiences of multilingual learners and their families are built into curriculum design, instruction, and classroom assessment.				
Adults throughout the school or district are student advocates who attend to students' languages and cultures.				
Linguistic and cultural sustainability draws from multilingual learners' "funds of identity" in and out of school.				
Professional learning offers ongoing opportunities for educators to dive deeply into multilingual, multicultural, and multiracial issues.				
Multilingual learners and their teachers form a community of learners who contribute to classroom and school decision-making.				
Multilingual learners are on a pathway of becoming agents of their own learning.				

Adapted from Gottlieb, 2024b, pp. 30–31.

This resource is available for download at https://companion.corwin.com/courses/Academic-Languaging.

Stop and Think

Spanish/Native Language Arts Materials Should Not Be Translations of Those From English Language Arts!

The development of high-quality culturally and linguistically relevant Spanish language arts materials is necessary for multilingual learners who participate in programs where Spanish is the language of instruction. It is critical for those students in dual language education immersion to adhere to its four pillars—bilingualism/biliteracy, high levels of achievement, sociocultural competence, and critical consciousness—by establishing strong literacy in English and Spanish, their partner language.

One of the primary considerations in the selection of language arts texts, whether literary or informational, is authenticity, ensuring that the text reflects the genres (discourse), cultures, and worldviews associated with the language of print. Materials that have been translated from English often retain the monoglossic or monolingual cultural perspectives, word choice, and grammatical constructions. Martínez (2023) names five areas of focus in considering rich authentic Spanish language arts materials when Spanish is the language of learning; these recommendations can readily apply to any additional language:

1. Materials value the richness and uniqueness of the Spanish language, as well as its varieties and cultures.
2. Materials reflect and maintain structures and traditions of Spanish literacy.
3. Materials value and utilize students' linguistic gifts, such as their use of translanguaging.
4. Materials represent the sociocultural and linguistic hybridity of U.S. multilingual learners and their families.
5. Materials promote the integration of assessment and instruction from a multilingual/multicultural perspective.

Facilitating Meaningful Discussion in the Language Arts Classroom

Fostering a sense of belonging in students is a key element in facilitating meaningful discussions while helping students develop their social and emotional competencies. For example, purposeful online multilingual discussion platforms encourage interaction among multilingual learners in multiple languages, promote collaboration among participants, and offer global perspectives. Students can exchange ideas with classrooms that have been tapped around the world, sharing their final products and seeking different perspectives.

As a community of learners, students have both oral and written options to partake in discussion; in fact, the students should decide their preferred mode (and language) of presentation. High school students who are steeped in a capstone project, after viewing exemplars on YouTube, for example, may wish to engage in TED Talks of their own. To stimulate creativity and interaction among students, you might wish to set up an author signing where student authors of poems, raps, short stories, and videos share their production and have their original work reproduced for other students and family members.

When students nominate books or articles for their Multilingual Book Club, more than likely they will choose those that resemble and appeal to them. One student can take the lead in assigning page numbers or accompanying videos so that everyone in the class can participate. Other students can generate questions to ask about the selection—the characters, events, and storyline. Over the year, students might even create a set of posters of each book and display them around the room. Having multimodal options, even for discussions, enables all students to participate and be proud of their accomplishments.

Considerations in Teaching and Learning Language Arts for Multilingual Learners

In examining language arts as a content area, we gain a perspective of conceptual expectations and skills attainment grade by grade. In this section we present some overall influences on the field of language arts, with attention to multilingual learners. Specifically, we focus on standards-related instruction and the impact of national organizations on literacy-related policy. Language arts teachers can be change agents by leading the charge to infuse reading and writing into every content area. Equally important is not limiting the content of language arts to text-dependent materials, but expanding its horizon to include images, multimedia, data visualization, and even content from social media (in other words, multimodalities).

The Contribution of the Standards Movement to Literacy Development

Three sets of standards influence the education of multilingual learners in the language arts classroom: (1) language arts standards, (2) language development standards, and (3) technology standards. For Latine students who constitute the majority of multilingual learners, all these standards are available in English and Spanish. Therefore, in speaking to standards, there should be parity for those Latine students who participate in dual language and bilingual Spanish–English programs.

The standards movement of the 2010s introduced a new vision for enacting English language arts curriculum across the educational arena and suggested that literacy instruction be the collective responsibility of all teachers. As a result, emphasis has shifted to student participation in literacy-related activities in four related areas: (1) engaging with complex texts, (2) using evidence in writing and research, (3) presenting ideas through speaking and listening, and (4) examining and analyzing language (Bunch et al., 2012).

For multilingual learners, what is notably absent from English language arts standards is any recognition and advantaging of the multilingual multicultural assets that these students bring to learning in school. Put another way, it appears that English language arts standards have a rather restricted monoglossic stance—English—without any admission, let alone acceptance, of the heteroglossic nature (the presence of a variety of language perspectives) of our growing multilingual student population.

English language arts and Spanish language arts standards form complementary pathways to student success. A similar relationship exists between English and Spanish language development standards. Although both are centered in language and required by federal law, there are stark differences between language arts and language development standards (see Table 3.4).

Table 3.4 Comparing Features of Language Arts Standards and Language Development Standards

LANGUAGE ARTS STANDARDS	LANGUAGE DEVELOPMENT STANDARDS
Encapsulate the domains and skills of the content area of language arts	Articulate the language domains and process of language development
Showcase what students should achieve at each grade level	Showcase student growth by language proficiency levels
Focus on disciplinary knowledge, skills, and concepts articulated in the language arts curriculum	Focus on effective and meaningful use of language within and across the content areas
Underscore learning theory	Underscore applied linguistic and psychological theory
Anchor curriculum, instruction, and assessment of language arts	Anchor curriculum, instruction, and assessment of language development
Are designed for all students	Are designed for multilingual learners for whom English is an additional language

While state academic content and language development standards are unique in their student expectations, together they strengthen instructional practices for any educator serving multilingual learners. In fact, the integration of content and language is a Big Idea or ideology that overlays the WIDA (2020, 2023) English and Spanish language development standards frameworks. The weaving of concepts, practices, and two languages makes for a seamless, coherent experience for multilingual learners and teachers alike.

The increasing role of technology in education and life is cause for states to adopt the International Society for Technology in Education (ISTE) standards for students, teachers, and coaches. Grounded in learning science research, these standards, designed to empower students to drive their own learning, intentionally build in thinking practices. For example, empowered learning (Standard 1.1) encourages multilingual learners to leverage technology to explore topics and access information in their multiple languages. Global collaboration (Standard 1.7) pushes multilingual learners to connect with others who share their language and culture through technology, such as participating in online forums, collaborating on projects, and gaining new perspectives through shared videos. In promoting a technology-rich learning environment by leveraging students' existing language skills and cultural knowledge, ISTE standards are a contributor to and an expression of multiliteracies.

Look Closer

Standards-Related Resources in English and Spanish

For standards-related resources revolving around language for multilingual learners, you might wish to refer to the following:

Council of Chief State School Officers. (2012). *California Common Core State Standards in Spanish language arts and literacy in history/social studies, science, and technical subjects.* Common Core en Español. https://www.sdcoe.net/common-core-espanol/ca-ccss-en-espanol

International Society for Technology in Education. (2016). *Estándares ISTE: Estudiantes.* https://cdn.iste.org/www-root/Libraries/Documents%20%26%20Files/Standards-Resources/ISTE%20Standards_One-Sheets-Students_Bilingual.pdf?

International Society for Technology in Education. (2024). *ISTE standards: Students.* https://iste.org/standards/students?

National Governors Association Center for Best Practices & Council of Chief State School Officers. (2010). *Common Core State Standards for English language arts and literacy in history/social studies, science, and technical subjects.* https://www.thecorestandards.org/ELA-Literacy/

WIDA. (2020). *WIDA English language development standards framework, 2020 edition: Kindergarten–grade 12.* Board of Regents of the University of Wisconsin System.

WIDA. (2021). *Marco de referencia de las artes del lenguaje del español de WIDA: Aplicación para la enseñanza (Marco ALE).* Board of Regents of the University of Wisconsin System.

WIDA. (2023). *Marco de los estándares del desarrollo auténtico del lenguaje español de WIDA (Marco DALE).* Board of Regents of the University of Wisconsin System.

Professional Organizations' Position Statements on Literacy and Multilingual Learners

In 2018, the NCTE issued a position statement that counteracts the dominance of monoglossia in schools and teacher preparation institutions by supporting the cultural wealth and community-based literacies of multilingual learners. Their position showcases multilingual learners' "verbal dexterity, multimodal ways of knowing, textual analysis, racial literacy, criticality, and multiple perspectives." Three dimensions position heterogeneity as a strength to encapsulate the ideals of parity and advocate for humanizing approaches to teaching and learning:

1. Literacy pedagogy and curriculum development (incorporating community assets into literacy learning to help shape the classroom culture)
2. Teacher preparation and professional development (centering and reflecting on pedagogical practice to better understand different contexts)
3. Assessment (valuing students' lived experiences, communities, languages, and literacies in the assessment experience) (NCTE, 2018)

TESOL International Association has long endorsed literacy development that recognizes students' multiple languages and cultures. In its position paper on language and literacy development for young multilingual learners, the association recommends the following features of literacy programs for young multilingual learners:

1. Oral language and literacy development is supported by the student's native language to build a connection between home and school.
2. Literacy learning is an ongoing process that requires time and support to fully develop.
3. Instruction and literacy-related materials are linguistically, culturally, and developmentally appropriate.
4. Literacy programs are meaning-based that foster comprehension, relying on students' experiences and literature from a variety of cultural backgrounds (2010).

In 2023, two organizations, the Reading League and the National Committee for Effective Literacy, issued a joint statement that outlines the commonalities and differences between the Science of

Reading and the literacy needs of multilingual learners. Overall, there is agreement that the assets of multilingual learners should be foundational for literacy instruction; however, their orientations and approaches are distinct. Basically, the neuroscientific research that undergirds the Science of Reading has roots in dyslexia and manifests in the content area of language arts (Gottlieb, 2023). Effective literacy practices for multilingual learners center on their attributes, experiences, languages, and cultures, which together are folded into reading and writing, as well as oral language, to promote ongoing language development in multiple languages across content areas.

Stop and Think

The Recognition of the Seal of Biliteracy

There was a 12-year span from the time California issued the first Seal of Biliteracy, an award granted by a school, district, or state in recognition of students who have attained proficiency in two or more languages by high school graduation, until its adoption by all 50 states in 2023, thus becoming a nationally recognized accomplishment by multilingual learners (and other students). A credential issued to bi-/multilingual learners in more than 100 languages along with English, the seal acknowledges the value of bilingualism and biliteracy in school and society (see https://sealofbiliteracy.org).

While overall considered a positive educational language policy and pride for multilingual learners, there has been some criticism and controversy of the initiative regarding the extent to which marginalized or minoritized students benefit. That is, there have been claims that the Seal of Biliteracy promotes or favors students participating in "foreign" or world language education (Subtirelu et al., 2019). Additionally, on some level, the Seal speaks to the gentrification of dual language education by students of more privilege than those it has historically served (Gándara, 2021; Valdez et al., 2016).

- To what extent do you think the Seal of Biliteracy promotes biliteracy for multilingual learners?
- To what extent are multilingual learners motivated to get the Seal of Biliteracy in your district or state?

The Language for Language Arts

Academic languaging in language arts means accepting multilingual learners' histories, experiences, and varieties of expression as legitimate. Furthermore, it stresses that multilingual learners do not have to aim to be "native speakers" or reach the full monolingual norm as their end goal (Valdés, 2023). Rather, several factors, including the context, audience, and topic, dictate how language is shaped and communicated. Given those premises, what becomes important is what multilingual learners can do with language. Of equal value is using students' language resources to critically examine, expand, and act on their worldview. In this section we examine the dimensions of language and their contributions to academic languaging.

Discourse

In a more traditional sense, discourse entails the oral or written exchange of ideas with a defined purpose. Awareness of discourse structure (how ideas are organized and their coherence) and variation across text types, genres, and content areas informs comprehension (Grabe & Yamashita, 2022) and related academic literacies. In another sense, discourse can refer to different communication modes as in spoken (oral), written, interactive, and multimodal (film, video, photography, graphic design).

Ways of expression vary by culture; it is said, for example, that in the United States, oral and written text in English is direct, starting with a thesis and then getting right to the point, while other cultures tend to approach text in a more circular fashion. Likewise, in some cultures, conversations are more circuitous. For example, "Your presentation was unclear because . . ." is direct feedback, while "You covered some pertinent points—perhaps you still need to work on other points" is indirect feedback. Multilingual learners often navigate within and across cultures (and, thus, partake in cross-cultural communication) in their speaking and writing styles, and their teachers should be accepting of all language and cultural varieties.

Sentences

Individual sentences, even those contextualized within a larger chunk of language, may be problematic for multilingual learners. Complex sentences, in particular, add density to text. The following are examples of how multilingual learners might be stumped by different sentence configurations.

- **Passive voice** occurs when the subject of the sentence is acted on by the verb (e.g., *She was kissed by the prince*).
- **Multiple meanings** (polysemous words) occur when a single word has more than one connotation (e.g., *light*, *bank*, *mole*, *mouth*); such words require the context of a sentence or discourse to decipher their meaning.

- **Multiple noun groups** begin with an article (e.g., *the, a, an*) or a determiner (e.g., *this, that, these, those, my, your, his, her, its, our*) and attach **multiple adjectives** to describe a person, place, or thing (e.g., *The run-down, inner-city, two-story, stone Victorian house is for sale*).

Words/Phrases

Words and phrases in English may be challenging for multilingual learners to decipher, but even those that are contextualized within a chunk of language may prove tricky for multilingual learners.

- **Nominalization** involves changing a word from one part of speech to a noun (e.g., *pronounce* → *pronunciation* or *pronouncement*) or multiple related nouns (e.g., *produce* → *product* and *production*). Nominalizations can prompt cross-linguistic transfer across romance languages (e.g., producir- producto- producción).
- **Idiomatic expressions** are nontranslatable chunks of language with unique meanings (e.g., *take a bath*; *pull my leg*; *under the weather*; *raining cats and dogs*).
- **Collocations** are words that go together in a specified order, such as food items (e.g., *peanut butter* and *jelly*; *fish* and *chips*) or colors (*black* and *blue*; *red*, *white*, and *blue*).
- **Cognates** are words in different languages that are similar in form and meaning (e.g., *technology*, *tecnología*, and *technologie*; *father* and *pater*; *democracy* and *demokratia*).
- **Complex noun groups** are created when a set of unrelated nouns bears its own meaning (e.g., *teachers' fall professional development workshop*; *football news commentary*).

Symbols

Unlike the other content areas, for language arts, symbols are a powerful tool, in essence a mental map for conveying complex ideas, emotions, and themes. Often conveyed in objects, settings, or characters, these symbols frequently transcend their literal meaning to represent more abstract concepts. As concepts, symbols in language arts are often culturally loaded, and may signify distinct interpretations. In Western cultures, symbols in literature might include any of the following:

- A dove, representing peace and purity, versus a raven, representing an ill omen
- A hero, portraying goodness and courage, versus a villain (or antihero), being evil
- A garden (as in the Garden of Eden), symbolizing paradise or innocence
- Different colors, noting a range of emotions—red standing for outrage or passion, blue epitomizing peace and tranquility, or black casting a dismal outlook or sense of evil

Symbols for language arts are often quite nuanced within a work of literature or poetry. Although they may add depth or symbolism to text, they may be totally incomprehensible to older multilingual learners due to their cultural implications. It might be worthwhile for students to compare symbols associated with their own cultures, such as their emblems on flags, land animals (e.g., dragons vs. bulls), birds (e.g., doves vs. cranes), or flowers (e.g., rose vs. lotus), to become more cross-culturally aware.

Using Model Texts in the Language Arts Classroom

Creating and/or analyzing model texts helps teachers communicate content and language to students in a meaningful context. The first example is a historical narrative written for the Chicano community by a Chicano activist about the plight to preserve a neighborhood park (see Figure 3.4) and its people. Its beauty lies in its colorful depiction of the contrasts that are so evident to the author but may be masked to the average visitor to the park. This compassionate story conveys a central message or theme, offering insights into the human experience and its emotions. You should note how translanguaging, or the use of Spanish (highlighted in blue), is purposefully interspersed in the park's description to add linguistic and cultural authenticity.

Model Text 1: The Story of Chicano Park, a Historical Narrative

Figure 3.4 Hasta La Bahia!!

Source: Photo by M. Gottlieb, February 2024

In many ways Chicano Park in San Diego, California, is like any other park. It's where families gather to have a reunion or enjoy a picnic. Where the delicious smell of carne asada on the grill floats in the air. Where the high-pitched giggles of niñitos y niñitas reverberate against the tall cement pillars. Where kids climb, slide, and swing on a playground that had been carved out by friends in the neighborhood.

It's a park where youngsters bounce a basketball on the court or challenge each other to a round of handball. Where couples exchange wedding vows in the Kiosko in the middle, just like in the placita of their Mexican hometown. Where a nana gently pushes a stroller along the walkways to pacify a grinning baby.

Unlike other parks, however, el Parque Chicano pulsates when trumpeting shells, throbbing drums, and percussive rattles proclaim the beginning of a Danza Azteca ceremony. Unlike other parks, Chicano Park displays on its colossal pillars one of the largest assemblages of public murals in North America. These awe-inspiring murals are giant mirrors of Chicano Mexicano history. And unlike other parks, Chicano Park was taken by militant force by a community angered by decades of neglect, ignorance, and racism.

The birth of the park is the story of a barrio tragedy transformed into triumph. It is the history of the Chicano Mexicano people struggling to reclaim their heritage and right to self-determination. The park is where history is enshrined in monumental murals. It is where we keep making history as we fight to preserve and defend a small piece of Aztlán in el Barrio Logan.

(Excerpt adapted from Anguiano, M. [n.d.]. *The battle of Chicano Park: A brief history of the takeover*. Chicano Park Steering Committee. http://www.chicano-park.com/cpscbattleof.html)

In the broadest sense, by analyzing this model text according to the dimensions of academic language, students can gain a better understanding of its meaning, its impact, and the interaction of language arts (the story) with historical concepts. Students may wish to contemplate the power of language and the actions taken to gain control of the park—in essence, how academic languaging made the story come to life. Here's a beginning of an analysis of this model text by its dimensions of language.

The *discourse* of this sophisticated narrative is organized around vivid description of a vibrant park and its untold history. Elements of storytelling are combined with rich details to paint a stunning picture of a unique place, Chicano Park, and its strong cultural heritage. The themes of each paragraph are quite distinct. To grasp the discourse of the excerpt in its entirety and gain insight into the human experience, you may wish to have students first discuss the significance of each paragraph in small groups and then summarize the entire reading either orally or in writing.

The next step in the analysis is to evaluate how the *sentences* in each paragraph build on each other to contribute to the overall effect of this powerful text. The author utilizes vivid details that appeal to the senses (the sight of families strolling or picnicking, the sound of young children's high-pitched giggles, the smell of carne asada on the grill) to create a multidimensional experience for the reader. Figures of speech—in particular, the repeated conjunction *where*—are used for author effect, reinforcing and accentuating a place, situation, or condition. Equally impactful is the prepositional phrase beginning with *unlike* that is applied repeatedly as a contrast or comparison.

Stop and Think

Challenging Sentence Types in English Language Arts

Being a multilingual learner has benefits and challenges when interpreting text. We have mentioned that having metalinguistic and metacultural awareness indeed is advantageous as students can connect one language to another. However, there are many syntactic or grammatical forms in English at the sentence level that just are not equivalent in another language. By not being translatable, they can cause misunderstanding; the more sophisticated forms can be highly nuanced. The following forms of language are the more challenging ones:

Figurative language: Similes, metaphors, personification—"I was *kissed* by the sun."

Idiomatic/colloquial expressions: Terms used mostly in casual conversations—"Did you *catch* a cold after you *took* your bath?"

Collocations: A predictable combination of words—"It's a *heavy* rain with a *strong* wind."

Double entendres: Phrases with double meanings, usually one with an innocent meaning and one that is risqué—"He's *hot!*"

Irony: Phrases that are said that imply another meaning—"What a *beautiful* day" (meaning it's really miserable).

Sarcasm: A form of irony that inflicts pain or is insulting to someone—"Well, *that's* a surprise."

Satire: A parody on words—"It's a *catch-22.*"

Lastly, strong feelings are portrayed in this model text through the choice of *words and phrases*. Compelling action verbs and precise nouns create movement and evoke clear mental images of the past and present. The strategic use of translanguaging strengthens the message of the fight for power and control by the Chicanos and denotes the important role of language and culture in their story.

Most published curricular materials are devoid of multiple languages. With growing numbers of multilingual learners in our schools, materials should recognize and celebrate bilingualism and multiculturalism, giving students and teachers opportunities to see themselves and engage in translanguaging exploration and practices. Teacher guides, not only for language arts but for all content areas, should encourage and respect students' voices and identities so that teachers understand when and how to encourage translanguaging (Martínez, 2023).

As an extension of the model text, you may have your multilingual learners experiment with translanguaging as a means of relating their own experiences with emotionality. You may have students consider that whenever they are relating a personal event or relationship, they may wish to use all their linguistic resources. In that way, multilingual learners can take control over their creativity of expression and exhibiting academic languaging.

Stop and Think

Translanguaging as an Expression of Culture and Equity in Language Arts

Model texts that contain multiple languages offer opportunities for multilingual learners to see their languages, and often cultures, side by side. Translanguaging has a specific purpose and effect in this excerpt model text, describing the plight of the Chicano community in trying to preserve their heritage amidst a concrete jungle of a major U.S. city. Having read and dissected this story aloud with students, teachers should ask multilingual learners how the natural insertion of Spanish words (often related to foods, places, and people) makes the story more familiar, realistic, and reflective of their cultural life. If applicable, invite Latine students to discuss the following questions with each other:

- How do you see yourself in this story?
- How do you see your language in this story?
- Which words and phrases do you relate to, and why?
- How visible is your culture in this story? Can you give some examples?
- How does this story make you feel proud of your heritage?
- How long of a list of activities in the park can you produce?
- How does the *mezcla* (mixing) of languages reinforce the story's message?
- How would the power of the story diminish if it was only written in English?

Young children enjoy fairy tales and imaginative narratives. The following model text is one to which all can relate, as bread in all its varied forms (Figure 3.5) is a universal food. This story with the anthropomorphic traits of its main characters, the two crumbs (attributing human characteristics to nonhumans), can stimulate interesting and creative conversation among the students.

Model Text 2: An Adventure of Two Breadcrumbs, a Fictional Narrative

Figure 3.5 Bread at the Bakery

Source: Photo by Gisela Ernst-Slavit

Once upon a time there was a busy bakery filled with wonderful smells of different breads from around the world. The baker wanted everyone who came to the store to be happy and buy their favorite bread. One day, two large breadcrumbs fell onto the wooden floor. Before they knew it, the baker brushed the crumbs outside with a broom. Off went the breadcrumbs on an exciting adventure!

As soon as the crumbs left the bakery, they were in the middle of a celebration! There was loud music playing, balloons floating in the air, and people singing and dancing. The streets were filled with wonderful, strange smells from different kinds of food. How much fun to see the world!

But then the sun began to set, and the sky became darker and darker. It was nighttime! The music stopped, the smells disappeared, and the people no longer crowded the streets. The crumbs became very sad. They didn't know what to do.

Just then a street cleaner came by and took the crumbs away. Luckily, the breadcrumbs were able to stay together, and they lived happily ever after.

Stop and Think

Infusing Linguistic and Cultural Relevance Into Stories

This model text was inspired, in part, by Ann Morris's 1989 book *Bread, Bread, Bread,* one we have read often to our students.

There are so many ways in which multilingual learners can participate in this model text—for example, by imagining being a breadcrumb, describing breads from different cultures, and sharing breads with their classmates. Student pairs could recount, draw, or reenact a festival or celebration they might have attended with their family. A more adventuresome class could even make bread or have a multicultural festival of their own!

Analysis of the Model Text According to the Dimensions of Academic Language

Introducing students to the dimensions of language should always begin with the big picture of how text is organized and the overall message—in other words, its genre (in this case, a fairy tale) or discourse. Thus, we venture from the top down, folding in sentences and words/phrases along the way.

Discourse: For young learners, one of the classic organizing features of a story is that it contains a beginning, middle, and end. In this model text it is readily detected as there is a specific event, time, and place that together create the narrative's sequence and flow. The genre of fairy tales in English is easily discernible as it typically begins with "Once upon a time" and ends with "and they lived happily ever after." As illustrated in Chapter 2, most cultures have unique openers for fairy tales, from Polish to Korean to Spanish, that multilingual learners can readily provide to become engaged in the story (see Wallace, 2024).

Sentences: In this model text, the conjunctions *and* and *but* serve as connectors between related ideas. Expressive punctuation, namely the exclamation mark, relates the emotionality of the crumbs on different occasions. Some sentences in this fairy tale denote different feelings; see if your students can identify them and share a time when they experienced the same feeling.

Words/Phrases: Much of the model text is in simple past tense. Gerunds are used to denote actions in the street festival, such as music *playing*, balloons *floating*, and people *singing* and *dancing*. There are also many colorful adjectives in the story. Students may first identify adjectives within sentences and then compare their placement with that of their other language to increase their metalinguistic awareness.

Look Closer

A Storytelling App

Technology has surely enhanced the storytelling experience of students! There is one educational app that is particularly applicable to fictional narratives. Toontastic 3D, launched by Google in 2017, is a multimedia app that adds three-dimensional animated characters and environments to students' stories (Contreras, 2023). Imagine the breadcrumb story coming to life and being shared with classmates. What an empowering experience for multilingual learners!

Strategies for Moving Language Arts Learning Forward With Multilingual Learners

All teachers can boost literacy for multilingual learners and simultaneously address curricular parity. Some strategies include teachers elevating the status of multiple languages and cultures through literature while other strategies engage students in taking ownership of their language learning and becoming more agentive. The following are some ideas for infusing activities into language arts routines to help create classrooms that promote a multilingual multicultural community of learners.

Here's what language arts teachers might do to instruct in linguistically and culturally relevant ways:

- Recast required readings in the curriculum to incorporate multicultural nuances, perhaps by choosing books with the same storyline or theme but from different cultural perspectives.
- Select multicultural books that are written by multicultural authors and illustrators; do not rely on translations from English.

- Incorporate culturally diverse texts into the classroom through books on tape featuring titles chosen by students.
- Uncover biases inherent in the literature and discuss the reaction by students.
- Account for multicultural voices, including Indigenous languages and varieties of English, in discussions around literature and storytelling.

Here's what students can do to show evidence for learning:

- Offer fresh insights and feedback on classroom readings based on their own experiences, languages, and cultures.
- Hold conversations with classmates on their reactions to characters, events, and circumstances from their vantage point.
- Express their opinions and insights from different text genres in multimodal ways.
- Act out interpretations of stories, poems, or raps of their liking.
- Create and perform puppet shows, plays, performances, and reenactments.

Chapter Summary

Multilingual learners are a tremendously heterogeneous population as are the educators with whom they interact. One of the most effective ways to support multilingual learners' literacy is to ensure that all teachers are familiar with and draw from language standards and language development standards, as together they can be a powerful duo for underscoring and reinforcing the value of languaging in content learning.

Additionally, we have emphasized how multimodalities—visual, graphic, linguistic, and kinesthetic avenues to learning—and oral language development must be incorporated into curriculum, instruction, and assessment as these critical literacy components aim to increase accessibility and fairness, especially for multilingual students. Linguistic and cultural relevance of materials coupled with multilingual learners' increased access to their full linguistic and cultural resources helps fortify the language arts classroom as well as more fully characterize students' language and literacy development.

Extensions

For Reflection

1. In states that have enacted legislation mandating the Science of Reading, structured literacy has tended to usurp the language arts block in classrooms in the lower grades. Remembering that literacy for language development is distinct from literacy for language arts, what else is needed so that multilingual learners can fully benefit from their literacy experience?
2. You and your grade-level team might consider revisiting your language arts curriculum, its textbooks, and supplemental resources through the lens of your multilingual learners in search of inherent biases. To what extent do your materials have linguistic and cultural relevance for multilingual learners, and how might it truly be sustained?

For Action

1. How might you begin to expand your exploration of multiliteracies? What does it look like in your classroom, your school, or your district? What strategies might you use to optimize access for your multilingual learners to succeed in the language arts classroom? How might you describe multiliteracies to your colleagues or administrators, and what steps might you plan to take to advance multiliteracies as part of your language arts curriculum?
2. What ideas from this chapter might you bring to your grade-level team to make your language arts curriculum more accessible and meaningful for your multilingual learners? Might you consider designing a policy or a set of principles that embrace the languages and cultures of your multilingual learners? How might you treat translanguaging?

Resources

Castro, M., & Gottlieb, M. (2021, October). Multiliteracies: A glimpse into bilingual language arts classrooms. *WIDA Focus Bulletin*. Board of Regents of the University of Wisconsin System. https://wida.wisc.edu/resources/multiliteracies-glimpse-language-arts-bilingual-classrooms

National Council of Teachers of English. (2019). *Position statement: Definition of literacy in a digital age.* https://ncte.org/statement/nctes-definition-literacy-digital-age/

Teachers of English to Speakers of Other Languages. (2010). *Position paper on language and literacy development for young English language learners (ages 3–8).* https://www.tesol.org/media/brtdsnng/literacyyoungell2010.pdf

WIDA. (2021). *Marco de referencia de las artes del lenguaje del español de WIDA: Aplicación para la actualización y desarrollo de estándares.* Board of Regents of the University of Wisconsin System https://wida.wisc.edu/sites/default/files/resource/Marco-ALE-Estandares.pdf

4 Academic Languag*ing* for Mathematics

MULTILINGUAL LEARNERS IN THE MATHEMATICS CLASSROOM

- May be well versed mathematically yet not be able to communicate effectively in English (i.e., older newcomers with consistent schooling may already have grade-level mathematical knowledge or beyond)
- May need extra time to think through a problem mathematically when unfamiliar with the written and oral language
- May show evidence for learning in different ways
- May be more comfortable showing mathematical solutions through multimodalities (e.g., tallies, graphs, spreadsheets, manipulatives, diagrams)
- Should have opportunities to explore and discuss mathematics in the language(s) of their choice

MULTILINGUAL LEARNERS IN THE MATHEMATICS CLASSROOM

- Should have access to resources in multiple languages to increase their accessibility to solve mathematical problems
- Should be able to choose from a variety of mathematics classes, including advanced courses

SPOTLIGHT ON MATHEMATICAL CONTENT

- Mathematics literacy revolves around three integrated components: mathematical proficiency, mathematical practices, and mathematical discourse.
- Mathematical practices and discourse utilize
    - Multiple symbol systems (e.g., written text, numbers, graphs, tables)
    - Multiple modes of communication (i.e., interactive, interpretative—reading, listening, and viewing—and expressive—writing, speaking, and representing)
    - Multiple representations (e.g., manipulatives, gestures, tables, drawings, symbols, graphs)
    - Multiple language registers (e.g., technical mathematical language, home languages, everyday language)

SPOTLIGHT ON LANGUAGE AND CULTURE

- Although there are many similarities among number systems across the world, mathematics (particularly as taught in schools) is far from being a universal language.
- Some students may be familiar with the metric system and different monetary denominations.
- Some students come from places where decimal numbers are represented with commas instead of periods, or where large numbers are written using periods instead of commas.
- Many familiar words and expressions take on different meanings in the mathematics classroom (e.g., *range*, *value*, *place*).
- Mathematical processes may be different around the world (e.g., division).
- The origin and development of mathematics have been traced to different cultures (e.g., African, Arabic, Aztec, Egyptian, Chinese, Eskimo, Greek, Inca, Indian, Mayan, Native American, Roman).
- Ethnomathematics examines how different cultural groups use mathematics to solve day-to-day problems in clever, contextualized, and unique ways.

Introduction

Linguistic variability has become the norm in classrooms worldwide, and the ability to live and work in multiple languages is increasingly regarded as a social and economic asset. Recent research in mathematics education (e.g., Barwell et al., 2019) highlights how multilingualism shapes students' mathematical thinking, emphasizing the need to leverage students' linguistic repertoires in mathematics instruction. In addition, the National Council of Teachers of Mathematics (NCTM) calls for equitable instructional practices, including noticing students and learning about the worlds they live in.

The first section of this chapter outlines three key topics in teaching mathematics for multilingual learners: a review of the eight Standards for Mathematical Practice, essential teaching strategies for language-responsive mathematics instruction, and recommendations for fostering meaningful discussions in mathematics classrooms (such as the one shown in Figure 4.1). Following a discussion of dimensions of academic languaging for mathematics—discourse, sentences, words/phrases, and symbols—the chapter analyzes two model texts: a story problem and a science, technology, engineering, and mathematics (STEM) assignment. These analyses illustrate the potential linguistic and cultural nuances that everyday mathematics tasks may pose to multilingual students' conceptual understanding. Toward the end of the chapter, specific teaching practices are suggested, offering strategies that integrate both linguistic and mathematical perspectives to better support multilingual learners in developing deeper comprehension and engagement.

Figure 4.1 ***Matemáticas* in Ida Crocamo-Farley's Dual Language Middle School Classroom**

Source: Photo by Steven J. Morrison

Current Perspectives on Teaching and Learning Mathematics for Multilingual Learners

Eight Standards for Mathematical Practice

The eight Standards for Mathematical Practice (SMPs) describe essential mathematical habits of mind and action that can guide K–12 curriculum, pedagogy, and assessment.

SMP 1. Make sense of problems and persevere in solving them.

SMP 2. Reason abstractly and quantitatively.

SMP 3. Construct viable arguments and critique the reasoning of others.

SMP 4. Model with mathematics.

SMP 5. Use appropriate tools strategically.

SMP 6. Attend to precision.

SMP 7. Look for and make use of structure.

SMP 8. Look for and express regularity in repeated reasoning (National Governors Association Center for Best Practices & Center for Chief State School Officers, 2010).

For the SMPs to be meaningful to multilingual learners, they must be couched within equitable instructional practices. The NCTM is quite adamant in its demand for equity.

> Equity-based mathematics teaching requires more than implementing new curriculum or using specific practices because it involves taking a stand for what is right. It requires mathematics teachers to reflect on their own identity, positions, and beliefs in regards to racist and sorting-based mechanisms. It involves noticing students, learning about the worlds they live in, and building mathematics that comes from these worlds. And finally, it involves engaging other educators in partnerships to build equity-oriented communities. (Chao et al., 2014)

The NCTM calls on all educators to take an equity stance. In this book, we position academic languaging for mathematics as a goal for teachers and school leaders.

Stop and Think

Mathematical Autobiography

Have you had your students do a mathematical autobiography? It is a wonderful way to learn about your students' feelings toward—and experiences with—mathematics. At the end of the chapter, you will find ideas for math autobiographies (see Figure 4.7). As appropriate, you can model this activity by sharing your own math autobiography!

The language for mathematics plays a pivotal role in the implementation of each recommended SMP. For example, "attend to precision"

(SMP 6) focuses on precise communication in speech, written symbols, and other representations (e.g., graphs and diagrams). The term *precision*, however, can be interpreted differently, particularly in reference to multilingual learners. Judit Moschkovich (2013) cautions teachers to consider when and how to focus on precision. She reminds us that "precise claims can be expressed in imperfect language and that attending to precision at the individual word meaning level will get in the way of students' expressing their emerging mathematical ideas" (Moschkovich, 2013, p. ix). Teaching 10 important words for the topic will not help students understand mathematical concepts and develop critical thinking skills; however, giving students voice to reason abstractly and construct viable arguments will.

In the next section we discuss two additional current topics from the mathematics education literature that focus on teaching mathematics in classrooms with multilingual learners. The first topic summarizes work by German Professor Susanne Prediger on language-responsive teaching. Her work demonstrates how effective mathematics teaching must address not just numerical concepts but also the specific language demands inherent in mathematics discourse. This work is especially timely due to the increasing linguistic heterogeneity in classrooms worldwide. The second topic, connected to SMP 3 (i.e., "construct viable arguments and critique the reasoning of others"), highlights the need for discussion-oriented classrooms that draw on students' languages, cultures, and communities and validate students' ideas. This section also outlines broad strategies for facilitating classroom discussions.

Language-Responsive Mathematics Teaching

In her analysis of effective teaching practices when working with multilingual students, Professor Prediger (2019) examines the skills teachers need to integrate language support into mathematics education effectively. Prediger emphasizes that language in mathematics is not only for communication but also plays a critical role in students' cognitive development and conceptual understanding.

The study outlines five essential teaching practices, referred to as "jobs," for successful language-responsive mathematics teaching:

- **Noticing** students' language use and identifying their linguistic needs
- **Demanding** participation in activities that require both cognitive and language engagement
- **Supporting** students' language use with scaffolds, such as word/phrase walls

- **Developing** students' language skills over time by bridging different language registers
- **Identifying** the critical language demands in mathematical content to focus efforts effectively

These teacher jobs, according to Prediger (2019), will be effective in mathematics classrooms if teachers have the following four orientations or assumptions:

1. Accepting and valuing language and cultural diversity
2. Sharing responsibility for students' language learning
3. Advancing instead of reducing language
4. Integrating language and mathematical learning, instead of just adding language learning

For further information in English about Prediger's research on conceptually oriented and language-responsive instructional approaches and their theoretical and empirical foundations, review the materials listed as follows.

Look Closer

Professor Susanne Prediger's Work on Language-Responsive Mathematics Teaching

Erath, K., Ingram, J., Moschkovich, J., & Prediger, S. (2021, February). Designing and enacting instruction that enhances language for mathematics learning: A review of the state of development and research. *ZDM: The International Journal on Mathematics Education, 53*(2), 245–262. https://doi.org/10.1007/s11858-020-01213-2

Prediger, S. (2019). Investigating and promoting teachers' expertise for language-responsive mathematics teaching. *Mathematics Education Research Journal, 31*(4), 367–392. https://doi.org/10.1007/s13394-019-00258-1

Prediger, S., & Buró, R. (2024). Fifty ways to work with students' diverse abilities? A video study on inclusive teaching practices in secondary mathematics classrooms. *International Journal of*

(Continued)

(Continued)

Inclusive Education, *28*(2), 124–143. https://doi.org/10.1080/13603116.2021.1925361

Prediger, S., & Neugebauer, P. (2023). Can students with different language backgrounds equally profit from a language-responsive instructional approach for percentages? Differential effectiveness in a field trial. *Mathematical Thinking and Learning*, *25*(1), 2–22. https://doi.org/10.1080/10986065.2021.1919817

YERME MathEd. (2021, February 4). *YERME interview series: Interview with former ERME President Susanne Prediger* [Video]. YouTube. https://www.youtube.com/watch?v=q5RAHh7lvf0

Meaningful Discussions in the Mathematics Classroom

The third SMP highlights the importance of meaningful discourse. For this standard, students are expected to "construct viable arguments and critique the reasoning of others," both of which lend themselves to classroom discussions. When students are encouraged to talk about their mathematical ideas or listen to and engage with the details of others' mathematical ideas, they are being mathematicians (Franke, 2014). Classroom conversations are a powerful strategy that allows students to see themselves as valued mathematical thinkers (Huinker & Bill, 2017).

Today's mathematics classroom conversations need to look very different from the kind of conversations (or lack thereof) that pervaded mathematics teaching in the last century. Walter (2018) offers a comparison of traditional classroom dialogue versus discourse focused on student meanings:

TRADITIONAL CONVERSATIONS	MEANINGFUL DISCOURSE
Low-level questions (e.g., "What is . . . ?" or "Which . . . ?")	High-level questions (e.g., "How . . . ?" or "Why . . . ?")
Questions that ask for a yes/no response	Open-ended questions or statements
Leading questions (e.g., "Is the next step ____ or ____?")	Nonleading questions (e.g., "How should we approach the problem?")
Focus on procedures, steps, solutions	Focus on thoughts, strategies, discussions
Depth of Knowledge (Levels 1 and 2 of 4)	Depth of Knowledge (Levels 3 and 4 of 4)
Teacher-centered	Student-centered

Adapted from Walter, 2018, p. 182

In discussion-oriented classrooms, students' responses inform the teacher's questions and shape the course of classroom talk. In particular, the teacher validates specific students' ideas by incorporating their responses into subsequent questions. In addition, drawing on students' languages, their cultures, and their communities' use of mathematical concepts can generate student interest and classroom engagement. For example, in a geometry class with several students from Algeria, Pakistan, and Somalia, Ms. Hodnett wanted her students to discover the mathematical concepts hidden in Islamic art and understand the practical use of mathematics through these explorations. Following a short slide presentation of Islamic art, Ms. Hodnett provided some background information about the culture and art, wrote some open-ended questions, encouraged discussion, and presented a list of resources. Next, she again showed a few of the slides while highlighting patterns and geometrical designs, asking questions, and hearing students' ideas. By the time students joined their small groups, they were curious about both the cultural and the mathematical aspects of the design. The small-group activity had a twofold goal: (1) to discover the patterns on their assigned photograph and (2) to replicate those patterns on paper using basic tools (e.g., compass, triangular ruler, protractor). Both activities required active discussion and engagement on the part of the students. The lesson was a success. Students gained an understanding of different concepts of plane geometry, used cartesian coordinates to draw on a plane, realized how polygons were used in Islamic art, and learned an appreciation for Islamic culture. Further, many of Ms. Hodnett's students felt validated to see some of their families' history included in the teaching of mathematics while other students had opportunities to "teach" their peers about their culture.

Look Closer

Islamic Arts and Mathematics

For more information, see the following resources:

- Metropolitan Museum of Art. (2004). *Islamic art and geometric design: Activities for learning.* https://www.metmuseum.org/-/media/files/learn/for-educators/publications-for-educators/islamic_art_and_geometric_design.pdf
- The Art of Maths, Co-funded by the Erasmus+ Programme of the European Union. (2020). *Tool 2: Islamic art and geometry.* https://artofmaths.eu/wp-content/uploads/2020/02/TOOL_2.pdf

Stop and Think

Mathematics Is Not Just Solving for x and *y*

Observing and reflecting on student participation in classroom discussions can offer insights into what students can do in terms of, for example, talking, listening, connecting with others, interpreting text, and solving problems. It can also offer clues about how some structures and routines might encourage or inhibit participation for students. Examples of questions to explore include the following:

1. Which students participate, and in what ways?
2. Which students are most active, and when?
3. What opportunities do all students have to make meaningful mathematical contributions?
4. What can teachers do or say that might expand students' access to meaningful participation (e.g., modeling, offering resources in multiple languages)?
5. What specific norms, routines, task structures, classroom arrangements, and visuals support or inhibit participation for some students?

The Language for Mathematics

> "Mathematics is not about numbers, equations, computations, or algorithms: it is about understanding."
>
> —William Paul Thurston (Cook, 2009, pp. 76–77)

The language for mathematics is the system used to communicate mathematical ideas. This language includes a variety of representational forms beyond oral and written language, such as symbol systems and visual displays. The semantic web in Figure 4.2 offers a visual representation of the complexity of academic languaging needed for mathematics that consists of layers of (1) everyday language, (2) technical terms and symbols, (3) grammatical conventions unique to mathematical discourse, and (4) oral and written language tailored for different purposes and audiences. This variety of registers and multimodalities used during mathematics instruction can play a role in affording or restricting access to the content to be learned.

The ability to develop understanding and communicate understandings in the mathematics classroom requires that students recognize and use discourse, sentences, words/phrases, and symbols. Each of these aspects

Figure 4.2 Engaging With the Language for Mathematics

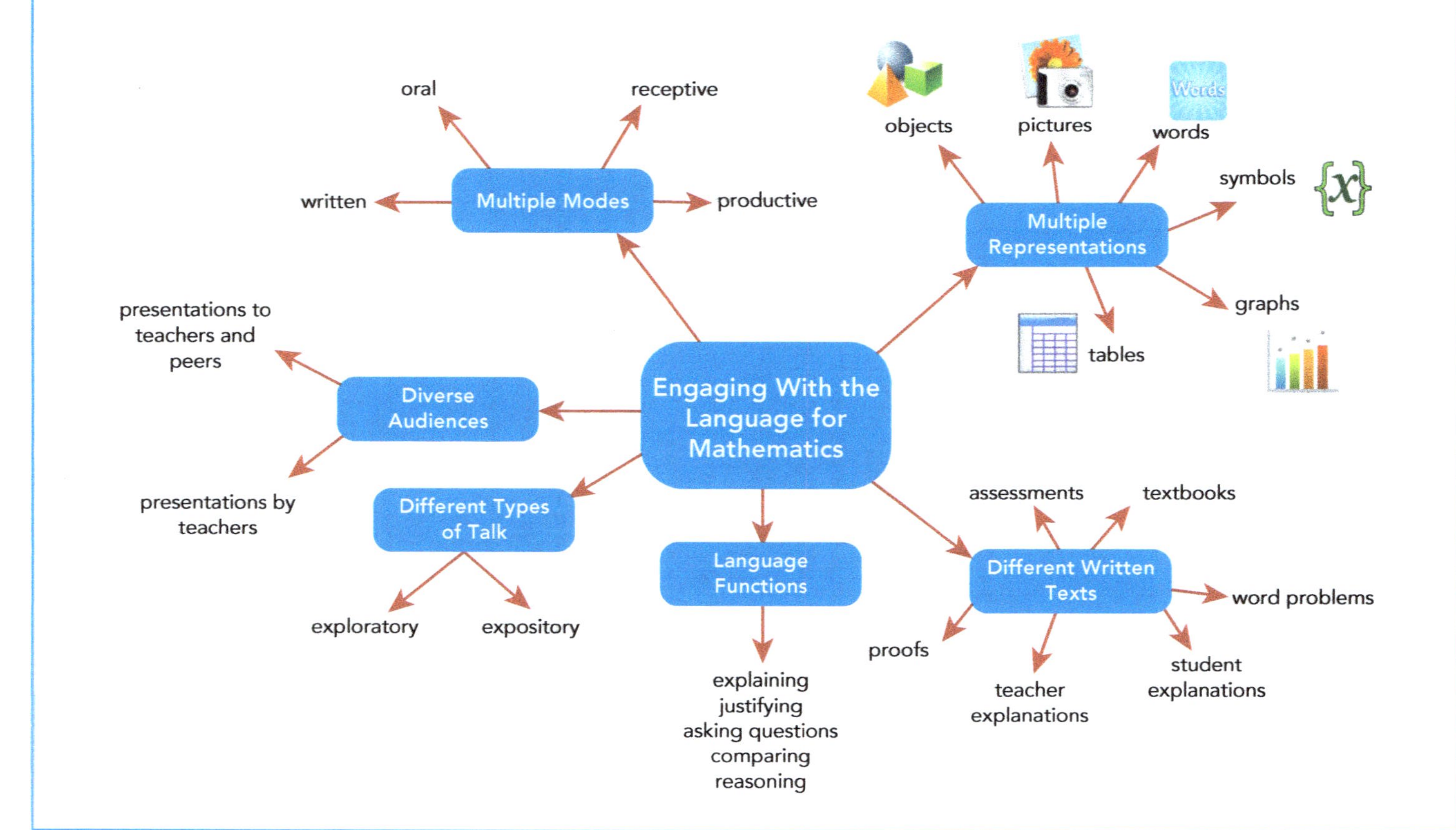

Adapted from Gottlieb & Ernst-Slavit (2014)

of the language for mathematics is explained as follows, accompanied by pertinent examples.

> "We must leave behind simplified views of language as vocabulary, embrace the multimodal and multi-semiotic nature of mathematical activity, and shift from monolithic views of math talk or dichotomized views of everyday and mathematics registers."
>
> —Judit N. Moschkovich (2024, p. 469)

Discourse

As discussed earlier, discourse refers to the larger bodies of oral and written language—their organization, coherence, and cohesiveness—that are tied to purposes for communicating, such as describing, explaining, and debating, within social contexts. Mathematical discourse encompasses various modes of communication, involving both written and spoken expressions for mathematical explanations, proofs, definitions, and text types such as word problems.

Utilizing a range of language forms is crucial for effectively conveying mathematical ideas and reasoning. Supporting the development of mathematical discourse entails providing students with ample opportunities to articulate their thoughts. Therefore, and as stated in the section on "Current Perspectives on Teaching and Learning Mathematics for Multilingual Learners," facilitating discussions and using language-responsive instructional approaches are key for learning how to language in mathematics classrooms.

Stop and Think

Did You Know That Fractions Are Not Read the Same Way in All Languages?

Bussi and collaborators (2014) highlight differences in reading orders between languages as significant for mathematical understanding. In European languages, fractions like $\frac{2}{3}$ are read from top to bottom, focusing first on the numerator (2) and then the denominator (3). Conversely, many Asian languages reverse this order, reading the denominator first, emphasizing the whole before the part. The authors suggest that this approach may enhance conceptual understanding, as it aligns with the idea that the whole must be divided before identifying its parts.

Sentences

There are language patterns and grammatical structures present in sentences specific to mathematics. Just as sentences in English and in other languages have verbs and state a complete thought (e.g., "The bird is green."), so do mathematical sentences (e.g., $y = 2x$). The following are examples of mathematical sentences presented in two different ways:

Eighteen minus ten equals eight	$18 - 10 = 8$
Ex equals three	$x = 3$
Two times ex equals six ex	$2x = 6x$
Tee plus four is equal to four plus tee	$t + 4 = 4 + t$

The "verb" in all the preceding sentences is the *equals* sign, and its presence makes each sentence a complete thought. Important to mention is that students can be misled when they attempt to read and write mathematical sentences in the same way they read and write everyday written text. For example, many students try to literally translate a mathematical concept expressed in words into a concept expressed in symbols. Dale and Cuevas (1992) demonstrated this type of linear, one-to-one translation with the algebraic phrase "the number a is five less than the number b." In their research, they found that students tended to represent this phrase with the mathematical expression $a = 5 - b$, when it should be $a = b - 5$.

Other language features may also complicate students' understandings at the sentence level. These include the use of logical connectors (e.g., *consequently*, *however*) that in everyday language indicate a logical relationship between parts of a text. In mathematics, however, they signal similarity or contradiction. Along the same lines, the use of comparative structures (e.g., *greater* or *less than*, 5 *less than* 9, n *times as much as*) and prepositions (e.g., the temperature fell *by* 12 degrees, *from* 24 degrees, *to* 12 degrees) may present snags for students trying to learn English and mathematics at the same time.

Look Closer

Building Your Cross-Cultural and Cross-Linguistic Knowledge

Educators at all levels can benefit from understanding the similarities and differences between various cultures and languages. The following three

(Continued)

(Continued)

books delve into essential aspects of specific cultures and languages that are crucial for understanding students, families, and communities.

Egbert, J., & Ernst-Slavit, G. (2017). *Views from inside: Languages, cultures, and schooling for K–12 educators*. Information Age.

Gannon, M. J., & Pillai, R. (2015). *Understanding global cultures: Metaphorical journeys through 34 nations, clusters of nations, continents, and diversity*. Sage.

Yoon, B., & Pratt, K. L. (2023). *Primary language impact on second language and literacy learning: Linguistically responsive strategies for classroom teachers*. Lexington Books.

Words/Phrases

English number names are highly irregular. For example, we say *fourteen*, *sixteen*, *seventeen*, *eighteen*, and *nineteen*. Shouldn't we also say *oneteen*, *twoteen*, *threeteen*, and *fiveteen*? In counting by tens, we have a similar discontinuity. There are *forty* and *sixty*, which resemble *four* and *six*. But there are also *twenty*, *thirty*, and *fifty*, somewhat related to *two*, *three*, and *five*. If we keep counting up, the numbers above *twenty* will have the tens first (e.g., *fifty-six*) whereas for the numbers below *twenty* we put the ones first (e.g., *thirteen*).

Mathematics languaging has cultural implications in how students understand and use mathematics. For example, Japanese, Korean, and Chinese use a more logical counting system than what is used in English. Eleven is *ten-one*, twelve is *ten-two*, and so on. Thus, the irregularity in English number names may have important consequences in basic computations. If during a Number Talk (see the following discussion) a teacher asks third graders to add *four-hundred-thirteen* plus *sixty-seven* in English, they will need to convert those words to numbers (413 + 67) and then do the computation. In Japanese this same request would sound like *four-hundreds*; *one-ten*; *three* plus *six-tens*; *seven*. Thus, Japanese students do not need to do the extra step of translating the words into numbers because the place value ideas are embedded directly into the number words (Ernst-Slavit & Slavit, 2013; for additional examples of multidigit computation methods across cultures, see Fuson, 2020).

Stop and Think

Number Talks

A **Number Talk** is a strategy, often embedded at the beginning of a mathematics lesson, designed to engage students in "mental math" through grappling with straightforward numerical exercises. Number Talks enable teachers to engage students in discussions of the connections among different approaches, errors, and misconceptions (see, e.g., Fuson & Leinwand, 2023).

Another important aspect of the language for mathematics at the words/phrases level is that many common English words have unique meanings in mathematics (e.g., *plane*, *face*, *bring down*, *net*, *negative*, *column*, *table*) and can be a source of confusion for multilingual learners. The example in Figure 4.3 (Moschkovich, 2008) underscores the need to help students learn the meaning of everyday words like *find* in the context of mathematics. The student did not know that "find x" within this mathematical context means "solve for x."

Figure 4.3 Finding x vs. Solving for x

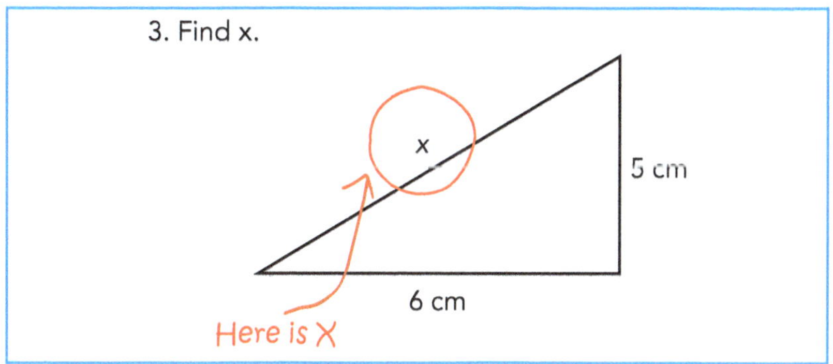

Adapted from Moschkovich (2008).

In general terms, the mathematics register includes diverse words, phrases, and expressions that can be grouped into three categories: everyday language, cross-disciplinary language, and technical language. Definitions and examples for each category are presented in Table 4.1.

Balancing rigor and comprehension implies careful attention to the kinds of words and phrases used during mathematics instruction. In mathematical word problems, specific words and phrases can suggest the kind of procedure that needs to be applied. For example, the word *and* often

Table 4.1 Types of Vocabulary and Examples

WORD/PHRASE	EXAMPLES	DEFINITION
Everyday language	*headphones* *healthy food* *buy*	Terms and phrases used in almost any setting
Cross-disciplinary language	*compare* *distribute* *table*	Terms and phrases used across content areas, including mathematics
Technical language	*data table* *irrational numbers* *polygons*	Terms and phrases specifically used with mathematics

means addition while the word *change* may mean subtraction. However, teachers should remain careful and flexible, as different students can identify different operations for the same problem. A key word approach to solving word problems is not recommended, although visuals with common words and phrases used in mathematics problems can be helpful for multilingual students (see the anchor chart in Table 4.2).

Table 4.2 Key Words and Phrases Used in Mathematics Problems

+	−	×	÷
add	are not	area	average
added to	difference	array	between
addend	decreased by	columns	cut up
altogether	dropped	double	distribute
and	exceed	each	divided by
both	farther	equal groups	dividend
combined	fewer	factor	divisor
in addition	greater than	in all	each
in all	how many more	multiple	each part
increased by	left	multiplied by	equal groups
join	left over	multiply	half
more than	less than	product	same
plus	minus	rows of	separate
sum	remain	times	shared equally
together	reduced by	total	split
total	take away	twice	quotient

This resource is available for download at https://companion.corwin.com/courses/Academic-Languaging.

Symbols

Mathematics uses symbols to represent and communicate concepts, values, or structures (e.g., sequences). As depicted in Table 4.2, those small symbols have enormous meanings. Furthermore, without symbols it would be very difficult to express procedures or relations. For example, solving an equation using words would take several paragraphs. However, words must accompany the introduction and use of mathematical symbols given that their purpose is to consolidate meaning. In doing so, they can hide meaning. Making the general and specific role of symbols explicit as a multimodal resource offers support to multilingual learners, such as the following.

There are the 10 digits: 0, 1, 2, . . . 9

There are symbols for operations: $+ - \times / \sqrt{} \pm$

There are symbols that "stand in" for values: x, y, . . .

There are many special symbols: $= \neq \approx \infty < \leq$, . . .

The next section will offer a closer examination of the language for mathematics by first pointing out the language demands of two model texts. As discussed earlier, a model text is an example of a text type. It can be a short text, a teacher- or student-created example, an excerpt of a longer text, a test item, or a story problem that has been analyzed to make visible the construction of the text and the use of certain language features. Model texts help mathematics teachers become aware of linguistic subtleties and can be used to demonstrate to students how specific language features work.

Using Model Texts in the Mathematics Classroom

As mentioned earlier, model texts can be used to examine the language used in assignments, videos, textbooks, assessments, and other tasks and materials. Model texts can also be helpful when collaborating with other educators, as examples for students, and to highlight important aspects related to letter conventions, symbols, vocabulary, grammatical structures, and discourse in language-responsive mathematics classrooms. In this section we provide two examples of typical mathematics activities and analyze the language students need to understand and use in order to succeed in mathematics classrooms. More specifically, we will scrutinize a lower elementary word problem and a middle school STEM assignment with multilingual learners in mind.

Model Text 1: Lower Elementary Word Problem

Also called story problems, word problems are used for mathematics teaching and assessment across all grade levels. Although word problems can be a powerful tool for learners to make sense of and reason with mathematical concepts, they can also be taxing for students since they have to be able to decode words and phrases to understand the context of the problem, identify the question that needs to be addressed, and finally create an equation or other mathematical representation to support their solution strategy. Here is a word problem suitable for students in the early grade levels.

A music store is having its "Black Friday" sale. The store will give $5 off for the second item a customer purchases. Emma wants to buy a pair of headphones for $25 and a CD for $18. How much does she need to pay in total?

As you read this word problem, ask yourself the following questions (please reflect on these questions before looking at Figure 4.4):

1. What are some of the language challenges, particularly for multilingual learners?
2. What are some of the mathematical challenges, particularly for multilingual learners?
3. What are some sociocultural features in this problem that may hinder understanding, particularly for multilingual learners?

Figure 4.4 Model Text 1: A Story Problem

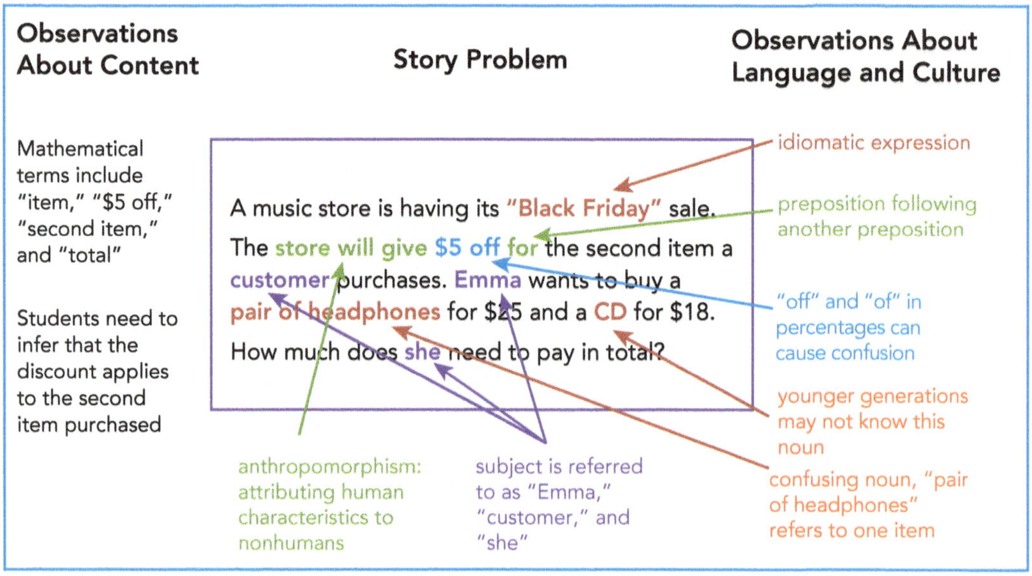

Like many word problems, directions can appear unclear and the choice of terms confusing, especially if the problem includes idiomatic expressions (e.g., "Black Friday"), unfamiliar words (e.g., "CD"), and a singular object referred to as "a pair of headphones." In addition to words and phrases, at the sentence level we notice that multiple terms are used to refer to the subject—that is, "Emma," "customer," and the pronoun "she." Likewise, when discussing percentages, the terms "off" and "of" can add some confusion since the percentage *of* something is quite different from the percentage *off* something. Finally, the use of anthropomorphism, as in "the store will give," can result in ambiguity and misleading communication.

In sum, for students to solve this word problem they have to understand numeric values, recognize mathematical operations, interpret discount language, apply arithmetic skills, engage in sequential reasoning, recognize the context, comprehend relevant words and phrases, and apply mathematical knowledge to a real-world situation. Making visible or removing some of these demands and supporting learners through work with others can often produce more meaningful learning experiences in classrooms. Later in the chapter, in the section on "Strategies for Moving Mathematics Learning Forward With Multilingual Learners," we offer selected strategies to support students in their work with word problems.

Supporting Elementary Students With Word Problems

For mathematics fluency a student must have the ability to solve a variety of word problems. However, as Model Text 1 illustrates, solving math problems is not just about math; it's also about reading multiple lines of text, identifying what is being asked, selecting the numbers to use, eliminating additional information, and setting up the equation—all before "doing any computation." The following are selected strategies to support students with the language for word problems:

1. Utilize visual representations (e.g., use visuals to represent a CD and a pair of headphones).
2. Connect to real-world contexts (e.g., relate mathematical concepts to stores in the neighborhood).
3. Use scaffolding techniques (e.g., break a problem into small parts).

4. Incorporate culturally sustaining strategies (e.g., use scenarios that reflect students' languages and cultures).
5. Plan for peer interaction and collaboration (e.g., work in small groups).
6. Provide student-constructed word and phrase walls, sentence frames for expressing mathematical thinking, and step-by-step student word problem strategies (e.g., see Tables 4.3 and 4.4).

Table 4.3 Example 1 of Step-by-Step Word Problem Strategies

MULTISTEP WORD PROBLEMS		
1	Read and visualize	*The monkeys picked 13 bananas. They ate 6. Later they picked 2 more. How many bananas do they have now?*
2	Write an answer statement	*The monkeys have ____ bananas.*
3	Write a number statement	*13 – 6 + 2 = ?*
4	Chunk and solve	*13 – 6 + 2 = ?* *(13 – 6) + 2 = ?* [chunk 13 – 6 and resolve] *7 + 2 = 9*

Table 4.4 Example 2 of Step-by-Step Word Problem Strategies

5-STEP WORD PROBLEM ATTACK PLAN	
STEPS	**THINK**
#1 **Read It**	What is this problem about?
#2 **Reread It**	What is this problem asking?
#3 **Plan It**	What is the best way to solve this problem?
#4 **Solve It**	What operation(s) should I use? + – × ÷
#5 **Check It**	Does my answer make sense? Is my math correct?

Model Text 2: Grade 6
STEM Assignment—Pollution Project

Plastic pollutes and harms our earth! What should we do with all our plastic? A group of sixth graders were asked to use mathematics to provide evidence to convince their principal to make a change. What math is necessary to tackle this part of their pollution project? How might you take on this issue?

Our school cafeteria is switching from using 500 plastic trays per day to degradable ones, where chemicals break down the material. Each degradable tray weighs $\frac{1}{4}$ pound or 4 ounces and decomposes, or comes apart, in 1 year. We estimated how much plastic waste our school could save in a 30-day month. Then we figured out how much plastic waste could be saved in a year (12 months). Explain why math is important for understanding the solution to pollution.

In this second model text we see the integration of mathematics, science, and language in a middle school STEM dilemma. How might you deconstruct the text to parse these three sources of academic languaging for multilingual learners? You and your grade-level team might use the following chart to jump-start your discussion of the interrelated issues in this STEM task.

THE LANGUAGE FOR MATHEMATICS	THE LANGUAGE FOR SCIENCE	THE LANGUAGE FOR LEARNING

There is potential misunderstanding for multilingual learners on all three language fronts (see Figure 4.5). In the area (a math term in and of itself) of mathematics, students must be conversant in weights and measures used in the United States, be able to apply fractions, and decipher multiple meanings of "figure." Examining the science portion involves understanding the concept of "degradable" and its relation to pollution of plastic waste. In terms of mathematics, the model text delves into the necessary calculations to estimate pollution reduction, including setting up and solving equations that are not explicit in the scenario.

Figure 4.5 Model Text 2: A STEM Assignment

<table>
<tr><th>Observations About Content</th><th></th><th>Observations About Language</th></tr>
<tr><td>Multilingual learners need to be familiar with "ounces" and "pounds."

The mathematical operations necessary for solving the problem are inferred.

Mathematical terms that may be confusing include "figure" and "figured out."</td><td>Our school cafeteria is switching from using 500 plastic trays per day to degradable ones, where chemicals break down the material. Each degradable tray weighs $\frac{1}{4}$ pound or 4 ounces, and decomposes, or comes apart, in 1 year We estimated how much plastic waste our school could save in a 30-day month. Then we figured out how much plastic waste could be saved in a year (12 months). Explain why math is important for understanding the solution to pollution.

The parentheses signal a definition for "year."

Explain why is asking for reasons.</td><td>"Ones" could be a math term for digits, but here it refers to "trays."

Here are phrasal verbs that are also idiomatic expressions — a double whammy for multilingual learners.

In this case, the conjunction "or" does not mean a choice but the equivalent.

Multilingual learners might question, "what is a day month?"</td></tr>
</table>

As the analysis of these two model texts indicates, languaging in mathematics classrooms includes understanding discourse, sentence structures, words/phrases, and symbols. For multilingual learners, it may also include learning new words and phrases (e.g., *ounces*), using conjunctions (e.g., *or* means "equivalent" in the STEM problem, not "choice"), overcoming particularly difficult phrasing (e.g., "switching from using 500 plastic trays per day to degradable ones"), and constructing explanations (e.g., providing a rationale about the importance of mathematics "for understanding the solution to pollution"). In other words, learning mathematics is not just learning the technical terms or practicing procedural fluency; it's about conceptual understanding, reasoning, communicating, and sensemaking.

Languaging Plays a Critical Role in STEM

David Slavit and his collaborators (2021) emphasize that language plays a critical role in fostering students' ways of thinking about STEM, especially through claim-making and reasoning. Their work highlights how interdisciplinary STEM activities require students to articulate their ideas clearly, engage in reasoning processes, and build on prior knowledge. Through collaborative discussions, students make claims and negotiate meaning (Slavit et al., 2021), validate their reasoning (Lesseig et al., 2023; Slavit et al., 2022), and adapt their thinking (Simpson et al., 2025).

These cognitive activities are all essential aspects of problem-solving in STEM contexts (English, 2023).

In addition, Slavit and collaborators (2021) argue that effective communication, including verbal, nonverbal, and written modes, is integral to STEM learning as it allows students to explore diverse perspectives and refine their understandings. These interactions align with the broader goals of STEM education (English, 2023; Honey et al., 2020), helping students become competent thinkers by encouraging them to reason through complex, open-ended problems. Language serves as both a tool for expression and a supportive framework for cognitive processes, facilitating deeper engagement with interdisciplinary concepts.

Strategies for Moving Mathematics Learning Forward With Multilingual Learners

Supporting and Expecting Mathematical Competence in Your Multilingual Learners

One goal in the mathematics classroom is to ensure that multilingual learners are actively engaged in conversation. This can be achieved by providing the students with opportunities to participate and fostering their confidence by finding ways to showcase their mathematical thinking.

There are several practical approaches to actualizing this goal. Here are a few suggestions:

1. Encourage multiple modes of expression of mathematical ideas, including verbal explanations in English and the home language, written descriptions, gestures, drawings, and diagrams.
2. Avoid interrupting the students to "correct" their English; instead, focus on the substance of their ideas.
3. Use a variety of talk moves, including wait time, as discussed later in Table 4.5.
4. Be prepared to adapt your teaching behavior, particularly by adopting a strategic, student-oriented approach to teacher talk.
5. Utilize available resources to facilitate students' participation, such as collaborating with other teachers (see "Collaborating

With Other Educators"), utilizing translation tools, engaging other students as translators, and leveraging technology.

6. Inquire about students' experiences with mathematics education, especially arithmetic, in their home countries, and invite them to describe their educational systems. Demonstrate a curiosity and appreciation for cultural differences to foster a positive environment for all students.
7. Connect the students' prior experiences with mathematics in their home cultures with those in school.

Using and Linking Multiple Representations

Researchers have found that students learn more conceptually from words and phrases reinforced by objects and pictures than from words alone (e.g., Malone et al., 2020). Using multiple representations or multimodalities to make connections between pictures, graphs, symbols, tables, objects, and verbal explanations of mathematical relationships will both enable and assist students to develop a greater understanding of mathematical concepts and connections (e.g., Roberts et al., 2022). In other words, it is not enough in the kindergarten classroom, for example, to write the number 5 on the board and show young students that the teacher has five fingers on her hand. What would help is that in addition to the teacher's five fingers, students could count their own fingers, put five cubes together, count five objects using their home language, get into groups of five, and grab five crayons while their teacher models explicit connections between the numeral and its representations.

Stop and Think

"Construct a rhombus with side lengths of 4 inches."

What Do You Need to Know to Solve This Problem?

Here are some thoughts. To understand what the problem is asking, you need to know what it means to "construct." Does it mean to physically cut a paper in the shape of a rhombus, to draw by hand, or to draw by using a ruler? You also need to know what kind of quadrilateral figure is a rhombus. Now, what happens if you are only familiar with the metric system? What else might your multilingual learners encounter?

Orchestrating Intentional Talk With Talk Moves

Teachers can play an active role in facilitating productive mathematical discussions by employing **talk moves**—that is, the intentional communication strategies employed by teachers during instructional interactions that can facilitate learning and promote student engagement. The authors of *Intentional Talk* (Kazemi & Hintz, 2014) discuss seven key talk moves that can guide both teacher talk and student talk: Revoicing, Repeating, Reasoning, Adding On, Wait Time, Turn-and-Talk, and Revise. These seven talk moves with pertinent examples are listed in Table 4.5.

Table 4.5 Mathematics Talk Moves, Examples, and Purpose

MATHEMATICS TALK MOVES	PURPOSE
Revoicing • *So I hear you saying . . .* • *Are you saying that . . . ?*	• To clarify meaning or a misunderstanding • To link everyday language with more precise language
Repeating • *Yo comprendo. Manuel is saying . . .* • *Can you repeat or rephrase what ______ said about ______?*	• To show that what someone said was heard and understood • To emphasize important points • To restate important parts of complex ideas
Reasoning • *What evidence did you use?* • *Please explain that further*	• To encourage students to justify or elaborate their own thinking by providing evidence • To expose students to the thinking of others
Adding On • *I agree (or disagree) with ______ because ______.* • *Does anyone have something else to add?*	• To connect students' ideas to what someone else is saying • To promote discussion and deeper reasoning by building on the ideas of others
Wait Time • *Take your time . . .* • *I'll give you some time to think before asking you to respond.*	• To allow students to organize their thinking before responding • To provide opportunities for multilingual learners to mentally translate

(Continued)

(Continued)

MATHEMATICS TALK MOVES	PURPOSE
Turn-and-Talk • *Turn and talk to the person next to you . . .* • *Share your thinking about . . .*	• To invite students to clarify and share their ideas • To allow students to orient themselves to each other's ideas • To have students build confidence before sharing with the whole group
Revise • *Would you like to change your strategy now? Why?* • *How has your thinking/ understanding changed?*	• To signal to students that it is acceptable to change their thinking • To provide opportunities to reflect on and review learning

Adapted from Kazemi & Hintz, 2014

Clearly, these talk moves help create a dynamic and interactive learning environment where students can make meaning by actively engaging in mathematics languaging to develop a deeper understanding of mathematics.

Collaborating With Other Educators

Mathematics teachers who work collaboratively with other education specialists, including those in special education, gifted education, instructional technology, and English language development, enhance opportunities for supporting students to maximize their success. In addition, teacher collaboration with colleagues to implement mathematics teaching practices prompt a growth mindset and establish a positive environment in their classrooms and school (Leinwand et al., 2014). For example, when a language specialist pairs with a mathematics specialist, two areas of expertise converge. Together the teachers can co-create an action plan along with their multilingual learners to optimize their students' learning opportunities.

Chapter Summary

Academic languaging for mathematics uses a combination of symbols, expressions, words and phrases, sentence constructions, discourse features, word order, conventions, idiomatic expressions, negations, and abbreviations. In today's world, everyone must know how to speak the language for mathematics as it is critical when interacting with technology and in solving common or complex real-world problems. Becoming aware of the richness of the language for mathematics is the first step in planning instruction that can increase all students' opportunities to learn, and subsequently impact, their understanding and mathematical achievement.

Extensions

For Reflection

1. In a Grade 3 classroom the teacher wrote on the board the following sentence:

   $$16 + 10 + 18 = x + 30$$

   Some students voiced that because the answer always follows the equals sign, the answer is 44. However, other students stated that x equals 14. As a teacher, what would you do in this situation?
   (a) Would you point at one of the students who got it right to come to the board and show the steps for solving the problem? (b) Would you model how to solve for x? (c) Would you have students work with a partner to discuss the two answers? (d) Would you encourage a whole-class discussion to help students understand the meaning of x? (e) Would you do something different? And, if so, what?

2. As we alluded to earlier, there are many mathematics homophones (words that sound the same but have different meanings). In addition to word walls, graphic organizers, and learning logs, how might you help students learn everyday words with multiple meanings?

3. Research consistently shows that one of the most influential factors in student success is the strength of the teacher–student relationship. When teachers build positive relationships, students are more likely to trust the process of productive struggle, stay motivated, and develop essential problem-solving skills. What activities have you used or observed your colleagues using to get to know your students?

For Action

1. Look at the seven talk moves in Table 4.5 designed to help getting discussions off the ground. Which talk moves are you currently using during mathematics instruction? What

additional talk moves would you like to add to your repertoire? In your next lesson, how might you incorporate new talk moves?

2. Read the following word problem. Do you think the context and sociocultural features of this problem will affect the understanding of your multilingual learners? If possible, try giving it to students, colleagues, and friends to find out.

   In the bustling market of Marrakesh, Ahmed is preparing to make a popular traditional Moroccan dish called Bstila for a family celebration. The recipe calls for $\frac{3}{4}$ kilograms of almonds to make the flavorful filling. Ahmed wants to make enough Bstila to serve to all the guests, so he decides to increase the recipe by making 5 batches. Almonds cost 450 dirham per kilo.

   Can you help Ahmed calculate (1) the total amount of almonds he needs for all the batches and (2) how much he will spend in Moroccan dirham?

3. World, state, and city flags offer great opportunities to examine shapes and symmetry in geometric figures. It might also help your multilingual students to share aspects of their own heritage. For example, if you ask Brazilian students to describe a rhombus, they will most likely describe the yellow rhombus on Brazil's flag (see Figure 4.6).

Figure 4.6 Flag of Brazil

Source: iStock.com/VanReeel

My Math Autobiography

Math autobiographies provide a platform for students to engage in self-reflection, connect emotionally with mathematics, and explore the personal significance of mathematical experiences. This autobiographical account can cover the student's history with mathematics, including early encounters with the subject, memorable experiences, challenges faced, achievements, and overall feelings toward mathematics. Multimodal approaches can be considered for the math autobiography: written text, visual representation (e.g., diagrams, graphs, timelines, collages), digital media (e.g., PowerPoint, video), mathematical artifacts (e.g., models), and interactive components. The following are examples of questions that can be included in a math autobiography. Ultimately, you can construct your own math autobiography based on your students' age, grade, and setting.

Figure 4.7

Potential Information to Include in a Math Autobiography

1. My home address (if applicable)
2. My age
    a. ______ years old
    b. ______ days old
    c. ______ months old
3. My height
4. My shoe size
5. Number of family members in my home
6. Number of pets in my home

7. Favorite or lucky number (draw and decorate it)
8. Number of doors in my house
9. Number of years until I am 50 years old
10. The time I have between waking up and arriving in school
11. Minutes per day I play video games
12. How many years I have played [soccer, football, lacrosse, basketball, or another sport]
13. How I spent my summer (design a pie chart)
14. How many times I used math over the weekend (e.g., baking a cake or cooking, going shopping, buying a sandwich, keeping score, counting laps, playing games, putting LEGO pieces together, organizing toys, planning a gathering)
15. A question I have about my neighborhood that relates to math (e.g., "How far is it to ________?")
16. How math could help people better understand me (explain)

Resources

Celedón-Pattichis, S., Lunney Borden, L., Pape, S., Males, J., Chapman, O. & Leonard, J. (2018). Asset-based approaches to equitable mathematics education research and practice. *Journal for Research in Mathematics Education, 49*(4), 373–389.

Civil, M., & Crespo, S. (2017). *Access and equity: Promoting high quality mathematics, grades 6–8*. National Council of Teachers of Mathematics.

Crespo, S., Celedón-Pattichis, S., & Civil, M. (2018). *Access and equity: Promoting high quality mathematics, grades 3–5*. National Council of Teachers of Mathematics.

de Araujo, Z., Orrill, C. H., & Jacobson, E. (2018). Designing communication-rich problem-centered mathematics professional development. *International Journal of Mathematical Education, Science, & Technology, 49*, 323–340.

de Araujo, Z., Roberts, S. A., Willey, C., & Zahner, W. (Editors). (2020). Special issue on multilingual learners: Translanguaging. *Teaching for Excellence and Equity in Mathematics, 11*(2). https://www.todos-math.org/assets/documents/TEEM/TEEM11-No2FINAL.pdf

Elliott, R., Loh, C. G., Psenka, C. E., Lewis, J. M., Kim, K.-Y., Haapala, K. R., Neal, D., & Okudan Kremer, G. E. (2022). Advancing transformative STEM learning: Converging perspectives from education, social science, mathematics, and engineering. *Journal of Integrated Design and Process Science*, *26*(3–4), 393–414. https://doi.org/10.3233/JID-220006

Gottlieb, M., & Ernst-Slavit, G. (2013a). *Academic language in diverse classrooms: Promoting content and language learning. Mathematics, Grades K–2*. Corwin.

Gottlieb, M., & Ernst-Slavit, G. (2013b). *Academic language in diverse classrooms: Promoting content and language learning. Mathematics, Grades 3–5*. Corwin.

Gottlieb, M., & Ernst-Slavit, G. (2013c). *Academic language in diverse classrooms: Promoting content and language learning. Mathematics, Grades 6–8*. Corwin.

Wilkinson, L. C. (2018). Learning language and mathematics: A perspective from linguistics and education. *Linguistics and Education*, *49*, 86–95. https://doi.org/10.1016/j.linged.2018.03.005

5 Academic Languaging for Social Studies

MULTILINGUAL LEARNERS IN THE SOCIAL STUDIES CLASSROOM

- May need time to become familiar with much of the material, particularly in the areas of U.S. history and geography
- May be able to make strong connections between cultural geography topics and their own lives and trajectories
- May be familiar with historical concepts presented around selected periods or dynasties, instead of in a linear manner

MULTILINGUAL LEARNERS IN THE SOCIAL STUDIES CLASSROOM

- May have a different understanding of what is considered ancient or old
- May not be acquainted with how to offer personal opinions or critical perspectives
- Should have opportunities to explore and discuss social studies topics in the language(s) of their choice
- Should have access to resources in multiple languages (e.g., Google Maps)

SPOTLIGHT ON SOCIAL STUDIES CONTENT

- The field of social studies comprises many different disciplines (e.g., economics, geography, history, psychology, archaeology).
- Many concepts (e.g., liberty, democracy, freedom) may be unknown by students coming from dictatorial regimes.
- Social studies textbooks and curricula are mostly written assuming that students have background knowledge on the topics—accumulated over time from one grade level to the next.

SPOTLIGHT ON LANGUAGE AND CULTURE

- Terminology in social studies can be abstract, culturally based, and difficult to translate.
- The perspectives and values present in textbooks and curricula might be very different from those of multilingual students' families and their home countries.

Introduction

The National Council for the Social Studies (NCSS, n.d.) emphasizes that the main objective of social studies education is to impart "content knowledge, intellectual skills, and civic values" that foster active and engaged citizenship both in the United States and globally. Social studies education seeks to help students understand domestic and global issues and guide them in making informed, thoughtful decisions. A major goal of social studies is to equip students with the skills and concepts needed to participate in a diverse democracy.

When teaching multilingual students, teachers must focus on students' cultural, linguistic, and civic knowledge and experiences to deliver impactful and meaningful social studies education (NCSS, 2016). Such education should be interdisciplinary, encourage critical and creative thinking, address issues of equity and social justice, and provide students with opportunities to actively engage in learning (Jaffee & Yoder, 2019).

In this chapter, we first present a summary of current perspectives on teaching and learning social studies, including the C3 (College, Career, and Civic Life) Framework developed by the NCSS. We then discuss how the variety of disciplines within social studies—each with its own content and specific language use—makes it one of the most perplexing subjects for multilingual students. We also highlight the importance of teachers being sensitive to students, as many topics can be controversial or may cause discomfort.

Next, we emphasize the importance of knowing your multilingual students and making social studies instruction meaningfully and powerfully connected to their lives and experiences. Following a review of the dimensions of academic language in social studies, we analyze two model texts to illustrate the distinct genres, complex grammatical structures, unfamiliar words and phrases, and patriotic symbols that may need deliberate instruction and support for multilingual learners to grasp. After the analysis of the model texts, at the end of the chapter, we offer specific suggestions for linguistic and culturally responsive instruction.

Current Perspectives on Teaching and Learning Social Studies for Multilingual Learners

The C3 Framework

The C3 (College, Career, and Civic Life) Framework, developed by the NCSS (2013), provides an essential structure for teaching social studies that emphasizes inquiry-based learning, disciplinary literacy, and civic engagement. This framework is particularly important for teaching social studies to multilingual learners for several reasons:

1. **Emphasis on Inquiry-Based Learning:** The C3 Framework promotes inquiry-based learning, which encourages students to ask questions, investigate issues, and construct their own understandings of social studies content, in essence, to engage in languaging. For multilingual learners, this approach provides opportunities for language development through meaningful interactions with content and peers. Figure 5.1 depicts two students working on preparing the content for their Google Slides presentation on the topic of *recursos enérgeticos* (energy resources) with Ms. Frederick's oversight.
2. **Integration of Language and Content:** The C3 Framework emphasizes the integration of language and content instruction, recognizing that social studies intertwines specialized vocabulary, academic language, and literacy skills. For multilingual learners, this integrated approach helps develop their language proficiency and content knowledge simultaneously to support their academic success in social studies.
3. **Focus on Civic Engagement:** The C3 Framework emphasizes the importance of civic participation and global awareness, encouraging students to understand their roles as active citizens in a diverse society. For multilingual learners, this focus provides opportunities to explore and discuss social issues, cultural perspectives, and civic responsibilities, which can enhance language development and cultural competency (NCSS, 2013).
4. **Development of Critical Thinking Skills:** Through its emphasis on inquiry, analysis, and evaluation, the C3 Framework fosters critical thinking skills essential for academic success and civic participation. For multilingual learners, this approach promotes deeper understanding and engagement with social studies content, as well as the development of language skills necessary for higher-order thinking (Lee & Buxton, 2013).
5. **Alignment With Language Proficiency/Development Standards:** The principles of the C3 Framework align with

language proficiency/development standards. This alignment ensures that social studies instruction for multilingual learners is both academically rigorous and linguistically appropriate (NCSS, 2013).

6. **Flexibility and Adaptability:** The C3 Framework offers flexibility for educators to adapt instruction to meet the diverse needs of students, including multilingual learners. Teachers can scaffold instruction, provide language support, and personalize learning experiences to ensure that multilingual learners have access to grade-level content while developing language.

In sum, the C3 Framework provides a comprehensive inquiry-based approach to social studies instruction that is well suited for multilingual learners. By emphasizing inquiry, integrating language and content instruction, fostering civic engagement, developing critical thinking skills, and aligning with language proficiency/development standards, the C3 Framework supports effective social studies education for all students, including in multiple languages for multilingual learners, as shown in Figure 5.1.

Figure 5.1 Students in Giovanna Frederick's Classroom Preparing a Presentation on *Recursos Energéticos*

Source: Photo by Steven J. Morrison

The Uniqueness of Social Studies Content

Three unique aspects of social studies deserve attention: (a) social studies consists of many disciplines; (b) social studies is often not treated like other disciplines; and (c) social studies includes themes that can be sensitive, confusing, or unfamiliar to multilingual students.

a. **Social studies encompasses multiple disciplines and courses.** According to the NCSS, at the elementary level, social studies includes the interdisciplinary study of history, geography, economics, and government/civics and is often integrated with the study of language arts, the visual and performing arts, and science, technology, engineering, and mathematics (STEM). At the secondary level, social studies can include, in addition to the above four areas, ethnic studies, psychology, sociology, philosophy, ethics, and law. Powerful and meaningful social studies is interdisciplinary, promotes critical and creative thinking, engages students in relevant and personal issues, and provides opportunities for students to be active in their learning (Jaffee & Yoder, 2019).

b. **Social studies is not treated in the same way as other content areas.** The marginalization of social studies has been well documented (e.g., Heafner & Plaisance, 2016) and is evident at three different levels: policy, accountability, and instructional time. At the policy level, school reforms such as No Child Left Behind legislation, Race to the Top funding, and the Common Core State Standards movement do not single out social studies as they do with other subjects, namely mathematics, reading/language arts, and science. In terms of accountability, social studies, particularly in elementary grades, is often not part of the high-stakes testing at state and district levels. This lack of accountability makes social studies vulnerable and prone to be integrated with other content areas or eliminated when other pressing activities and content areas pack the school day.

c. **Social studies includes themes that are sensitive, confusing, or unfamiliar to multilingual students.** Social studies deals with topics in history, politics, and current issues that can be controversial or make students feel uncomfortable. Multilingual students might come from nations with different historical narratives, political systems, or social and cultural norms, which can conflict with their prior knowledge or beliefs. In addition, topics like immigration, race, religion, human rights, and LGBTQ+ concepts and related issues can be particularly sensitive to some students, especially if these issues intersect with their identities or the experiences of their communities. For many multilingual students, especially those who are recent immigrants, discussions about immigration policies, border control, or refugee crises can be deeply personal and distressing. Students may have lived experiences related to displacement and family separation.

Additionally, discussions around citizenship, national identity, civic responsibilities, and democratic values can be stressful, particularly for newcomers and those coming from places with different civic structures. Finally, topics that touch on war, conflict, discrimination, and persecution may have a strong emotional impact on students who may have personal or family histories connected to these issues. For example, lessons about racism, segregation, or civil rights struggles in the United States can resonate deeply with multilingual students who may have experienced discrimination or racial bias, both abroad and in the United States. Table 5.1 lists potentially sensitive topics that may relate to the cultural backgrounds, immigration status, and historical events tied to multilingual learners' identities.

Table 5.1 Potentially Sensitive Topics in Social Studies for Multilingual Learners

Citizenship	National Identity
Colonialism	Racial and Ethnic Discrimination
Economic Inequality	Religions and Religious Persecution
Family Dynamics and Gender Roles	Slavery
Immigration	War and Conflict

Connecting Social Studies Instruction to Student Experiences

The presence of multilingual students in the social studies classroom "should impact what is being taught, in addition to *how* it is being taught" (Yoder et al., 2016, p. 31). Thus, educators need to first learn about their students and second connect social studies instruction to student experiences in meaningful and powerful ways.

As discussed in Chapter 2, knowing your students is fundamental, functioning as a foundation for all other classroom practices. Once teachers have gained insights into the lives of their multilingual students, they can use asset-based pedagogies, such as funds of knowledge (Moll et al., 1992) and community cultural wealth (Yosso, 2005) to build on students' strengths. For example, Morrison (2022) reports on a unit on myths and legends in a dual language program in the Pacific Northwest. As part of their mandated curriculum for seventh graders, two teachers decided to adapt a unit that integrated social studies with Spanish language arts. Since the unit emphasized the functional differences between the two literary genres by presenting a variety of Greek and Roman stories, the teachers decided to replace those with myths and legends from the Native peoples of the Americas. In that way, many Latine and Indigenous students could build on and expand their knowledge of stories that included Raven, La Llorona, Coyote, and Chupacabra.

"Given the inherently contested nature of most social studies content, students will benefit from planned opportunities to examine multiple perspectives."

—Ashley Taylor Jaffee and Paul J. Yoder (2019, p. 310)

Important to note is that multilingual students are representatives of a new globalized world and have unique understandings and knowledge of events, languages, and cultures beyond the U.S. borders. For example, your multilingual students and their families may have experiences with and knowledge of topics in social studies such as independence movements, civil wars, immigration, multiculturalism, border crossing, and a variety of current global events. While the knowledge and perspectives that students bring can be used in the classroom to scaffold new academic learning, it is important to proceed with caution and care since some of these topics may be a source of trauma and pain for students.

Look Closer

Supporting Students During Discussion of Sensitive Topics

For information about how to navigate and support your students during discussions about sensitive topics and political violence, consult the following resources:

Alter, G. T. (2017). Discovery, engagement, and transformation: Learning about gender and sexual diversity in social education. *Social Education*, *81*(5), 279–285.

Colorín Colorado. (n.d.). *Discussing political violence with ELLs, immigrants, and refugees*. https://www.colorincolorado.org/discussing-political-violence-ells-immigrants-and-refugees

Said, S. (n.d.). *Supporting students' ability to process conflict in our world*. Confianza. https://ellstudents.com/blogs/the-confianza-way/supporting-students-ability-to-process-conflict-in-our-world

Key to social studies instruction is being aware of the unique characteristics of the language for social studies and using this awareness to plan deliberate and systematic instruction that focuses on both content and language. The next section will shed light on the language for social studies.

The Language for Social Studies

Languaging in social studies instruction, where students have opportunities to take action based on specific topics, is often marked by an abundance of unfamiliar vocabulary, complex grammatical structures, and distinct genres. Consequently, for students learning English as a second, third, or fourth language—including those with advanced proficiency—languaging in the social studies classroom offers opportunities for student engagement. In this section, we delve into explanations and examples that highlight discourse features, sentence structures, vocabulary/phrases, and symbols.

Discourse

The discourse dimension, consisting of the organization, coherence, and cohesiveness of large bodies of oral and written language, has several issues related to teaching and learning for multilingual learners. We discuss three of these aspects: (1) lack of background knowledge on the topic; (2) difficulties presented by social studies textbooks and materials; and (3) use of diverse types of texts and modes (e.g., timelines, maps, essays, historical arguments) that students need to access and produce.

1. **Background knowledge about U.S. history and geography.** Multilingual students may be at a disadvantage regarding social studies content because they may not have "a working knowledge of American culture that can serve as a schema for new social learning" (Cruz & Thornton, 2013, p. 3). This is due to the heavy emphasis on U.S. history and geography where the concepts build upon each other beginning in the early grades up through high school. However, in terms of globalization, transnationalism, geopolitical conflict, and current international events, your multilingual students may have an array of knowledge and can make a strong contribution to the topic at hand. Students' languages and cultures embedded in their life experiences, are simply not tapped, thereby limiting student participation in learning activities (Sang, 2017).

2. **Social studies textbooks and materials.** Most social studies textbooks include complex language, cultural references, and limited visual support and assume background knowledge acquired in previous grade levels. Recent studies (e.g., August & Shanahan, 2017; Gay, 2023) identified issues social studies textbooks may pose for multilingual learners. Suggestions for how to overcome these issues are summarized in Table 5.2.

   Addressing these hurdles requires educators to use strategies that make content more accessible and relevant for multilingual students, such as accepting and incorporating diverse perspectives, providing additional support, and using a variety of multimodal resources. (Remember, your multilingual students can access information in more than one language!).

3. **Social studies' wide variety of genres.** Various types of social studies texts often require multilingual students to tackle content complexity and unfamiliarity with academic genres. We must not forget that the teaching of social studies varies significantly across countries and that some of your multilingual students may come from places where social studies is taught using more traditional methods (e.g., lecture-based, textbook-driven, and exam-focused). Examples of the text types and genres that students have to use, understand, and produce in U.S. social studies classes are presented in Table 5.3.

Table 5.2 Challenges Presented by Social Studies Textbooks and Materials for Multilingual Learners

KEY CHALLENGES	DESCRIPTION	OVERCOMING CHALLENGES
Assumed Background Knowledge	Materials may assume students have prior knowledge of historical events, cultural contexts, or political systems.	Accepting multiple perspectives can offset multilingual students' misunderstanding of assumed background knowledge when presented from an Anglocentric lens.
Cultural References	Textbooks may include cultural references, historical events, or idiomatic expressions unfamiliar to multilingual students.	Multilingual learners bring a wealth of cultural references; however, they may not have the background knowledge presented in U.S. textbooks.
Cultural Biases	Some materials may present biased or one-sided perspectives on historical events or cultural practices.	Students should be sensitized to content that does not reflect their own experiences or that presents skewed (monoglossic) views.
Limited Support	Some texts may lack sufficient visual aids, such as maps, diagrams, or pictures, to support comprehension.	Multimodal supports help students understand and visualize complex information.
Abstract Concepts	Social studies often deal with abstract ideas like democracy, justice, or economic systems.	Concrete examples and explanations offer ways for students to process abstract concepts.
Lengthy and Dense Text	Social studies textbooks can be lengthy and contain dense passages of information.	Chunking information into smaller amounts can avoid text complexity, which can overwhelm students and impede their ability to process and retain information.
Complex Language	Social studies texts often use technical vocabulary, complex sentence structures, and abstract concepts.	Students should develop strategies to tackle comprehension and grasp key ideas and details.

online resources This resource is available for download at https://companion.corwin.com/courses/Academic-Languaging.

Table 5.3 The Variety of Text Types Used in Social Studies Instruction

AI image generators	AI history chatbots	biographies
charts and tables	diagrams	digital (audio) books
digital maps	editorials	essays
graphic novels	historical arguments	journals
Minecraft	media analyses	personal accounts
photo essays	podcasts	primary sources
scenarios	slide presentations	theses
timelines	travelogues	virtual tours and field trips

Sentences

The following text comes from a McGraw-Hill social studies middle school textbook:

> The Bill of Rights was intended originally to constrain only the national government. For many years, local and state governments were not bound by its terms. As a result, states sometimes used their reserved powers to pass laws that violate, or disobey, civil liberties. In most parts of the country, for example, women and African Americans could not vote. Before 1865, many states had laws that sanctioned the enslavement of African Americans, who were treated as property and had almost no rights at all. (Remy et al., 2008, p. 134)

In addition to historical terminology (i.e., *Bill of Rights*, *national government*, *reserved powers*, and *civil liberties*) and the advanced specialized vocabulary (i.e., *sanctioned*, *enslavement*, and *disobey*) that may require contextual understanding for full comprehension, two other aspects of linguistic complexity in this short paragraph deserve attention. First, the text contains complex sentence structures with multiple clauses, such as "The Bill of Rights was intended originally to constrain only the national government," which may not be easy to parse for some readers, particularly those who are less proficient in English. Second, references to specific time periods such as "before 1865" add temporal complexity and require readers to understand historical timelines.

Aside from complex sentence structures and temporal complexity, social studies textbooks and materials often employ a variety of sentence types such as cause-and-effect relationships, compare-and-contrast constructions, argumentation, passive voice, idiomatic expressions, syntactic ambiguity, complex noun phrases, and multiple clauses that connect a series of facts, concepts, and ideas in one long sentence. These and other features may pose difficulties for students to navigate without explicit and contextualized instruction on grammatical structures. Figure 5.2 showcases two examples for supporting students as they learn how to construct compare and contrast sentences. While the photo on the left includes sentence frames in Spanish, the photo on the right lists key words in English.

Figure 5.2 Key Words and Sentence Frames for Compare/Contrast and *Comparar/Contrastar*

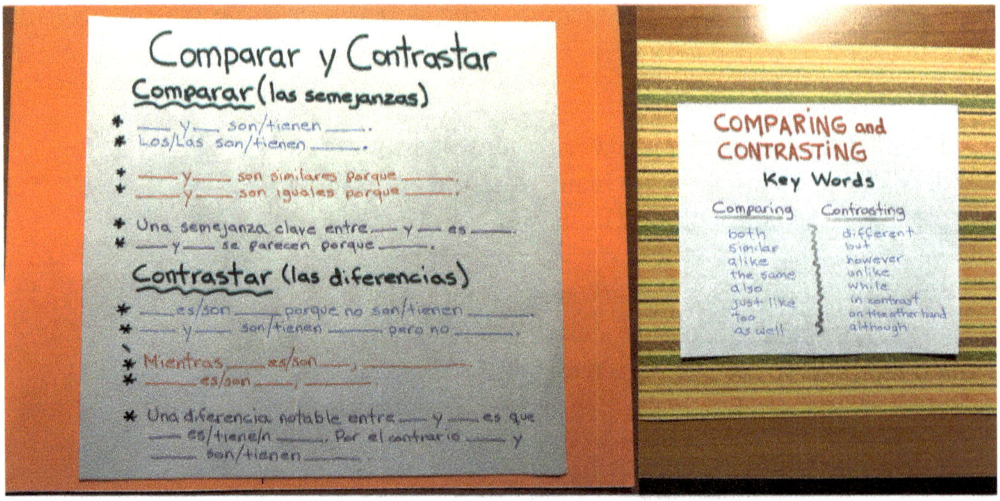

Words/Phrases

Teachers need to be deliberate and systematic in helping students learn the words and phrases in the social studies classroom. First, the range of words, phrases, and expressions used across the various disciplines within social studies is extensive. Second, many of these terms may carry different meanings or lack a direct translation in students' other language (Egbert & Ernst-Slavit, 2010). These two aspects are further explained as follows.

Vast vocabulary

The variety of disciplines within social studies makes its content-specific vocabulary more extensive when compared to other disciplines. Carleton and Marzano (2010) collected information from selected districts and states and compiled a list of vocabulary targeted for each grade-level band (lower elementary, upper elementary, middle school, and high school). Their partial results, in Table 5.4, show how social studies curricula expose students to approximately five times the number of words when compared to other content areas.

Table 5.4 Number of Targeted Vocabulary Words by Content Area and Grade-Level Band

LEVEL	LANGUAGE ARTS	MATHEMATICS	SCIENCE	SOCIAL STUDIES
Lower Elementary	96	96	96	**330**
Upper Elementary	251	190	179	**1,268**
Middle School	253	204	218	**1,166**

Direct translation

Words, phrases and expressions may have a different meaning or may not have a direct translation. Multilingual students may also encounter words, phrases, and expressions with meanings that are culturally based (and biased); therefore they may have a different meaning or may be difficult to translate. For example, terms like *democracy*, *colony*, *revolution*, *cultural diffusion*, *gun rights*, and *civil rights* require background knowledge and abundant context information. Additionally, some terms may have a different meaning (e.g., *colony*), can be controversial for some students (e.g., *immigration*), or may not have a direct translation to their home language. For example, *challenge*, *privacy*, and *efficiency* have no direct translation in the Russian language. Terms like *awkward*, *insight*, and *bully* cannot be translated into most languages with a single word.

Stop and Think

Checks and Balances

The concept of "checks and balances" is key for understanding the three branches of the U.S. government. Yet, "checks and balances" is one of those phrases that is difficult to translate to other languages. For example, translated into Portuguese using Google Translate as "freios e contrapesos" and into Spanish as "controles y contrapesos," this important concept makes no sense in the context of government. This is just one example of the many terms in social studies that do not have direct translations to other languages. Can you think of others?

Similar to other content areas, many everyday words in social studies have different meanings and can be especially troublesome for students who might know only one meaning. Consider, for example, the following polysemous terms: *left*, *market*, and *mole*. Multilingual students may know about directions, places where items are sold, and a small furry animal but may not know the meaning of those terms within historic, economic, or political contexts. Table 5.5 includes a list of selected polysemous words in social studies.

Table 5.5 Examples of Polysemous Words in Social Studies

VOCABULARY	EVERYDAY MEANING	SOCIAL STUDIES MEANING
capital	The city where a government is located	Wealth or assets, financial resources (e.g., cultural capital)
draft	A preliminary version of a written document	A system for selecting individuals for compulsory military service

(Continued)

(Continued)

VOCABULARY	EVERYDAY MEANING	SOCIAL STUDIES MEANING
house	A building where people live	Bicameral legislative body
interest	A stake or involvement in an issue or activity	The cost of borrowing money, usually expressed as a percentage
movement	The act of changing physical location or position	A group effort or campaign for social or political change
order	A command or directive	A structured arrangement or sequence (e.g., world order)
party	A social gathering or event	A political group or organization
period	A punctuation symbol used at the end of a sentence	A large segment or division of time

Stop and Think

Teaching Word Learning Strategies: Prefixes and Suffixes

As mentioned in Chapter 2, a large percentage of disciplinary language is derived from the Latin and Greek languages. Thus, your multilingual students may very well know the meaning of many of the word roots, prefixes, and suffixes when they see those in writing (although their pronunciation might be very different). Helping students build on that knowledge or learn how words are formed will help students unlock the meaning of additional words. For example, Table 5.6 is an example of negative prefixes. Once students identify those prefixes while reading social studies and other content area materials, they will be able to realize the meaning of many technical words in context.

Table 5.6 Negative Prefixes

NEGATIVE PREFIXES			
A-	Apolitical, asocial, atheist	**IL-**	Illegal, illicit, illogical
AB-	Abdicate, abnormal, abuse	**IM-**	Imbalance, immobile, immoral
AN-	Analphabetic, anarchic, annul	**IN-**	Inactive, incorrect, inefficient
ANTI-	Antihero, antipathy, antithesis	**IR-**	Irrational, irrelevant, irreversible
DE-	Decry, denigrate, deprive	**MIS-**	Misfortune, misjudge, mislead
DIS-	Disagree, dishonest, dislike	**NON-**	None, nonsense, nontoxic
IG-	Ignoble, ignominious, ignorance	**UN-**	Unable, unaware, undo

Symbols

Understanding different kinds of symbols is integral to social studies instruction. While most students will be familiar with several of the peace signs that are used around the world (see Figure 5.3) and some of the map symbols, multilingual students will most likely not know the meaning of U.S. patriotic symbols (e.g., bald eagle, Liberty Bell, Uncle Sam) used regularly in the social studies class. Students can engage in academic languaging by suggesting new symbols for social studies concepts that are meaningful to them and explaining how they might publicize them throughout their school and community.

Figure 5.3 Peace Symbols From Around the World

Source: Artwork by Gisela Ernst-Slavit

Stop and Think

Do you know what the national mammal is?

In 2016 the American bison was made the first national mammal, underscoring its historical, cultural, and economic importance. For Native Americans, the American bison or buffalo symbolized their survival and well-being. Every part of the bison was used whether it was for clothing, food, shelter, or tools or as part of their rituals and traditions. Different tribes spoke different languages, and each tribe had a different name for this animal. A few of those names include *iinniwa* in Blackfoot, *tatanka* in Lakota, *ivanbito* in Navajo, and *Kuts* in Paiute. In fact, the Cheyenne alone used 27 different words for a buffalo, depending on its sex, age, or condition (Burns, 2023).

Because symbols hold different meanings for different people, your multilingual students may not know that the U.S. flag, national anthem, and bald eagle "help to convey American values such as liberty, freedom, democracy, and independence" (Brugar & Dickman, 2013, p. 17). When teaching about these patriotic symbols, and depending on students' grade level, teachers can begin with a discussion about symbols and later analyze the meaning of the symbols found in other flags (e.g., students can select a flag from their own country or a country they would like to visit). Other ideas include students designing their own flags or coats of arms and explaining the meaning of the symbols used. Listed in Table 5.7 are selected U.S. patriotic symbols.

Table 5.7 Selected U.S. Patriotic Symbols

Liberty Bell	U.S. Flag	Statue of Liberty
Washington Monument	Gateway Arch	White House
Bald Eagle	Jefferson Memorial	Uncle Sam
Mount Rushmore	Seal	MLK Memorial
National Anthem	National Motto	Pledge of Allegiance

The use of geographic representations, terms, and technology to process information from maps is also part of the social studies curriculum. Here, students should have access to cardinal directions, a compass rose, Google maps, and a physical map legend or key and then apply these representations to design their own ways of navigation.

Look Closer

Spatial Thinking and Map Skills

Spatial literacy is "the competent and confident use of maps, mapping, and spatial thinking to address ideas, situations, and problems within daily life, society, and the world around us" (Stinton, 2012).

Luckily, as citizens of the world, your multilingual students will most likely be interested in maps and geography. Here are some suggestions to make map symbols engaging for students and enhance their power of academic languaging:

- Have students use paper and pencil or tablets and computers to create and describe their own symbols to represent different features on a school or community map
- Have students use artificial intelligence (AI)–powered platforms (e.g., Kahoot!, Quizlet) to create a matching game, connecting symbols with their meanings.
- Visit National Geographic and select grade-level-appropriate activities from a collection of map activities designed to strengthen spatial thinking skills for preK–6 students at https://education.nationalgeographic.org/resource/map-skills-for-students/.

Using Model Texts in the Social Studies Classroom

As we have seen in previous sections, social studies materials frequently display complexity, featuring elements that differ from the language students typically encounter in their daily lives. These elements encompass extended noun phrases, nominalizations, discourse markers, time indicators, and a range of clauses, all commonly encountered in social studies texts. Two model texts showcasing different language features are included in this section. The first excerpt is from a well-used Grade 1 textbook.

Model Text 1: Grade 1 Social Studies Textbook—Family Budget

A budget is a plan for how to use money. A family makes a budget to keep track of how much money they spend. They make sure they have enough money for the things they need. And they try to save some money, too.

A family lists the money they have. Then they list all of the things they need. Groceries, clothes, and school supplies are some things they need to buy. These things are called expenses.

The family tries to save some money. They can use this money later on. They can also use it to buy things they want.

Source: *IMPACT Social Studies* (2020, p. 216).

As you read this Grade 1 excerpt from a social studies textbook, ask yourself the following questions (please reflect on these questions before looking at Figure 5.4):

1. What language challenges might multilingual learners encounter?
2. What concepts may vary across cultures, and how might you be more inclusive of all multilingual learners?
3. How might this passage be offensive to some students and families?

Figure 5.4 Model Text 1: Grade 1 Social Studies Textbook—Family Budget

Observations About Content		Observations about Language and Culture
The concept of budgeting and managing finances may vary across cultures. First graders may not have prior knowledge with these concepts.	A budget is a plan for how to use money. A family makes a budget to keep track of how much money they spend. They make sure they have enough money for the things they need. And they try to save some money, too. A family lists the money they have. Then they list all of the things they need. Groceries, clothes, and school supplies are some things they need to buy. These things are called expenses. The family tries to save some money. They can use this money later on. They can also use it to buy things they want.	compound sentences abstract concepts polysemous words idiomatic expression

Figure 5.4 highlights some of the unique language features for all first graders, particularly multilingual learners. These areas are further explained and expanded as follows.

Vocabulary: The text contains unfamiliar vocabulary to a first grader, such as *budget*, *expenses*, and *supplies*, which may require additional explanation and role play to ensure comprehension. In addition, there are polysemous words, such as *make*, *budget*, *track*, *list*, *save*, and *have*. Also, "make sure" is an idiomatic expression.

Words/phrases illustrating abstract concepts: The text introduces abstract concepts such as "budgeting," "expenses," and "saving money." These concepts may be outside the experiential realm of multilingual learners, especially without prior exposure in their other language.

Complex sentence structures: While the sentences are generally short, there are compound sentences, such as "A family makes a budget to keep track of how much money they spend. They make sure they have enough money for the things they need." Some first graders may find it challenging to figure out the meaning of these complex sentences.

Discourse of an explanation through sequential understanding: The text describes a sequence of events related to budgeting, such as making a budget, listing expenses, and saving money. First graders may struggle to understand this explanation—the sequence of events and the connections between them—without additional support (e.g., visuals) or clarification.

Cultural context: This topic can be sensitive for students experiencing poverty and homelessness. In addition, the concept of budgeting and managing finances varies across cultures, and multilingual first graders may not have prior knowledge or experience with these concepts in their cultural context.

Stop and Think

Consider the various meanings of the terms *make* and *have*.

Yes, there are many definitions for each of these words! For example, *make* is a highly versatile verb in English with over 60 primary senses, with many subsenses and variations. Moreover, *make* is used in many idiomatic expressions (e.g., "make sure"). The word *have* is another versatile verb in English. The *Oxford English Dictionary* lists around 20 major senses for *have*, with numerous subsenses depending on the grammatical or situational usage (Oxford University Press, 2025). The English word with the most meanings is the verb *set*, which has 430 senses listed in the second edition of the *Oxford English Dictionary* (Simpson & Weiner, 1989). Therefore, it is important for multilingual learners to understand the context in which these words are presented.

Supporting Grade 1 Students' Access to This Material

You may wish to discuss how different families may manage money and make budgets. Note students' sensitivities with the text to make it more relatable.

- Encourage students to share their own experiences or stories about saving money or buying things, including food, by integrating their personal experiences with the text's content. Remember that not all students have handled money or know the meaning of "piggy bank."
- Use visual strategies, such as a Picture Walk. Before reading the segment, show illustrations of concepts mentioned in the text, such as family, money, groceries, clothes, and school supplies. You may also want to ask students what they see in the pictures and how

these items relate to each other. Then you might have students partner to create their own oral or written stories from the pictures.

- Model oral reading of the text using expression and emphasizing key words. Demonstrate how to use different kinds of clues (e.g., visualization, translation) for comprehending new words and phrases.
- Have students role-play creating a budget, perhaps by setting up a store. Use play money and items they might need to buy. Help them figure out the concept of planning and saving.
- Have students sequence pictures to explain the steps a family might take when making a budget while using sequencing language (e.g., first, second, then, last).

The next example is from a Grade 5 project for students at the end of a unit on life in colonial America.

Model Text 2: Grade 5 Project—Exploring Colonial Life Through Primary Sources

1. Choose one primary source document from the provided selection, such as a diary entry, letter, advertisement, or newspaper article, that relates to colonial life.
2. Read your selected document carefully, paying attention to details about daily routines, social customs, economic activities, or political events.
3. Write or record a brief summary of the document, including information about the author, date, and context.
4. Analyze the content of the document, considering the following questions:
    a. How do the experiences described in the document compare to your own life today?
    b. What insights does the document provide about life in colonial America?
    c. What challenges or opportunities did people face during this time period?
5. Create a visual representation of the information from the primary source document. This could be a timeline, a poster, a collage, or a digital presentation.
6. Present your findings to the class, sharing your analysis and discussing the significance of the document in understanding colonial life.

Again, as you read this excerpt, ask yourself the following questions (please reflect on these questions before looking at Figure 5.5):

1. What language challenges might multilingual learners encounter? Why?
2. What concepts may vary across cultures and therefore be unfamiliar to multilingual learners?

Figure 5.5 Model Text 2: Grade 5 Project—Exploring Colonial Life Through Primary Sources

Observations About Content	Instructions:	Observations about Language and Culture
A variety of genres, texts, and tasks are used in social studies.	1. Choose one primary source document from the provided selection, such as a diary entry, letter, advertisement, or newspaper article, that relates to colonial life.	
	2. Read your selected document carefully, paying attention to details about daily routines, social customs, economic activities, or political events.	variety of genres
	3. Write or record a brief summary of the document, including information about the author, date, and context.	abstract concepts
	4. Analyze the content of the document, considering the following questions:	polysemous words
	a. How do the experiences described in the document compare to your own life today?	text structures
	b. What insights does the document provide about life in colonial America?	controversial terms
	c. What challenges or opportunities did people face during this time period?	referents
	5. Create a visual representation of the information gathered from the primary source document. This could be a timeline, a poster, a collage, or a digital presentation.	
	6. Present your findings to the class, sharing your analysis and discussing the significance of the document in understanding colonial life.	

As depicted in Figure 5.5, there are a variety of linguistic and socio-cultural aspects that deserve attention in this model text.

Controversial terms: For many in the United States, the term *colony* is associated with pride in reference to the 13 colonies, the Great Revolutionary War, the independence from Great Britain, and the onset of the United States. However, for many immigrant, African American, and Native American students, terms like *colonization*, *colonial*, and *colonialism* are associated with imperialism, oppression, enslavement, loss, and violence.

Abstract concepts: Analyzing primary source documents and discussing insights into colonial life require understanding abstract concepts such as historical context, daily routines, social customs, economic activities, and political events.

Diverse written and oral genres: First, although there are a variety of genres for students to select from, students will need to know what those options entail. Second, producing a summary, conducting an analysis, and planning a presentation involve knowing specific writing and oral conventions. Multilingual students should be offered multimodal options in addition to expressing their ideas in written and spoken form, especially if they are in the early stages of English language development.

Cultural context: Multilingual students may have limited exposure to U.S. history, let alone relate to the content and perspectives presented in primary source documents.

Comparison to own lives: Comparing the experiences described in primary source documents to their own lives today may be onerous for multilingual students who have different daily routines, social customs, and economic activities.

Compare-and-contrast structure: Students will need to use specific clauses, beyond *because* and *so*, to signal how their life is different or similar when compared to the insights they gained from the primary source document (as required in item 4a).

Polysemous words: *Primary*, *letter*, and *content* are words with several meanings.

Reflecting on this fifth-grade model text, students will need to engage in several tasks and identify a variety of text types to fulfill the assignment (see Table 5.8).

Table 5.8 Model Text 2: Tasks and Text Types Involved in the Project

TASKS	TEXT TYPES
Choose a document Read the document (and related resources) Write or produce a summary Analyze the content Answer questions Identify insights or new knowledge Compare and contrast Create a presentation Orally present findings and analysis	Primary source document Diary entry Letter Advertisement Newspaper article Timeline Poster Collage Digital presentation Oral presentation

The following is a list of strategies that may be helpful to support Grade 5 students in completing this project.

Supporting Grade 5 Students to Complete This Project

- Throughout the unit, review and have models available of the different text types.
- Provide or have students generate sentences to express their ideas orally and in writing.
- Encourage ongoing student participation throughout the unit in constructing and using a word/phrase/sentence wall.
- Break complex tasks into smaller, more manageable steps during the instructional unit while offering guided practice before expecting students to work independently.
- Make films, videos, and other visual material available to provide background information and facilitate students' understanding of colonial life and the historical context of the primary source documents.
- Offer students opportunities to collaborate. For example, by pairing multilingual students with peers, students can compare their own thoughts before addressing item 4a, which asks for a comparison of colonial life with their own lives.

Strategies for Moving Social Studies Learning Forward With Multilingual Learners

Relating Large-Scale Historical Events to Local Lives

> I didn't like social studies . . . it was all about the U.S. and every year we did the same thing . . . I tried to memorize facts but that didn't work. Nothing that we read or talked about was related to me or my family or my friends.
>
> —Aisha, student from Somalia

Even though social studies covers topics such as culture, race, identity, language, religion, social justice, and community that can connect with students' lives and communities, students like Aisha often feel disconnected from its content. Ladson-Billings (1995) contends that a key factor in teaching is to utilize students' "rich and diverse array of cultural and linguistic resources that are currently vastly underutilized and systemically devalued in schools" (Alim & Paris, 2015, p. 80). Culturally relevant teaching and culturally responsive pedagogy (as well as its various incarnations; see Chapter 2) calls for teachers to bridge cultural divides by utilizing "students' culture as a vehicle for learning" (Ladson-Billings, 1995, p. 161) in partnership with the class community (Gay, 2023). Connecting students' home and community with the school content fosters academic success (Au, 2011) and facilitates academic languaging, enabling multilingual learners to take action.

A clear example of how a Grade 4 teacher validated her students' home languages and cultures is presented by Ernst-Slavit and Morrison (2019) in their analysis of a unit on 19th-century westward migration. Within this unit, narratives are crafted by teacher and students to showcase regional examples of linguistically and ethnically diverse communities, linking global immigration trends to local history. These narratives are later employed in a culminating lesson on immigration, which integrates—and, in doing so, validates—students' family stories as an ongoing part of U.S. history.

Stop and Think

Why is the term *westward migration* problematic?

Traditionally, the term *westward migration* has been used to exemplify the successful movement of white settlers from the eastern United States to the western frontier. However, this narrative is problematic because it oversimplifies the complexity of this movement, overlooking the expansion of slavery down into the Southwest and the profound impact on Indigenous communities—including racism, violence, loss of lands, and widespread devastation.

During this three-week unit, students in the classroom, including 13 multilingual students, collected and shared oral histories of their families and connected that information with source material related to immigration and the United States. By doing so, all students in the classroom affirmed their identities as a product of immigration, whether they came a few years ago or as descendants of immigrants. Embedded in this unit were two important aspects that deserve attention: (1) the creation of interactive contexts conducive to academic languaging (e.g., expert groups proposing different viewpoints) and (2) treating students as researchers. The significance of these activities cannot be overstated; students engaged in genuine research about their families' trajectories and connected the reasons and context of that migration with those that took place during the 19th century (for more information, see Ernst-Slavit & Morrison, 2019). Additional strategies for, and examples of, linking large-scale historical events to local lives are presented as follows.

Involving parents, families, and community.

Topics such as immigration, 9/11, the Korean War (known as the "625 War" in South Korea), the Vietnam War (known in Vietnam as the "American War)", world religions, and current events can be linked to students' families and communities by tapping the knowledge and resources of individual members.

Incorporating place-based education in your teaching.

Place-based education is a pedagogical approach that emphasizes the experiential, community-based, and ecological learning to enhance the students' connection to local cultures, contexts, and environments (Gruenwald & Smith, 2014). Even though standards, district curricula, and textbooks tend to focus on national and international topics and not on local issues, topics such as food, housing, and family are relevant to students and their communities, both in the past and in the present (Resor, 2017).

Comparing historical places to modern locations familiar to students.

Comparing historical and modern maps gives students insight into how a city or region changes over a period of time. For example, students in Boston can compare and contrast maps of Boston from different periods of time and identify how humans have altered the physical landscape (see "Comparing Historical Maps" at National Geographic: https://education.nationalgeographic.org/resource/comparing-historical-maps/).

Bringing current events into the social studies classroom.

Students can discover that they are not the first ones to wrestle with a particular issue and thus may be able to learn from experiences in previous times. For example, when studying the significance of geography in shaping the development or decline of civilizations, a video or a picture of Kiribati, a Pacific island nation that is slowly disappearing due to rising temperatures and increasing ocean levels, can serve to link past events with the urgency of current situations. Students could perhaps better understand forced migrations in the past while tinkering with questions such as these: What will happen with the people if the islands become submerged in the ocean? Where will the inhabitants have to move? How might they become environmental refugees? Will we or should we host these people in our local refugee centers?

Relating historical journeys to modern travel.

All your students might better understand the endurance required of epic journeys made by foot, horseback, wagon, river, or sea when comparing the timeline, mode of transportation, and routes of a historical trip to what is required to make the same trip today (Resor, 2017). For example, when studying the Oregon Trail—a wagon road trip of 2,170 miles from Missouri to Oregon—students might compare and contrast the type of routes, transportation modes, equipment, costs, and stops they would need to take in order to repeat the trek done by thousands during the 1840–1880 period.

Stop and Think

Roman Numerals

Roman numerals are symbols used in several other languages (e.g., some Romance and Slavic languages) to label centuries, dynasties, events, and book chapters instead of Hindu-Arabic numbers. If your older students write "XIX century" and "IV Egyptian dynasty," a probable explanation is that in their home language they use Roman numerals to describe periods of time.

Modeling Oral Language

Multilingual learners need ample opportunities to hear and take action using language to be successful in school. Social studies, with its variety of disciplines, the nature of its content, and multilingual students' trajectories, lends itself to small-group interaction and whole-class discussions. Hence, teachers need to model the oral language skills we want students to develop and practice. Just as students cannot learn to sing, paint, or play basketball just by watching videos of Taylor Swift, Bob Ross, or Steph Curry, students cannot engage in academic languaging simply by reading or observing. As educators, we must first be aware of the language we use and second make sure that we are systematic and intentional in modeling the language we want students to learn and use.

In addition to being aware of how we provide explanations and ask questions, teachers need to be conscious of the language we use when addressing students, providing feedback, and encouraging participation during whole-classroom discussions. Table 5.9 showcases in the left-hand column examples of the language teachers should model to elevate the status of their students and in the right-hand column language teachers might want to avoid.

Table 5.9 Modeling Academic Languaging

MAKE AN EFFORT TO	AVOID
Use the following terms to refer to students: Researchers Scientists Artists Historians Scholars Mathematicians Authors	*Using the following terms to refer to students:* Guys Niños Boys and girls Chicos Folks Kiddos
Provide constructive and helpful feedback: • That is a very thoughtful explanation of why . . . • I appreciate your insights on this topic and your precise language to express them. • Thank you. Perhaps you can elaborate some more on what you mean by. . . .	*Unhelpful feedback:* Correct. I don't think so. Thank you. Interesting. Hmm. Good job. Not exactly. Yep.
Encourage a professional contribution: • Thank you. Please use your inside voice. • Please repeat and project your voice. • Thank you for speaking loudly and clearly.	*Ways of asking students to speak louder:* Huh? Can't hear. Say it louder. ¿Qué? Didn't get that. Say that again. What did you say?
Ask students to contribute: • Who has a different conclusion? • Who would like to respond to that statement? • What additional sources did you use?	*Asking students:* • Who wants to start? • OK, can someone get us going? • Who wants to share? • Who can tell me the answer?

This resource is available for download at https://companion.corwin.com/courses/Academic-Languaging.

While teachers need to model language, we must afford students plenty of opportunities to hear themselves using new words and putting those words and phrases into sentences, as they practice with their peers how to ask questions, construct explanations, and prepare arguments. Oral language provides a foundation to literacy development; hence, purposeful talk leads students to develop and deepen their understanding of concepts and ideas that can also be reinforced through print (Gottlieb & Ernst-Slavit, 2014).

Making Text Features Visible

Many educators expect students entering the upper grades to have a clear understanding of the text features that characterize informational texts. However, this may not be the case for many students, including multilingual students. Although text features in U.S. textbooks and materials are designed to help readers navigate, understand, and retain information, the sheer variety of text features (see Table 5.10) can really puzzle students who may be accustomed to materials with fewer features, pictures, and colors.

Table 5.10 Examples of Different Kinds of Text Features Found in Social Studies Texts

PRINT FEATURES	GRAPHIC AIDS	INFORMATIONAL AIDS	ORGANIZATIONAL AIDS
Bold print	Charts/graphs	Boxed texts	Appendices
Bullet points	Electronic menu	Captions	Chapter titles
Colored print	Icons	Footnotes/endnotes	Glossaries
Font types/ sizes	Illustrations/ photos	Labels	Headings/ subheadings
Italics	Maps	Numbered steps	Indices
Underlining	Tables	Timelines	Tables of contents

There are a variety of ways of helping students learn from text features. The following are suggestions you can use depending on students' grade level and their level of English language proficiency.

- Have students use sticky notes or software to label and define selected text features.
- Before students read an assigned text, do a scavenger hunt for the different features and reflect on their potential applications.
- Display on a large screen a page or two of the assigned reading and review features.
- Ask students to discuss the text features in pairs and discuss their purpose, their placement, and whether or how they enhance their understanding.
- After reading material, have students evaluate which features were helpful, which ones were confusing, and which ones they ignored.
- With your students, create an anchor chart with different text features, definitions, and examples.
- Have students apply some of the reviewed text features in their writing.

Chapter Summary

Social studies may be the most difficult content area for multilingual students due to the variety of disciplines—each with its own content and unique ways of language use, and because social studies includes topics that may be unfamiliar, confusing, or sensitive to students—including multilingual students. Knowing your multilingual students and having insights into their lived experiences should impact the content and how the content is taught. In other words, social studies instruction needs to be connected to students' lives and experiences in meaningful and powerful ways.

The language for social studies is vast and is marked by distinct genres, a variety of complex grammatical structures, an abundance of unfamiliar words and phrases, and symbols that may be difficult to grasp. Becoming aware of the unique linguistic and cultural aspects of social studies—and intentionally modeling and engaging students in academic language use—can empower multilingual learners. Creating opportunities for them to take individual or collective action in response to an issue or to improve a situation is a powerful way to guide them toward success.

Extensions

For Reflection

1. Can you recall a time when a teacher went out of their way to understand you personally? What actions did the teacher take? How did that experience make you feel, and what effect did it have on your learning? How do the efforts of that teacher connect to the strategies for multilingual students discussed in this chapter?
2. Every morning, across the nation, many students in public schools stand, place their hands over their hearts, and recite the Pledge of Allegiance. Do you think your students understand the meaning of the Pledge of Allegiance? Have you checked what they think about this ritual? Did you know that not all states require teachers and students to recite the pledge and that in many states students can opt out of saying it?
3. Most maps place north at the top, but this orientation is arbitrary. It became standard during the European exploration in the 16th century, possibly because Europeans used the North Star and magnetic compasses for navigation or preferred to position themselves at the top of the map. This convention has influenced how people perceive geography, leading to phrases like "above" or "below" certain places, or traveling "up" or "down." Since being "at the top" is often linked with importance, the north or up orientation can imply that northern countries are more significant than those in the south. Reversing the map, with the South Pole at the top, offers a fresh perspective on the world. If you have not tried this before, turn a globe or a world map upside down. What do you notice? What will your students think?

For Action

1. Are you aware of the language you use during social studies instruction? How do you address your students? What kinds of oral feedback do you provide students? Do you clarify the meaning of polysemous words? How much wait time are you allowing after you ask a question? If you do not already know the answer to these questions, then it is time to record yourself teaching using audio or video. Video recording is a great option because it allows you to look at several aspects of your interaction, including body language, identifying who is

speaking, and where you generally stand. When video recording yourself, focus your analysis on one or two strategic areas.

2. If you do not live in the same neighborhood as your students, learn about your students by doing home visits (for suggestions on planning home visits, see Ernst-Slavit & Mason, 2012). If home visits are not possible in your district, attending your students' sporting events, shopping and eating in neighborhood stores and eateries, walking your dog around the school neighborhood, and talking to people associated with community resources and organizations (e.g., Boys and Girls Club, library, and churches) are excellent ways of familiarizing yourself with your students' community.

3. Use timelines or graphic organizers to offer historical insights, showing how cultures emerge, develop, and intersect with other cultures within the same region and around the world. This kind of global perspective will help your students make connections with other cultures (which they may have some prior knowledge of) and critically analyze the trajectory of different cultures in relation to issues and events.

Resources

de Oliveira, L. C. (2023). *Teaching social studies to multilingual learners*. Routledge.

Ernst-Slavit, G., & Morrison, S. J. (2019). "Unless you were Native American . . . everybody came from another country": Language and content learning in a Grade 4 diverse classroom. *The Social Studies, 109*(6), 309–323. http://dx.doi.org/10.1080/00377996.2018.1539700

Jaffee, A. T. (2016). Community, voice, and inquiry: Teaching global history for English language learners. *The Social Studies, 107*(3), 1–13. https://doi.org/10.1080/00377996.2016.1140626

Jaffee, A. T. (2018). Developing culturally and linguistically relevant historical thinking skills: Lessons from U.S. history teachers for newcomer English language learners. In L. C. de Oliveira & K. M. Obenchain (Eds.), *Teaching history and social studies to English language learners: Preparing pre-service and in-service teachers* (pp. 7–37). Palgrave Macmillan.

Schell, E. M. (2020–2021). Cultivating global citizenship. *Social Studies Review*, 2–6. bit.ly/3mnC5du

6 Academic Languag*ing* for Science

MULTILINGUAL LEARNERS IN THE SCIENCE CLASSROOM SHOULD

- Access all their language and cultural resources to make sense of science and connect their life experiences to phenomena in meaningful ways
- Approach science from different perspectives and cultural orientations to show evidence for learning
- Collaboratively engage in scientific inquiry with classmates to research, examine, and solve scientific issues
- Be motivated to pursue their own scientific interests through apprenticeships, including STEM and STEAM projects

SPOTLIGHT ON SCIENCE CONTENT

- Scientific literacy revolves around understanding and applying the three dimensions of scientific learning—practices, cross-cutting concepts, and disciplinary core ideas—both in and out of school.
- Scientific practices and discourse utilize
  - Multiple modes of communication: interpretive—reading, listening, and viewing; interactive—among students and between students and technology; expressive—writing, speaking, and representing
  - Multimodalities: e.g., visual, technological, linguistic, and graphic representation
  - Acronyms for symbol systems, complex compounds (e.g., DNA, RNA), chemical formulas, as in carbon dioxide and water (e.g., CO_2, H_2O), or processes, such as photosynthesis ($6CO_2 + 6H_2O \rightarrow C_6H_{12}O_6 + 6O_2$)
  - Multiple ways of languaging, such as incorporating technical scientific language (e.g., *phototropism*), cognates (e.g., *la calidad del aire- air quality*), or raps (search YouTube for examples)

SPOTLIGHT ON LANGUAGE AND CULTURE

- Science is shaped by the culture/context in which it is practiced, such as medical practices.
- The views of science by some multilingual learners and families are steeped in Indigenous cultures while others see science through an Eastern holistic lens. All perspectives are valid, are to be honored in the science classroom, and should jump-start discussion of scientific issues from students' understandings and perspectives.
- Some multilingual learners are familiar with unique natural phenomena that occur outside of the U.S. mainland, such as volcanic eruptions, tsunamis, and typhoons; these experiences can be shared (if students have not been traumatized) and used as points of comparison.

Introduction

The classroom is the ideal place for content area teachers to highlight the language for science as state academic content standards—in particular, the Next Generation Science Standards—are language-rich statements of what students can do. Understanding that these standards represent three-dimensional learning of real-world phenomena offers teachers, coaches, and other educators opportunities to make curriculum more authentic and of interest to students. As part of this redesign effort, multilingual learners' languages, cultures, and perspectives should be taken into account to promote academic languaging in science, enabling students to be critical creative thinkers and users of language for specific purposes.

Current Perspectives on Teaching and Learning Science for Multilingual Learners

Much of science education in today's classrooms can be traced to the influence of the National Research Council's 2012 *Framework for K–12 Science Education*. It states that as educators, we should "provide all students with the background to systematically investigate issues related to their personal and community practices . . . frame scientific questions pertinent to their interests, conduct investigations and seek out relevant scientific arguments and data, review and apply those arguments to the situation at hand, and communicate their scientific understanding and arguments to others" (National Research Council, 2012, p. 278). The *Framework* is inclusive of rich opportunities for language use during science learning. You might wish to read the quote again, this time looking for the visibility of language and its integration with content.

A second report, the National Academies of Sciences, Engineering, and Medicine's *English Learners in STEM Subjects* (Francis & Stephens, 2018), has also been influential in steering a new course in science education for multilingual learners (referred to as English learners in the document). Specifically, the report states that students "develop science, technology, engineering, and mathematics (STEM) knowledge and language proficiency when they are engaged in meaningful interaction in the classroom and participate in the kinds of activities in which STEM experts and professionals regularly engage" (Francis & Stephens, 2018, p. 55).

These accounts of the state of the art of science education have stimulated a shift in thinking in the field. No longer is language viewed as separate from content; rather, science and language learning are now perceived as integrated, with the *Framework*'s Science and Engineering Practices spearheading rich potential for language use (National Research Council, 2012). Concomitantly, there has been an increased awareness of the important roles of equity and science literacy (Stoll, 2022).

Three-dimensional learning proposed in the science standards emphasizes real-world phenomena and design problems that are relevant to students' communities and lives. Learning in the science classroom is no longer envisioned as transfer of knowledge, but rather is considered transformational. To underscore the growing contribution of multilingual learners to science education, we present several topics prominent in K–12 settings.

1. Attending to Science and Engineering Practices
2. Promoting Multilingual Learner Identity in Science
3. Including Students' Languages and Cultures in Science
4. Connecting the Science Curriculum to the Local Environment
5. Facilitating Meaningful Oral Discussion in the Science Classroom
6. Fostering Linguistic and Culturally Responsive Science Teaching

Attending to Science and Engineering Practices

The National Research Council's 2012 *Framework* was the foundational document for the development of the Next Generation Science Standards (National Research Council, 2013), which have been adopted or adapted by the majority of states. In it, eight Science and Engineering Practices are the grounding for essential science habits of mind and action that guide K–12 science, technology, engineering, and mathematics (STEM) and science, technology, engineering, art, and mathematics (STEAM) curriculum, instruction, and assessment:

1. Asking questions and defining problems
2. Developing and using models
3. Planning and carrying out investigations
4. Analyzing and interpreting data
5. Using mathematics and computational thinking
6. Constructing explanations and designing solutions
7. Engaging in argument from evidence
8. Obtaining, evaluating, and communicating information

The Science and Engineering Practices exemplify the interweaving of scientific concepts and the language for science in elementary and secondary classrooms. After all, students don't use language in isolation, but rather use it for specific purposes, and these are tied to the disciplines or content areas. Relying on the progressions from the Next Generation Science Standards, Appendix F (National Research Council, 2013, pp. 1–33), Table 6.1 dissects examples of scientific understandings from their associated language for the Science and Engineering Practices. Teachers of science may find this distinction helpful for their multilingual learners as they invite students to use all their language resources to access, make sense of, and apply these essential practices during their daily routines.

Table 6.1 Uncovering Content and Language in the Science and Engineering Practices

SCIENCE AND ENGINEERING PRACTICE	SCIENCE UNDERSTANDINGS (Examples of what students do with science)	LANGUAGE UNDERSTANDINGS (Examples of what students do with language)
1. Asking questions and defining problems	Conducting research involving natural phenomena	Eliciting and responding to the who, what, where, when, how, and why of natural phenomena
2. Developing and using models	Designing diagrams, physical replicas, analogies, and computer simulations	Comparing and evaluating different models of the same tool, process, mechanism, or system
3. Planning and carrying out investigations	Identifying appropriate tools; collecting data to serve as the basis for evidence	Forming testable explanations based on prior experiences
4. Analyzing and interpreting data	Refining design solutions for objects, tools, or processes based on analysis	Describing, comparing, and contrasting information
5. Using mathematics and computational thinking	Measuring or graphing quantities; showing patterns and relationships	Describing or estimating quantities; expressing patterns and relationships
6. Constructing explanations and designing solutions	Making quantitative and/ or qualitative claims from evidence	Stating the why, how, or explaining the sequence of steps in investigations
7. Engaging in argument from evidence	Stating research findings and citing accompanying evidence	Evaluating the claims, evidence, and/ or reasoning; critiquing evidence and posing questions related to a position
8. Obtaining, evaluating, and communicating information	Integrating qualitative and/or quantitative scientific and/or technical information	Relating scientific and/or technical information orally, in writing, or in multimodalities formats

Stop and Think

Highlighting Languaging and Cultural Relevance in Science Materials

Often there is a disconnect between the underlying principles of a discipline and linguistically and culturally relevant materials. The English Learners Success Forum (2024) is an organization dedicated to "expand(ing) educational equity for multilingual learners by increasing the supply of high-quality instructional materials that center their cultural and linguistic assets . . . to ensure every multilingual student engages in learning that allows them to thrive academically and choose their path for success" (p. 2). In that vein, it has crafted a set of guidelines with five focal areas that direct language use for specific purposes for science and engineering materials underscoring the language(s) for doing science (Suárez, 2020):

1. Interdependence of science and language learning
2. Leveraging students' assets
3. Assessment for science and language learning
4. Supports and structures for science and language learning
5. Metalinguistic and metacognitive awareness

A growing number of books and articles offer a culturally responsive perspective of science through the lens of multilingual learners—in particular, that of Indigenous communities. In addition, sharing lesser-known biographies of scientists from an array of cultures helps multilingual students feel seen and represented (Joshi, 2023).

Not only do we hold languaging as transformative across the content areas, but in the case of the Science and Engineering Practices, languaging is considered social interaction with language as action. Students should engage in the language for science, as for all content areas, through dynamic *languaging*—"the process of making meaning and shaping knowledge and experience through language" (Swain, 2006, p. 98). Oral language is a critical component of multilingual learners' development and a primary mode for languaging as students gradually assume agency.

Promoting Multilingual Learner Identity in Science

Within the multilingual education community, researchers often refer to *A Framework for K–12 Science Education* (National Research Council, 2012) and the Next Generation Science Standards (National Research Council, 2013) as the impetus for positive change in bringing about fairness in science education. As a result, sensemaking in science has elevated student voice and participation with increased student interaction and collaboration while instruction and assessment have been reoriented around the interests and identities of the learners.

As introduced in Chapter 1, multilingual learners' identities are influenced by a number of factors present inside and out of school. Denver Public Schools has designed a culturally responsive and sustaining evaluation tool that, in part, focuses on students' science identity and how minoritized voices must be present in all courses and materials. Table 6.2 shows how identity is treated in the rating scale.

Table 6.2 Science Identity in the Denver Public Schools' Science Evaluation Tool

INDICATOR	NO EVIDENCE	SOME EVIDENCE	STRONG EVIDENCE
Students are prompted to connect home and community-based knowledge related to phenomena.	Students are not asked to share home or community-based knowledge related to phenomena.	Cursory connections are made between students' home and community-based knowledge and phenomena.	Students' home and community-based knowledge are communicated and recorded in the classroom and used to make progress toward explaining phenomena.
The contributions of scientists with different racial, ethnic, and gender identities are promoted in the curriculum.	Materials center only on traditionally promoted science identities.	Contributions of scientists with different racial, ethnic, and gender identities are acknowledged but lack depth.	Contributions of scientists with different racial, ethnic, and gender identities are meaningfully centered and presented as originators of scientific practices.

Source: Clarissa Deverel-Rico and Erin Marie Furtak, *How Do We Get to Culturally Responsive and Sustaining Approaches to Classroom Assessment? Perspectives and Approaches.* 2024 Classroom Assessment Conference, Chicago, September 19–20. https://drive.google.com/file/d/1RRfydGYjhfvlpDB1vHV76D5VWETClw6l/view

Researchers in science education have seen changes in the last decade. Lee (2021) has pointed out a necessary shift from traditional to contemporary approaches of science teaching along with a shift from a deficit-oriented view to an asset-oriented view of students. Soto et al. (2023) attribute equity moves that support multilingual learners in science to the integration of language scaffolds with culturally responsive scaffolds. Grapin (2023) has dichotomized the notion of equity for multilingual learners in content area classes, specifying the following:

1. Equity can mean that students have access or opportunities to participate in (content-based) learning according to grade-level norms.
2. Equity can mean that educators engage in transforming (or disrupting) the dominant education paradigm with the goal of elevating the status of the language and knowledge base of minoritized students.

In a similar vein, Calabrese Barton and Tan (2020) have proposed a justice-oriented or a "rightful presence" that "challenges and transforms what participation in the disciplines entails" (p. 436). A similar view comes from the National Academies of Sciences, Engineering, and Medicine (2022), whose synthesis of research in STEM education focusing on minoritized students, including multilingual learners, reveals equity and social justice along a continuum from "increasing access [at one end of the spectrum] to redressing injustices and disrupting systemic oppressions [at the other end]," ultimately concluding that multiple conceptions are necessary to "genuinely and fully work toward disrupting systemic oppression" (p. 27).

Look Closer

Resources From the National Science Teachers Association

If you are curious about the perception of equity in science education, you might refer to the following resources:

Coppens, K. (2022). Equity in science: Starting the conversation with your class and yourself. *Science Scope, 46*(1). https://www.nsta.org/science-scope/science-scope-septemberoctober-2022/equity-science

Penuel, B. (2022). *To promote equity, prepare students for what science could be. Science Scope, 46*(1). https://www.nsta.org/science-scope/science-scope-septemberoctober-2022/equity-science

Reigh, E., Miller, E. A., Simani, M. C., & Severson, A. (2023). Toward equity for multilingual learners: The standards offer a new opportunity to engage multilingual learners in science. *Science and Children, 60*(4), 26–29. https://doi.org/10.1080/00368148.2023.12291867

Including Students' Languages and Cultures in Science

For the Science and Engineering Practices to be meaningful to students and their teachers, they must be couched in instructional and assessment practices grounded in multilingual learners' languages and cultures, our third topic of discussion. Science and STEM/STEAM teachers of multilingual learners, often in collaboration with language specialists, must be aware of and implement equity moves in classrooms. Equity moves are research-based strategies that include language and culturally responsive supports to advance multilingual learners' conceptual and language development (Soto et al., 2023).

Yet as members of the multilingual education community we must always be cautious of how science is portrayed. Graves et al. (2022) present a case of how inequalities are pervasive in science and have negative effects on "racial, ethnic, gender, identity, ability, and other types of diversity" (para. 10). They argue that there is no agenda-free science and that the organization of science content itself may reflect hidden or biased agendas reflective of white angiocentric norms.

Stop and Think

Multilingual Learners' Cultures and Science

Having multilingual learners share their connections to different scientific topics through their languages and cultures can enhance the learning experiences of all students. Here are some questions for exploring and discussing different cultural perspectives of science with multilingual learners:

1. What personal beliefs do you bring to the scientific community on topics of investigation? How might your family's "funds of knowledge" contribute to these perspectives?
2. In what ways do your lived experiences contribute to your understanding of scientific knowledge?
3. What opportunities do you have to support science in personally meaningful ways?
4. How do your multiple languages and cultures enrich your scientific insights?
5. What are the views of Indigenous peoples or those from Eastern cultures (e.g., Asia), and what are their contributions to the phenomena being studied?

Educational organizations have been making a concerted effort to bring parity to the forefront by accentuating the role of language and culture in shaping science. WIDA, a consortium of 41 states, territories, and entities devoted to advancing teaching and learning for multilingual learners and their educators, in collaboration with the National Science Teaching Association, has crafted a set of design principles for engaging multilingual learners in three-dimensional science with attention to language and culture (MacDonald et al., 2020). Table 6.3 names these principles and gives a summary of each.

Table 6.3 Scientific Design Principles for Multilingual Learners

SCIENTIFIC DESIGN PRINCIPLE FOR MULTILINGUAL LEARNERS	WHAT IT SAYS
1. Students have the right to learn science.	Students should access science through familiar issues in their lives and communities. Science education supports engaged civic participation and provides students opportunities to seek STEM-related careers.
2. The legacy of disparities in science can be disrupted.	When educators view the teaching and learning of science from multiple perspectives and attend to historical and contemporary disparities in power, authority, and status, science education can then treat and engage multilingual learners in more equitable ways.
3. Phenomena matter for sensemaking.	When working with phenomena related to real-life events and experiences, students are encouraged to collaborate by delving into questions, analyzing problems, designing solutions, building claims, evaluating evidence, and communicating their findings with others.
4. Student contributions matter for sensemaking.	Teachers are to value students' ideas, languages, cultures, and multiple ways of making sense of science; when students see themselves as capable learners and users of science, they cultivate more interest. Student-generated models keep meaning-making at the center of their scientific practice and serve as representations of thinking.
5. Science and Engineering Practices matter for sensemaking.	Students build scientific understanding and develop language by engaging in Science and Engineering Practices. Supporting students to gather evidence, discuss evidence with others, and weigh strengths of that evidence allows for shared sensemaking about phenomena. The Science and Engineering Practices allow students to critique different ideas while building their knowledge base alongside developing language.
6. Positioning students to have agency and authority matters.	Students can express complex, precise, and explicit ideas with everyday language. Supporting students to elicit their ideas is central to their becoming competent members of a learning community. Creating opportunities for students to exercise agency as capable inquirers and problem-solvers fuels their efforts to become authors of scientific explanations, builders of models, and designers of innovative solutions.
7. Educators must leverage and sustain students' cultural and linguistic assets.	Equitable science education leverages students' assets—their experiences, ways of knowing, and cultural and linguistic resources—to make sense of science and the world around them. In sharing, exploring, and communicating within a learning community, students develop science and language simultaneously in culturally sustaining ways.
8. Students learn through expanding science and linguistic repertoires.	Linguistic and culturally responsive science invites students to explore ideas and questions in the language(s) of their choice. Science teaching that fosters a broad range of language resources and multimodalities, including translanguaging, gestures, and visual representations, helps students expand their repertoires of language use.

Connecting the Science Curriculum to the Local Environment

Science classrooms have been slowly shifting away from following a formulaic "scientific method" to having students engage in the practices of scientists: asking, investigating, and answering questions with evidence about the natural world (Osborne & Quinn, 2017). In accord with this vision, teachers are anchoring their science units and lessons in exploration of natural phenomena. In experiencing observable events, students come to understand scientific ideas that they, in turn, can explain or challenge (Lowell & McNeill, 2019). In this way, the science curriculum is moving more toward students' personal interaction with the world around them while academic languaging suggests what students can do with scientific phenomena rather than just learning its facts.

Look Closer

Virtual Trips

One way the science classroom can come alive, even if vicariously, is through virtual field trips by exploring Google Earth or through video tours. There are so many options to choose from, including the following:

- Students can check out the NASA (2012) international space station at https://www.youtube.com/watch?v=doN4t5NKW-k.
- Science On a Sphere® (https://sos.noaa.gov) offers students tours of the solar system where they can explore rocketry, engineering, robotics, weather, or even Mars.
- The American Museum of Natural History in New York invites middle school students to inspect plate tectonics in the formation of the Earth's oceans, continents, and mountains in the Hall of Planet Earth (https://www.amnh.org/exhibitions/permanent/planet-earth).
- The Smithsonian National Air and Space Museum on the National Mall in Washington, DC, offers students and teachers alike a collection of YouTube videos (https://www.youtube.com/@airandspace/videos).

Multilingual learners who are newcomers to U.S. schools (having attended for less than three years) should be exposed to grade-level content that is scaffolded to meet their individual interests and needs. However, we realize that it's challenging for students who have been subject to trauma, may not yet be literate, are highly mobile, or may have had interrupted education. One way for students to become familiar with their new surroundings and make connections to their own life experiences is through place-based education.

Stop and Think

Place-Based Education

As discussed in Chapter 5, place-based education engages students in exploring their local environment through real-world science projects that extend content and cultural learning beyond the classroom. The Milan Urban Food Policy Pact (2015), for example, has an international agreement with select cities worldwide to involve students in helping build sustainable urban food systems that are inclusive, safe, and diverse (see www.milanurbanfoodpolicypact.org/the-milan-pact).

You might look for languages and cultures in participating cities in the Milan Urban Food Policy Pact that match those of your students to see how you might replicate some of their efforts. Another place-based idea is to work with community organizations to generate solutions to local scientific problems, such as air or water pollution.

Additionally, place-based education can be designed to provide students with authentic learning opportunities to foster connections between a place and its cultural roots. In Hawai'i, place-based education serves as a call to action to increase environmental stewardship coupled with community improvement (Regional Educational Laboratory Pacific, 2025).

If you can't take science learning outdoors, you might bring literature or rich informational text about places to the classroom to discuss sustainability and environmental issues, such as ones suggested by E. Bailey (2024) in *Language Magazine*.

For multilingual learners connected to Indigenous heritages, there are several pathways to acknowledge and pursue their cultural roots within the content area of science. A sampling of Indigenous contributions and perspectives are presented in the following topics:

- Agriculture—realizing the important role of maize (corn), rice, or potatoes for food production and consumption; developing sustainable farming practices, such as crop rotation, in different countries
- Medicine—using certain plants for promoting herbal remedies; initiating healing practices, such as acupuncture, to alleviate certain conditions

- Astronomy—applying astronomical knowledge of celestial bodies for navigation purposes, devising calendars, and keeping time
- Ecology—building irrigation and hydraulic systems (e.g., aqueducts)
- Ocean life—initiating a relationship between the ocean and climate to identify marine and coastal life

Facilitating Meaningful Oral Discussion in the Science Classroom

Research confirms that oral language is a vital component of multilingual learners' literacy development; however, student interaction historically has been absent from curriculum (National Academies of Sciences, Engineering, and Medicine, 2017). In the *Talk Science Primer* (2012), Michaels and O'Connor encourage and support productive talk by offering a variety of interactive formats and teacher moves. Participation formats include teacher facilitation of whole-group, small-group, and partner talk while orchestrating talk revolves around students thinking through questioning, such as in "Do you agree or disagree, and why?"

This strategy continues as teachers model a series of questions around a topic, inviting students to respond. Students then huddle according to their response, decide on various reasons for the "why," and share their rationale with other groups. Multilingual learners are encouraged to use the language(s) of their choice—English, their other language, or both languages, such as through translanguaging.

Talk among students stimulates their engagement in learning, confidence, and agency. Conversations can be extended when multilingual learners feel comfortable with and have opportunities to interact in multiple languages in the science classroom. For example, they might do any of the following:

- Propose creative solutions
- Give and receive targeted feedback
- Revise their thinking based on feedback
- Critique scientific models based on a set of criteria
- Recommend and defend other perspectives
- Reach consensus on next steps in their investigation

Learning science concepts through oracy enables multilingual learners to develop language and content concurrently. Structured talk can be built into daily routines—whether in a science classroom or during a literacy block around a science topic. Ideas for oral discussion can be found in language development standards frameworks (see WIDA's 2020 and 2023 editions in English and Spanish) in language expectations (goals for content-driven language learning) and their expressive functions. Table 6.4 suggests ways for students to interact and self-reflect based on grade-level cluster language expectations for Standard 4, the language for science, along with typical topics.

Table 6.4 Standards-Referenced Language Expectations for Explanations and Example Topics

GRADE-LEVEL CLUSTER	MULTILINGUAL LEARNERS WILL CONSTRUCT EXPLANATIONS THAT	EXAMPLE GRADE-LEVEL SCIENCE TOPICS
K–1	• Describe information from observations about a phenomenon • Relate how a series of events causes something to happen • Compare multiple solutions to a problem (WIDA, 2020, pp. 52, 77)	• Properties of water • Effects of motion (e.g., push and pull) • Growth in plants and animals
2–3	• Describe observations and/or data about a phenomenon • Develop a logical sequence between data or evidence and a claim • Compare multiple solutions to a problem considering how well they meet the criteria and constraints of the design solution (WIDA, 2020, p. 94)	• Weather around the world • Electrical models; forces and motion • Factors controlling ecosystems
4–5	• Describe observations and/or data about a phenomenon • Establish neutral or objective stance in communicating results • Develop reasoning to show relationships between evidence and claims • Summarize and/or compare multiple solutions to a problem based on how well they meet the criteria and constraints of the design solution (WIDA, 2020, p. 122)	• Systems of a human body • Structure and physical properties: mass, volume, and states of matter • Chemical changes • Challenges in aerodynamics & hydrodynamics

(Continued)

(Continued)

GRADE-LEVEL CLUSTER	MULTILINGUAL LEARNERS WILL CONSTRUCT EXPLANATIONS THAT	EXAMPLE GRADE-LEVEL SCIENCE TOPICS
6–8	• Describe valid and reliable evidence from sources about a phenomenon • Establish neutral or objective stance in how results are communicated • Develop reasoning to show relationships among independent and dependent variables in models and simple systems • Summarize patterns in evidence, making trade-offs, revising, and retesting (WIDA, 2020, p. 156)	• Environmental change • Predications based on geologic events • Comparison between pure substances and mixtures • Simple machines
9–12	• Describe reliable and valid evidence from multiple sources about a phenomenon • Establish neutral or objective stance in how results are communicated • Develop reasoning to illustrate and/or predict the relationships between variables in a system or between components of a system • Summarize and refine solutions referencing scientific knowledge, evidence, criteria, and/or trade-offs (WIDA, 2020, p. 194)	• Forces of nature • Properties of acids and bases • The flow of energy • Chemical change

Stop and Think

Makerspaces

Makerspaces are a global phenomenon where students construct and share their personal or collaborative inventions. In doing so, learners become creative producers rather than consumers (Hira & Hynes, 2018) and, thus, engage in academic languaging. While all students feel a connection to their environment, makerspaces legitimatize multilingual learners' relationships with their communities' languages and cultures. Language becomes alive as languaging becomes a means of exchanging perspectives in students' enactment of the science and engineering practices. The state of New Jersey celebrates Makers Day, featuring high school student STEM projects, such as marshmallow launchers, electric circuits, and homopolar motors driven by magnetic force fields (as reported in the *Essex News Daily* by Jackovino, 2024).

How might you initiate or extend this idea of science-, STEM-, or STEAM-motivated makerspaces that utilize the Science and Engineering Practices to your classroom, school, or district? How might you directly encourage participation of students' application of original ideas?

Fostering Linguistic and Culturally Responsive Science Teaching

Culturally responsive science curriculum empowers students to probe real-world issues in their local communities and pose solutions. When students see themselves, their cultures, and their community represented in the curriculum, they are more likely to be engaged and motivated and to gain confidence in learning. Curricular foundations in the Science and Engineering Practices all have linguistic and culturally responsive applications. The use and development of models, for example, allow students to explore scientific concepts through their families' funds of knowledge and explain content from varying perspectives (Brown, 2017).

Transitioning to a phenomenon-based approach to teaching science requires teachers to abandon being the primary holder and dispenser of knowledge to being more of a planner, facilitator, and guide (Lowell & Lowenhaupt, 2024). Students, in turn, must come to see science as relevant to their lives as a precursor to deepening their learning. To make science classrooms more culturally responsive, Joshi (2023) suggests the following:

1. *Encourage students to explore their own cultural identities.*

   Just as families' and communities' accumulated knowledge and skills are valuable educational resources, so too are students' identities, representing their cultural capital and lived experiences (Esteban-Guitard & Moll, 2014). When exploring science themes, whether climatic adaptation or genealogy, teachers should begin with students' positioning of and connection to their cultural heritage.

2. *Incorporate diverse perspectives and experiences into learning.*

   As educators, we should always begin new units of learning from the students' linguistic resources and perceptions before focusing on the overall goals for learning. When investigating changing environmental conditions and their impact on the earth, are you trying to project a neutral stance, or do you accept different cultural perspectives? When learning about human body systems, do you invite your students to investigate their familial healing practices and remedies according to various cultures? Assuming diverse perspectives leads to rich discussion around various cultural beliefs and practices, which, in turn, influence our scientific understanding.

3. *Facilitate student-led inquiry.*

   When students have choices in designing, implementing, and evaluating their scientific knowledge, their learning becomes

> relevant and meaningful. Better yet, when students collaborate either as partners or in small groups and decide how to pursue learning, their conversations lead to new discoveries and actions. In other words, students working together and interacting with each other gradually take on responsibility and ownership to become drivers of their own learning (Gottlieb & Honigsfeld, 2025). Inquiry and interaction are essential ingredients of academic languaging as they require students to engage in active learning and make their own discoveries.

In tandem with or as an extension of linguistic and cultural responsiveness, in science instruction there is also a focus on student-driven learning where students are directly involved in the Science and Engineering Practices. When students are at the helm, they become the sensemakers while teachers act as facilitators to support student learning. In this new vision of science education, learning revolves around students doing the practices of scientists by asking, exploring, and answering questions about the natural world, rather than memorizing a set of facts or following the "scientific method" (Osborne & Quinn, 2017). According to Granger et al. (2012), "transforming science learning through student-centered instruction that engages students in a variety of scientific practices is central to national science-teaching reform efforts" (p. 105).

The Language for Science

In being exposed to curricular practices based on content and language standards, students are simultaneously being exposed to prominent ways of using language; case in point, the science classroom is generally oriented around explanation and argumentation. In this section, we unpack the dimensions of language in science.

> "As [multilingual learners] engage in science and engineering practices (e.g., developing models, arguing from evidence, and constructing explanations), they use language for the purpose of making sense of phenomena and problems through interactions with peers and the teacher."
>
> —Okhee Lee (2021, p. 1075)

Discourse

Discourse includes consideration of genres in their interactional contexts; genres, in turn, are texts (oral, written, and/or multimodal) that are formed from specific organizational patterns to relay specific communicative purposes. In scientific investigation, discourse highlights making meaning, building understanding of phenomena, and designing solutions (Lee et al., 2013). As Science and Engineering Practices 6 and 7 highlight the role of explanation and argumentation, respectively, these two genres are strongly interwoven in the science discipline and are reflected in academic content and corresponding language development standards (see ELD/SLD standard statements 4 [WIDA, 2020, 2023] and genre (Key Language Use) distribution charts [WIDA, 2020]).

Scientific explanations are written, oral, or graphic expressions of language in response to questions where students analyze and interpret information prior to reporting their findings. In producing cause-and-effect chains, students often engage in discussions that entail explanations, including the following:

- Defining scientific concepts
- Asking and answering open-ended questions
- Describing processes, procedures, or cycles
- Comparing and contrasting information
- Evaluating ideas about the how and the why, using concrete or mental models
- Summarizing relationships or a series of events that lead to a conclusion

Argumentation is another important genre in science with its own organizational pattern, often described as process oriented, yet it works in conjunction with explanations for natural phenomena; in engineering, argument is a means to identify solutions to design problems. Students use the language for argumentation when they listen to, compare, and evaluate competing ideas and methods. In doing so, students provide reasoning for their ideas rather than just relying on the accuracy of the concepts. Inviting evidence-based counterarguments with counterclaims lends itself to student interaction and the deliberation of alternatives. The discourse contained in scientific arguments revolves around various purposes for language use:

- Describing the controversy and summarizing each side
- Posing scientific statements (or claims) backed by reasons
- Evaluating the claims with evidence from both sides
- Defending or confirming a position based on analysis of data and reasoning
- Convincing others of one of the positions
- Reflecting on a position based on the body of evidence (adapted from Gottlieb & Castro, 2017, pp. 121–122)

Stop and Think

Discourse in Science

The National Research Council in *A Framework for K–12 Science Education* (2012) underscores the role of discourse as students work with the three dimensions of science: Science and Engineering Practices, Cross-Cutting Concepts, and Disciplinary Core Ideas. The *Framework* states, "Students cannot fully understand scientific and engineering ideas without engaging in the practices of inquiry and the discourses by which such ideas are developed and refined" (National Research Council, 2012, p. 218). What does scientific discourse mean in this statement? How would you describe it? How do you apply scientific discourse to your classroom so that students have the freedom of exploration and taking action through academic languaging?

Sentences

Understanding the discourse or big picture of a genre's language patterns, such as the prevalence of explanation or argument in science, enables students to analyze oral or written text. The discourse of argumentation generally contains claims, evidence, and reasoning that pertain to an issue or problem with two definitive sides or positions. Sentences, whether independent or within a chunk of discourse, generally move in sophistication from simple to compound to complex as multilingual learners mature in age and language development.

Scientific inquiry revolves around questioning and having students investigate the world around them. Discussing and deciding on a universal controversial science topic that exemplifies argumentation with your students is a starting point for engaging in debate using powerful sentences. Table 6.5 presents a set of sentences illustrating the features of argumentation across grade-level clusters or different age groups—namely, claims, reasons, and evidence. The examples revolve around students' personal experiences with the issue "Are vaccinations safe or risky?"

Table 6.5 Deconstructing an Argument Into Sentences Illustrative of Claims, Reasons, and Evidence

DISSECTING AN ARGUMENT INTO ITS COMPONENT PARTS	SCHOOL LEVEL	EXAMPLE SENTENCES ADDRESSING THE ISSUE Are vaccinations safe or risky? Why? What are the advantages or disadvantages of getting vaccinations?
Claim	Elementary School	We need vaccinations to prevent us from getting contagious diseases.
	Middle School	Vaccinations provide us immunity against preventable diseases.
	High School	Vaccinations empower us to take responsibility for our health and contribute to herd immunity.
Reason	Elementary School	Vaccinations are important because they help protect us and our families.
	Middle School	Vaccinations are critically important as they allow us to remain healthy.
	High School	Vaccinations are vital as they protect us from potentially life-threatening diseases and contribute to our overall health.
Evidence	Elementary School	Children who are vaccinated don't get as many infectious diseases as children who are not vaccinated.
	Middle School	Vaccinated students miss fewer days of school due to illness than unvaccinated students.
	High School	Vaccinated students have a significantly reduced risk of contracting serious illnesses such as measles, mumps, and whooping cough, enabling them to stay focused on learning.

Words/Phrases

The topic or theme of a unit of study, its essential question, selected materials, and resources determine the words and phrases used during science instruction. Oftentimes publishers will highlight new concepts and define them within the text. If you are using such a text, make sure any new concepts are understandable for all students, checking for cognates that multilingual learners can discover and easily transfer from their other language. Polysemous words (those with multiple meanings, such as *cell*, *compound*, *attraction*, *root*, *base*, *organ*, and *change*) can be a challenge and need to be highlighted. There are also compound words in science (e.g., *thunderstorm*, *backbone*, *butterfly*, *greenhouse*, *bluebird*, and *sunflower*) with distinct meanings unique to English.

Speaking of compounds, referring to both grammatical and scientific references, let's examine how the language might play out in the science classroom. Compound phrases contain a mixture of nouns, verbs, adjectives, adverbs and prepositions. Table 6.6 is a sampling of different compound phrases that are common in science.

Table 6.6 Examples of Compound Phrases in Science

TYPE OF PHRASE	EXAMPLE IN THE SCIENCE CLASSROOM
Adjective	Aluminum is light, nontoxic, nonmagnetic, and silvery
Adjective + Noun	Red blood cells
Noun	Palpitations
Noun + Noun	Earth cross-section
Adverb	Every year, perennial flowers return
Preposition	In the spring
Number	Double-helix structure

Many scientific terms are rooted in Greek and Latin languages. For example, all living organisms are classified in Latin by their genus and species. Examples of Greek words in science are *gamma*, such as in *gamma rays*, and *biology*, meaning the study of living organisms. In addition, many scientific root words (e.g., *cardi* = *heart*, *bio* = *life*, *chlor* = *green*, *hydro* = *water*) are present across languages, facilitating cross-linguistic transfer.

Symbols

Scientific symbols provide a concise and universal way to represent complex ideas, quantities, and relationships. What most readily comes to mind when associating symbols with science is the periodic table and how combining elements produces many different chemical reactions. It's quite easy to show how chemical symbols such as two particles of H (hydrogen) and one of O (oxygen) combine to make up the compound known as water (H_2O) or how sodium (Na) and chloride (Cl) combine to form salt. Additionally, there are biological symbols, as in DNA and RNA; physical symbols in measurement, as in K for kelvin and A for ampere; and even astronomical symbols for the planets. Lastly, there are symbols that form scientific equations, one of the most well-known being $E = mc^2$.

Using Model Texts in Science

Ideally, model texts are student or teacher generated, but as we have mentioned, they can also represent grade-level content taken from other multimodal sources, such as video recordings, podcasts, and even textbooks. In analyzing the language of model texts according to discourse, sentences, words/phrases, and symbols, students gain insight into the use of language for distinct purposes or how language functions in different contexts—in this case, the science classroom. The following two model texts illustrate distinct ways in how a creative story (narrative) and an explanation interweave language and science.

Model Text 1: A Personalized Scientific Narrative

Students enjoy imagining the world around them that can be readily communicated through narration. Combining scientific facts with literature enables students to creatively engage in content-based language development through storytelling. Students can assume many identities in science—from entities in the solar system to organs in a body's system; in essence, in the stories, a nonhuman object can assume human traits, or become anthropomorphic. The first model text, intended for students in the lower grades, is one where a student chose to be a flower (see Figure 6.1); it can easily be accompanied by photos or labeled diagrams to unveil the life cycle of plants.

Figure 6.1 I Want to Be a Flower

Source: Photo by Gisela Ernst-Slavit

> I always wanted to be a pretty flower. One day my wish came true! I sprouted from a tiny seedling in the earth. Soon I became a flower and found out about my life cycle.
>
> As I grew into a young plant I met many friends. I played with other flowers, bees, and birds. I learned about photosynthesis, the process I use to take in sunlight, water, and carbon dioxide to produce oxygen and energy. I also found out about pollination where bees take pollen grains from me and bring them to another flower to produce new plant seeds. Then, one sunny day, I bloomed into a proud flower.
>
> I discovered that plants come in all shapes, colors, and sizes. Some tall trees, like the palms, grow in warm places, like where I live. Their leaves are always green. I like being a beautiful hibiscus flower. My cousins come in many colors, white, pink, and yellow, but I like my five coral petals the best.
>
> Flowers and trees have many different colors, shapes, sizes, and smells. They help make our world beautiful. I am proud to be a flower.

Having read this story aloud to your newcomers or younger students, you should ask yourself the following questions regarding the dimensions of language or discuss the integration of narration and science with colleagues:

1. Regarding discourse, how would you justify calling this science story a narrative? What pieces of informational text are embedded within scientific concepts?
2. How does using first person help the reader relate to the story? What are some examples?
3. What is some descriptive language that enriches the sentences in the story?
4. What are some cultural elements of the story that may favor multilingual learners from Hawai'i, the Caribbean, or the Pacific?
5. How might you encourage your multilingual learners to use the language they are familiar with (e.g., the names, shapes, or colors of plants) or to translanguage in describing a scientific phenomenon?
6. How are specific content (scientific) words interwoven in the story, and how can you ensure that they are meaningful for multilingual learners?

Model Text 2: A Sequential Explanation Based on a Recipe

Scientists who are living in outer space must have a special diet. The following model text is a recipe from the Smithsonian National Air and Space Museum (n.d., 2015) for astronauts at the space station that can be replicated in the science classroom. Your students might enjoy trying out this recipe and discovering a physical change (see Figure 6.2).

Figure 6.2 Eating Ice Cream . . . Just Like the Astronauts!

Source: iStock.com/PamelaJoeMcFarlane

Do you have a favorite frozen treat you like to eat? Could it be ice cream? Even in space some 220 miles above the earth, astronauts enjoy this treat. Do you realize that science is involved in making ice cream? In fact, combining the ingredients of this recipe produces a physical change. You can follow this science recipe to learn how to make ice cream in a bag. Then you might wish to taste your results (unless you have a lactose or milk sensitivity).

Ingredients:

- Sugar
- Half-and-half (cream and milk), milk, or heavy whipping cream
- Vanilla extract
- Salt
- Ice cubes

Materials:

- Measuring spoons
- Measuring cups
- Small, sandwich-size resealable plastic bags
- Large, gallon-size resealable plastic bags

- Oven mitts or a small towel
- A timer or clock

Procedure:

1. In a small resealable plastic bag, place 1 tablespoon (T) of sugar; $\frac{1}{2}$ cup (C) of half-and-half, milk, or heavy whipping cream; and $\frac{1}{4}$ teaspoon (t) of vanilla extract. Seal the bag tight.
2. Add 4 cups (C) of ice cubes to a large gallon-sized plastic bag. Then add $\frac{1}{2}$ cup of salt to the bag.
3. Put your small bag into the large bag with the ice cubes. Be sure both bags are tightly sealed.
4. Put on oven mitts or wrap the bag in a small towel. Shake the bag for five (5) minutes. Feel the smaller bag every couple of minutes while you shake it.
5. Open the bags. Taste what you made. Does it taste like ice cream? If so, you are now a physicist—combining the materials to create a physical change! If it didn't work, what can you do? Maybe you could use a different salt, try to shake the ingredients longer, or put more ice in the bag.

For a visual explanation of the process, you might wish to watch one of the videos available at www.youtube.com/results?search_query=making+ice+cream+in+a+ziploc+bag.

You should note the interaction among language, science, and mathematics in oral and written text in this integrated multidisciplinary activity. However, at times, you may wish to deconstruct the text to see the interplay between content and language as prompted by the ensuing questions:

- Following this recipe, how might you describe the physical change, the science concepts? (To do so, students need to understand the entire passage or discourse). The ice and salt mixture becomes colder than the ice without salt. This extra-cold mixture of salt and ice freezes the ingredients in the small bag and turns them into ice cream.
    - In creating ice cream, you also make an emulsion. In your ice cream, the fat molecules in the cream are perfectly mixed with water, ice, sugar, and air.
- Following this recipe, what is going on linguistically (the language for science)?
    - Procedural recounts are genres, illustrative of the *discourse* dimension of language, where students adhere to a process

through a series of steps. The "how" behind it, where students follow the set of directions, is an explanation.

- The *sentences* are in numerical order and are introduced with a command, a statement that directs you what to do in the series.
- Certain action *phrases* are associated with physical reactions (e.g., "seal the bag"; "add . . . salt to the bag [of ice cubes]").
- Certain *words* and phrases are associated with measurement in mathematics (e.g., *cup*, *tablespoon*, *teaspoon*) and can be noted through *symbols*, such as C, T, and t. Multilingual learners may be more accustomed to the metric system or to inexact measurement for recipes; therefore, they may be challenged by this measurement system.

Having read (and perhaps even followed) this recipe, students may ask themselves the following questions:

1. What makes the directions or steps of the recipe easy or difficult to follow? (Perhaps it's the commands at the beginning of the sentence that offer precise instructions. Also, the use of bullets that list the ingredients and materials make the language concise.)
2. At home, do you use measures like the ones in the recipe, do you use metric measures (i.e., grams), or do you just estimate the amount? Give an example of one of your family's recipes. (Different cultures apply measurement in distinct ways.)
3. In this activity, how might you describe yourself as a physicist? What steps have you taken that change the substance?
4. How might you alter a recipe—maybe you would like to add a flavor—or make up a recipe of your own where combining the ingredients causes a reaction, even something like making pudding?

Strategies for Moving Science Learning Forward With Multilingual Learners

Emphasize Student Interaction

Student–student interaction fosters deep content learning in conjunction with content-driven language development. This strategy is especially effective for promoting multilingual learners' active participation in the science classroom. Jeff Zwiers and Sara Hamerla (2018) consider three types of academic conversations for engaging multilingual learners in science discussions:

1. *Taking a side or position on a controversial science issue*

   Argumentation is one of the most prominent actions in state science and language development standards (National Research Council, 2013; WIDA, 2020). From the early grades through the most advanced courses in high school, students can take a stance and defend their position based on multimodal evidence and reasoning gleaned from scientific information and exploration.

2. *Collaborating in interpreting scientific data or information*

   Student collaboration in the sharing of information and ideas pertaining to scientific investigation not only builds relationships among classmates but offers opportunities for students to negotiate and come to consensus on the meaning and importance of data to support their claims.

3. *Role-playing that deals with scientific phenomena*

   Role-playing is a creative way for students to physically participate in science learning.

   Students—individually, in pairs, or in small groups—can use gestures, engage in dialogue, or simulate scientific discoveries, processes, or cycles. Be sensitive to students' interest in participating in such an activity and gauge each student's views and feelings in conjunction with observations of language and content.

Make Phenomena Authentic, Meaningful, and Accessible Through Multimodalities

We have noted how culturally sustaining science classrooms invite students to actively participate in learning by interacting with their peers, making their thinking visible using genre-based discourse as they engage in the Science and Engineering Practices. To do so, teachers tend to retrofit or modify existing science curriculum materials to better match their student populations rather than design universal experiences with embedded pathways to success (Curry et al., 2006). Inserting multimodalities, the combined use of different modes of communication (e.g., graphics, visuals, and technology), into the learning experience enhances access to meaning for all students.

Stop and Think

A Makeover With Multimodalities

In addition to oral and written modes in one or more languages, multilingual learners can communicate their understanding through multimodalities, using gestures, or through videos, diagrams, illustrations, and computer-mediated content. In science, students also interact with natural phenomena and instruments, such as microscopes or binoculars. Teachers must be cautious when introducing multimodalities presented in textbooks, as multilingual learners must then decode the text message as well as additional literacies, such as digital, visual, and graphic (Gottlieb & Ernst-Slavit, 2014). Which multimodalities do you find most effective for the content area of science, and how do you embed them into curriculum, instruction, and assessment?

Integrate the Language for Science and the Content of Science

A practice-oriented science classroom with multilingual learners can be a rich environment for boosting language learning alongside science learning (Quinn et al., 2012). Educators of multilingual learners must see the strong relationship between content and language across the curriculum and, subsequently, elevate the status of language within content area instruction. Ultimately, the recognition of content and language occupying a shared space did not occur until the turn of the millennium (Carr et al., 2006; Gottlieb, 2016, 2024a; WIDA, 2020). Today, the overlapping connections between content and language spark collaboration between teachers and between teachers and students, encouraging multilingual learners to actively participate in instructional and assessment activities (Gottlieb & Honigsfeld, 2025).

The WIDA 2020 and 2023 standards frameworks for English and Spanish language development amplify ways in which the language for science and other content areas can be directly applied to classrooms. Key Language Uses or purposes for language use, a major component of the standards frameworks derived from academic content standards, are useful for students to relate science stories, offer scientific ideas and information, sequence steps in scientific explanations, and engage in scientific arguments. Their application to the science classroom adds versatility and flexibility to language use within content instruction (Westerlund & Miller, 2023). Table 6.7 defines four Key Language Uses in English and Spanish along with science examples.

Table 6.7 Coupling Key Language Uses With Examples From the Science Classroom

KEY LANGUAGE USES	EXAMPLES FROM THE SCIENCE CLASSROOM
Narrate (Relatar): *language for conveying experiences*	• Biographies of famous scientists from around the world • Stories of scientific discoveries • The histories of a range of scientific fields
Inform (Informar): *language for providing facts related to definitions, descriptions, or comparisons of ideas, concepts, or phenomena*	• Describing different ecosystems • Relating impending weather-related disasters • Reporting accounts of scientific events
Explain (Explicar): *language for how or why things work, showing cause and effect or sequence*	• The steps in life or food cycles • How circuits work • Why rainbows occur
Argue (Argumentar): *language for justifying claims, using evidence, and providing reasoning*	• Is nature stronger than nurture? • Does climate change exist? • Should cloning animals be legal?

This resource is available for download at https://companion.corwin.com/courses/Academic-Languaging.

Chapter Summary

We present academic languaging as a means for students to build knowledge and take subsequent action to solve challenging problems resulting in personal confidence and agency. Nowhere is academic languaging more apparent than in the content area of science with its focus on multimodalities and technology to enhance scientific investigation and communication. The National Research Council's 2012 *Framework for K–12 Science Education* has been the impetus for the advancement of this discipline for more than a decade. Its vision for science learning integrates language-intensive practices and concepts, inviting all teachers to promote language use and learning in their science classrooms and beyond.

Today's curriculum must revolve around technology if we are to advance as a society; our growing reliance on STEM and STEAM will enable students to tackle complex issues and create imaginative new solutions. Becoming aware of the expanding vision of STEM that seeks justice-centered responses to societal dilemmas (Lee & Grapin, 2024) is a significant step for educators in planning science curriculum. Authenticity coupled with linguistic and cultural relevance are critical for multilingual learners in science classrooms where their interests are pursued, sparking a drive to contribute to the world around them.

Extensions

For Reflection

1. Science is all around us. Invite students to maintain an oral or written science log of their observations based on units of learning or a science journal of their reactions, feelings, or reflections on their scientific discoveries at home and in the community. In their noticings, have students take photos or make sketches and annotate their findings.

2. The International Society for Technology in Education (2017) standards for students, educators, education leaders, and coaches are a framework of technology-related competencies for learning, teaching, and leading. Available in multiple languages, these standards should work alongside state academic science standards and language development standards to underscore the increasing influence and impact of technology on what we do as a science and STEM community. You might wish to explore these standards in your professional learning communities or grade-level teams to see their representation in your curriculum. As you do so, make suggestions as to how you might focus on more student-centered ways to empower your multilingual learners during instruction and classroom assessment.

For Action

1. You may wish to review the Stop and Think boxes sprinkled throughout the chapter that pertain to makerspaces, place-based education, and linguistically and culturally relevant materials. With your multilingual learners, generate ideas for capturing their preferences and incorporate their ideas into curriculum, instruction, and classroom assessment. With your colleagues and students, brainstorm how you might connect the families' strengths at home and in the community to those of school.

2. To what extent are you familiar with the periodic table of elements? How many of the scientific elements can you and your students recognize from their symbols? Using your and their linguistic resources, what additional words can you and your students identify with the same origins? Do you realize that the table was created in the 19th century by a Russian, Dmitri Mendeleev, who used Latin as the identification scheme?

Figure 6.3 Periodic Table of the Elements

Periodic Table of the Elements

Atomic Number → 1 H ← Symbol; Name → Hydrogen; 1.008 ← Atomic Weight

State of matter (color of name): GAS LIQUID SOLID UNKNOWN

Subcategory in the metal–metalloid–nonmetal trend (color of background): Alkaline metal; Lanthanide; Transition metal; Alkaline earth metal; Actinide; Post-transition metal; Metalloid; Polyatomic nonmetal; Diatomic nonmetal; Noble gas; Unknown chemical properties

1 IA	2 IIA	3 IIIB	4 IVB	5 VB	6 VIB	7 VIIB	8 VIIIB	9 VIIIB	10 VIIIB	11 IB	12 IIB	13 IIIA	14 IVA	15 VA	16 VIA	17 VIIA	18 VIIIA
1 H Hydrogen 1.008																	2 He Helium 4.002602
3 Li Lithium 6.94	4 Be Beryllium 9.0121831											5 B Boron 10.81	6 C Carbon 12.011	7 N Nitrogen 14.007	8 O Oxygen 15.999	9 F Fluorine 18.998403163	10 Ne Neon 20.1797
11 Na Sodium 22.98976928	12 Mg Magnesium 24.305											13 Al Aluminium 26.9815385	14 Si Silicon 28.085	15 P Phosphorus 30.973761998	16 S Sulfur 32.06	17 Cl Chlorine 35.45	18 Ar Argon 39.948
19 K Potassium 39.0983	20 Ca Calcium 40.078	21 Sc Scandium 44.955908	22 Ti Titanium 47.867	23 V Vanadium 50.9415	24 Cr Chromium 51.9961	25 Mn Manganese 54.938044	26 Fe Iron 55.845	27 Co Cobalt 58.933194	28 Ni Nickel 58.6934	29 Cu Copper 63.546	30 Zn Zinc 65.38	31 Ga Gallium 69.723	32 Ge Germanium 72.630	33 As Arsenic 74.921595	34 Se Selenium 78.971	35 Br Bromine 79.904	36 Kr Krypton 83.798
37 Rb Rubidium 85.4678	38 Sr Strontium 87.62	39 Y Yttrium 88.90584	40 Zr Zirconium 91.224	41 Nb Niobium 92.90637	42 Mo Molybdenum 95.95	43 Tc Technetium (98)	44 Ru Ruthenium 101.07	45 Rh Rhodium 102.90550	46 Pd Palladium 106.42	47 Ag Silver 107.8682	48 Cd Cadmium 112.414	49 In Indium 114.818	50 Sn Tin 118.710	51 Sb Antimony 121.760	52 Te Tellurium 127.60	53 I Iodine 126.90447	54 Xe Xenon 131.293
55 Cs Caesium 132.90545196	56 Ba Barium 137.327	57 - 71 Lanthenoids	72 Hf Hafnium 178.49	73 Ta Tantalum 180.94788	74 W Tungsten 183.84	75 Re Rhenium 186.207	76 Os Osmium 190.23	77 Ir Iridium 192.217	78 Pt Platinum 195.084	79 Au Gold 196.966569	80 Hg Mercury 200.592	81 Tl Thallium 204.38	82 Pb Lead 207.2	83 Bi Bismuth 208.98040	84 Po Polonium (209)	85 At Astatine (210)	86 Rn Radon (222)
87 Fr Francium (223)	88 Ra Radium (226)	89 - 103 Actinoids	104 Rf Rutherfordium (267)	105 Db Dubnium (268)	106 Sg Seaborgium (269)	107 Bh Bohrium (270)	108 Hs Hassium (269)	109 Mt Meitnerium (278)	110 Ds Darmstadtium (281)	111 Rg Roentgenium (282)	112 Cn Copernicium (285)	113 Nh Nihonium (286)	114 Fl Flerovium (289)	115 Mc Moscovium (289)	116 Lv Livermorium (293)	117 Ts Tennessine (294)	118 Og Oganesson (294)

57 La Lanthanum 138.90547	58 Ce Cerium 140.116	59 Pr Praseodymium 140.90766	60 Nd Neodymium 144.242	61 Pm Promethium (145)	62 Sm Samarium 150.36	63 Eu Europium 151.964	64 Gd Gadolinium 157.25	65 Tb Terbium 158.92535	66 Dy Dysprosium 162.500	67 Ho Holmium 164.93033	68 Er Erbium 167.259	69 Tm Thulium 168.93422	70 Yb Ytterbium 173.045	71 Lu Lutetium 174.9668
89 Ac Actinium (227)	90 Th Thorium 232.0377	91 Pa Protactinium 231.03588	92 U Uranium 238.02891	93 Np Neptunium (237)	94 Pu Plutonium (244)	95 Am Americium (243)	96 Cm Curium (247)	97 Bk Berkelium (247)	98 Cf Californium (251)	99 Es Einsteinium (252)	100 Fm Fermium (257)	101 Md Mendelevium (258)	102 No Nobelium (259)	103 Lr Lawrencium (266)

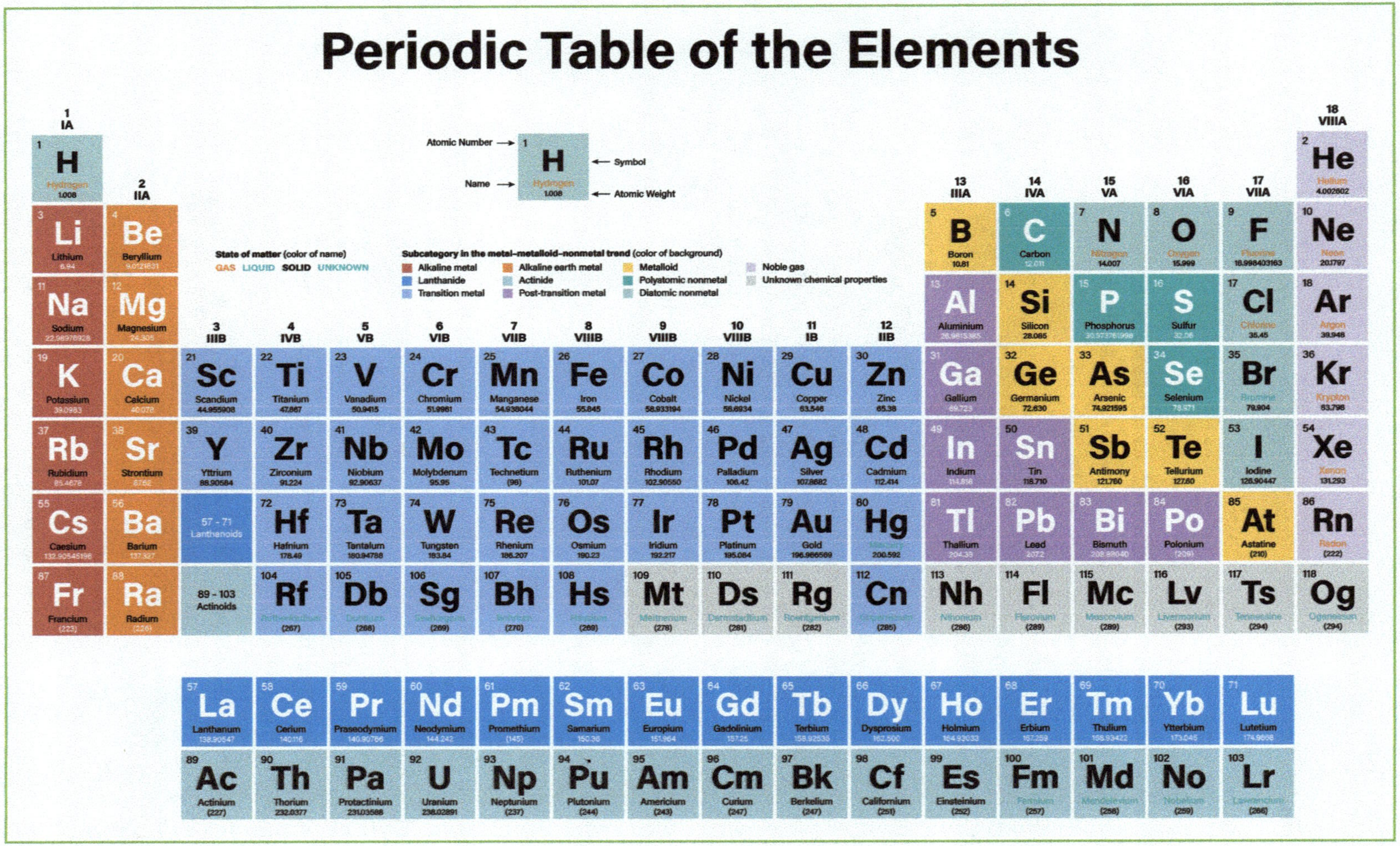

Source: iStock.com/duntaro

3. If your students were to create a scientific table or reorganize the periodic table, what would be its defining elements, and how might they describe their system to classmates?

Resources

Ernst-Slavit, G., & Pratt, K. L. (2017). Teacher questions: Learning the discourse of science in a linguistically diverse elementary classroom. *Linguistics and Education, 40*, 1–10. https://doi.org/10.1016/j.linged.2017.05.005

International Society for Technology Education. (2017). *ISTE standards for students, educators, education leaders, and coaches.* https://iste.org/standards

National Academies of Sciences, Engineering, and Medicine. (2017). *Promoting the educational successes of children and youth learning English: Promising futures.* National Academies Press. https://nap.nationalacademies.org/read/24677/chapter/2

National Academies of Sciences, Engineering, and Medicine. (2022). *Science and engineering in preschool through elementary grades: The brilliance of children and the strengths of educators.* National Academies Press. https://nap.nationalacademies.org/catalog/26215/science-and-engineering-in-preschool-through-elementray-grades-the-brillance

National Research Council. (2012). *A framework for K–12 science education: Practices, crosscutting concepts, and core ideas.* https://nap.nationalacademies.org/read/13165/chapter/1

National Research Council. (2013). *Next Generation Science Standards: For states, by states.* National Academies Press.

WIDA. (2020). *WIDA English language development standards framework, 2020 edition: Kindergarten–grade 12.* Board of Regents of the University of Wisconsin System.

WIDA. (2023). *Marco de los estándares del desarrollo auténtico del lenguaje español de WIDA: Kinder al 12° grado.* Board of Regents of the University of Wisconsin System.

7 Taking a Dynamic Stance

Academic Languag*ing* for Multilingual Learners and Educators

In this book we have invited you to contemplate a shift of mindset, weighing the juxtaposition of content and language in your teaching and how your multilingual learners can take ownership of their language choices in each content area. In centering what to do with language, teachers and students alike move from academic language to academic languaging. In this transition, we envision movement from use of a stationary or fixed corpus of language to one of verbal, written, and multimodal action taken by you, the language user. Taking on a languaging perspective is dynamic and flexible, always evolving, and being shaped and reshaped, depending on the context and communicative purpose. We emphasize how multilingual learners are positioned to engage in academic languaging, as these students have opportunities to exhibit their full linguistic resources accumulated from school, home, and community.

Framed within a sociocultural perspective, the shift from *language* as a noun to *languaging* as a verb moves our understanding of the construct away from prescriptive, static, and exclusive notions of lists of skills to learn or the vocabulary for a lesson. Shifting our understanding of language from a noun to a verb also reinforces our belief that educators should see academic languaging as an ongoing process, shaped by the lived experiences of multilingual learners and their interactions with others, texts, and technologies.

We have not taken our movement toward and acceptance of academic languaging lightly. In positioning academic languaging as a verb or a gerund, our intent is to give language back to the students as language users, and we accept the linguistic repertoires of our students in making sense and taking ownership of their learning. This reconceptualization of academic language has been spurred by several impactful educational movements involving multilingual learners of the last decade. We elaborate on these three trends, sprinkled throughout the book, and then close this chapter with revisiting the 10 anchors:

- The growing acceptance and use of multiliteracies, including translanguaging, and multimodalities as pedagogical practices
- The rise of dual language education as an avenue to bilingualism and biliteracy
- The advancement of student agency for developing self-autonomy

In approaching academic languaging in this last chapter, you should have a firm sense of what it is and how to apply it in your setting. Table 7.1 is a Frayer model that serves as a recap for defining the construct and offering examples. You might consider using the figure as a call to action for educators in jump-starting a schoolwide professional learning day on defining, exploring, and applying academic languaging.

Table 7.1 Depicting Academic Languaging Across the Content Areas

What It Is	What It Isn't
Examples	**Nonexamples**

Prominent Trends Leading to Academic Languag*ing*

Multiliteracies and Multimodalities

We reintroduce the two phenomena that constitute multiliteracies and their influence on academic languaging—the coupling of technological advances through expanded communication modes with connectedness among linguistic and cultural societies worldwide—to underscore its global and continual impact (The New London Group, 1996). As you remember from Chapter 3, the traditional vision of equating text with print is no longer tenable (van Leeuwen & Jewitt, 2001) as, with the advancement of technologies at such a rapid pace, the breadth and depth of learning experiences have broadened significantly. Consequently, methodologies and pedagogies, in essence schooling, must be redefined and reshaped to adapt to the overflowing sources of accessible knowledge (Chan et al., 2017). Couple the gaining of meaning beyond the printed word with the hypergrowth of multilingual learners (totaling more than 11.5 million in U.S. public schools and growing worldwide), and you have a sense of the growing expanse of multiliteracies (Kids Count Data Center, 2022).

After almost three decades since the groundbreaking 1996 paper by The New London Group, educators are beginning to question and reformulate what constitutes literacy for their multilingual learners. In essence, this broader vision of multiliteracies is in response to societal demands; it includes a range of technology platforms, modalities, discourses, and symbol systems, components that shape academic languaging across content areas. In school, multiple modes are deemed essential for engaging in disciplinary practices that are articulated in state academic content standards, allowing multilingual learners to draw from a variety of meaning-making channels (Grapin, 2019). As we have emphasized, through multiliteracies, the school, home, and community become interconnected through multiple modes of communication.

What is emerging from this trend is a vision of inclusion, where the cognitive-based skills, such as those grounded in the Science of Reading, are subsumed within a nested model where literacy and biliteracy are expanded to form multiliteracies (see Figure 3.3). Here instructional contexts, learning environments, social interactions, and cultural practices inform and shape oral language, reading, and writing practices within and across the content areas (Gottlieb, 2023; Hull & Moje, 2012). Academic languaging emerges from multiliteracies when there is intent, a reason for using language for a specific purpose when integrating language domains within the content areas.

To reiterate, for multilingual learners, multiple modes or multimodalities (visual, graphic, kinesthetic, auditory, and linguistic representation in combination with oral and written text) are natural and authentic ways of communicating information and ideas. Unfortunately, these multimodalities are often equated with scaffolding, defined as a temporary structure that is removed when students grasp grade-level content or language. We note, however, that scaffolding, when thought of and applied as a transient strategy, often carries a deficit connotation, noting student dependence and their lack of ability to access information and comprehend text.

Instead, educators of multilingual learners should conceptualize multimodalities as a means of increasing opportunity for students to have choices throughout the instructional and assessment cycles (Gottlieb &

Honigsfeld, 2025). In essence, incorporating and maintaining multiliteracies and multimodalities in curriculum, instruction, and assessment enable students to engage in learning through an array of outlets. Thus, we point out multiple expressions of and pathways to academic languaging. You are invited to use Table 7.2 as a stimulus for brainstorming with grade-level colleagues those modalities that are applicable within and across the content areas you teach.

Table 7.2 Applying Multimodalities Across the Content Areas as a Springboard for Academic Languaging

CONTENT AREA	VISUAL, GRAPHIC, TECHNOLOGICAL, AUDITORY, LINGUISTIC (MULTIMODAL) WAYS TO ACCESS THE CONTENT	EXAMPLE OF HOW STUDENTS MIGHT MAKE USE OF MULTIMODALITIES TO ENGAGE IN ACADEMIC LANGUAGING
Language Arts		
Mathematics		
Social Studies		
Science/ STEM		

This resource is available for download at https://companion.corwin.com/courses/Academic-Languaging.

Multimodalities afford multilingual learners options in learning coupled with a variety of ways to show evidence for their learning. As we have illustrated, each content area represents multimodalities in distinct ways. For example, in science, *multimodality* refers to linking discourse with different means of representation (e.g., verbal, graphic, and numerical) to express scientific reasoning and findings (Waldrip et al., 2006); in mathematics, multimodality allows students to deepen their learning by manipulating real-life objects, drawing numerical representations, or creating graphic displays. Universal Design for Learning (UDL) also offers various avenues for multilingual learners to pursue learning, especially those students with individualized education programs (Cohan et al., 2020; Gottlieb, 2021a). In summary, teacher and administrator adoption of multiliteracies is foundational in building a strong base for pursuing academic languaging.

Stop and Think

What impact have multiliteracies and multimodalities had on you and your colleagues, personally and professionally?

As mentioned in Chapter 3, multiliteracies is a multidimensional construct that inherently pertains to multilingual learners. It encompasses and builds on an array of literacy philosophies and approaches while it extends across a wide range of multimodalities, including translanguaging and technologies. How might you explain to colleagues the significance of multiliteracies and multimodalities for multilingual learners in today's educational world? As a school or district, how might you incorporate multiliteracies into curriculum, instruction, and assessment? In what ways do multiliteracies extend to you and your home life?

Translanguaging

Equally important in our discussion of academic languaging is the acceptance of translanguaging not only as a bona fide authentic and natural means of communication among persons who share two or more languages, but also as a contributor to student identity and agency. In other words, translanguaging directly draws from and is equated with bi-/multilingualism, where the world is seen through a heteroglossic (multilingual) lens. For example, the model text about Chicano Park in Chapter 3, ripe with translanguaging, is an excerpt from a larger narrative illustrative of action taken by a group of activists in defense of their cause. Similarly, just as model texts serve as a catalyst for teachers to help analyze classroom materials and identify the interaction between language and content for multilingual learners, the careful analysis of student writing can help teachers recognize students' strengths in both English and their other languages.

As you read this writing sample from Montserrat, a third grader, consider the following questions:

- What strengths does this student demonstrate in her writing?
- How can we nurture this student's language development?

Spring

Some adults don't get a spring vocachon but we do.

Y a veces when I get a spring vocachon and it is worm outsia I ask mi mamá if I could go out to the park. Sometimes if it is worm she seys yes and if it is a cold she seys no.

She seys no porque hace frío.

When the leaves start to growe frome the tree is becases spring is hear.

Gracias.

Clearly, Montserrat's writing shows many strengths, which we will highlight, followed by strategies to support her language and conceptual development.

Strengths Evident in Montserrat's Writing

- **Clear Organization:** The writing follows a logical sequence, beginning with spring break and progressing to personal experiences and observations about the season.
- **Effective Use of Translanguaging:** Montserrat skillfully blends Spanish (highlighted in yellow) and English, demonstrating bilingual proficiency. Her use of phrases like "*Y a veces*" and "*porque hace frío*" supports communication and reflects authentic bilingual speech patterns.
- **Accurate Spelling in Spanish:** She spells Spanish words correctly, including those with accents (e.g., *mamá*), indicating a strong command of Spanish spelling conventions.
- **Understanding of Sentence Structure:** Montserrat constructs simple but mostly complete sentences that include a subject and verb (e.g., "*She seys no because it is cold outside.*").
- **Vocabulary Development:** She effectively conveys ideas related to spring, using words such as *park, tree, leaves,* and *growe.*

Strategies to Nurture Montserrat's Language and Conceptual Development

Leverage translanguaging as a strength:

- Encourage bilingual expression: Allow Montserrat to draft ideas in Spanish and gradually incorporate more English, retaining translanguaging for emphasis, as appropriate.

- Provide Montserrat with bilingual books and videos related to seasons and weather.
- Model translanguaging strategies: Show how multilingual speakers can use both languages strategically and effectively.

Foster writing confidence through scaffolding:

- Offer concrete feedback for student revision of drafts.
- Rely on peer assessment based on criteria for success.
- Use interactive writing: Co-construct sentences with Montserrat allowing her to take the lead in explaining how or why she translanguages.
- Encourage revision: Instruct Montserrat how to reread and edit her writing.

Make learning meaningful and culturally sustaining:

- Incorporate personal experiences: Have students write about their own spring traditions.
- Engage in oral storytelling: Encourage students to describe seasonal changes, as applicable, in their own words and share with others before writing.

By integrating these strategies, we can support Montserrat's English language and conceptual development while affirming her voice and valuing her multilingual identity.

Translanguaging as a legitimate communication tool is commonplace in multilingual homes and throughout multilingual communities but is also present in school. To support students like Montserrat, school leadership must take a translanguaging stance and practice in their design of policies and structures to support their multilingual learners and families (Castro & Henn-Reinke, 2024). For translanguaging to become a schoolwide norm, newcomer students to the United States as well as bi-/multilingual students born and raised here need to feel empowered to set their own course of learning (Hernández García et al., 2023).

Just like multimodalities, translanguaging is not confined to the language arts classroom, but rather is present in all content areas and instructional programs. For example, research accentuates its valuing in literacies (Seltzer & de los Ríos, 2021), sensemaking in science education (Martell & Yangua-Peña, 2024), understanding mathematical concepts (LópezLeiva & Argüello de Jesús, 2024), and gaining agency through engagement in social studies inquiry (Hernández García et al., 2023). Through translanguaging, "multilingual students can engage in literacy in ways that deepen their understanding of texts, generate more diverse texts, develop students' confianza in performing literacies, and foster their critical metalinguistic awareness" (García & Kleifgen, 2019, p. 9). Thus, *translanguaging* can serve as a stimulus for *academic languaging*.

Look Closer

Translanguaging

Since 2009, the body of research and references for translanguaging has grown exponentially in the United States and worldwide. The following are some influential articles and books related to the topic. You might further pursue specific resources for your specialty or content area.

Castro, M. (2020, September). Translanguaging: Teaching at the intersection of language and social justice. *WIDA Focus Bulletin*. Board of Regents of the University of Wisconsin System. https://wida.wisc.edu/sites/default/files/resource/Focus-Bulletin-Translanguaging.pdf

CUNY-NYS Initiative on Emergent Bilinguals. (2021). *Translanguaging guides*. https://www.cuny-nysieb.org/translanguaging-resources/translanguaging-guides/

García, O., Johnson, S. I., & Seltzer, K. (2017). *The translanguaging classroom: Leveraging student bilingualism for learning*. Brookes.

Leung, C., & Valdés, G. (2019). Translanguaging and the transdisciplinary framework for language teaching and learning in a multilingual world. *Modern Language Journal, 103*(2), 348–370. https://doi.org/10.1111/modl.12568

Vaish, V. (2020). *Translanguaging in multilingual English classrooms: An Asian perspective and contexts*. Springer.

Artificial Intelligence

With the acceptance of multiliteracies has also come the explosion of technological devices at home and in school. With the meteoric rise of technologies during the COVID-19 years of 2020–2022, artificial intelligence (AI) has come onto the scene as a most relevant and impactful mode of communication that now occupies a prominent space in every facet of schooling. Students are being exposed to myriad apps and modalities and are being invited to indulge in creative ways to utilize content and show evidence for learning. Concurrently, teachers are experimenting with AI's many creative applications, from curriculum and lesson generation to interpreting original student work.

"With the increased adoption of AI systems, inferencing, verbal reasoning, problem-solving, and decision-making will become major aspects of the curriculum."

—Meghan Hargrave et al. (2024, p. 4)

AI not only has altered the lives of educators; AI has also changed how students pursue learning. When working with multilingual learners in school, you might set up some guardrails for its use. For example, you might consider using AI to

- Generate integrated learning targets for units of learning
- Facilitate translation into multiple languages
- Produce model texts that are linguistically and culturally relevant
- Add illustrations or graphs to increase student accessibility to content
- Offer multilingual resources for students and families
- Craft communication for and exchange information with family members

Stop and Think

Integrating Artificial Intelligence Into Instruction and Assessment

AI is a multimodal literacy-dependent support for students and educators that is becoming indispensable in every aspect of education and our lives. It is a powerful tool that is rapidly transforming how we learn, communicate, and interact. Our ability to process and analyze vast amounts of data across various formats (text, image, audio, video) instantaneously helps support multiliteracies.

But how might AI be integrated into classroom instruction and assessment? The first rule of thumb is to engage students as part of the decision-making process.

Empowering students will give them ownership; in turn, they will more than likely pay heed to policies and practices that they are vested in. Together, teachers and students can

- Set up boundaries, such as a classroom or school policy, for use of AI
- Make provisions for multilingual learners to use their multiple languages
- Craft a plan for personalizing learning
- Investigate questions related to a specific content area topic
- Evaluate the extent that AI is being used (or abused)
- Form a classroom council to make judgment on conditions for AI applications
- Understand the pros and cons of AI for specific purposes and applicable apps (see the third model text, on AI, in Chapter 1)
- Protect student (and family) integrity and identities

Technology has opened language doors for multilingual learners, their families, educators, and society. There are online sites in numerous languages, and AI's potential as an instant translator cannot be denied. Multimodal resources, such as videos (YouTube and more) and even podcasts, are available, and a variety of sites enable students to record dialogue or their individual voices. Thus, through technologies, multilingual learners can be enriched, further their learning, and share their transcultural and linguistic expertise with their peers. With technologies, teachers can be more confident in their multilingual moves, students can become more agentive, and thus both can promote academic languaging.

Multimodalities and multiliteracies are not the wave of the future—the future is here! Admittedly, AI is constantly changing and advancing, and, as educators, we must be aware of how it can advantage multilingual learners. In bi-/multilingual education contexts, AI is useful for promoting biliteracy and bilingualism, two goals of dual language programs. After all, academic languaging is not just confined to one language, but is more impactful when multilingual learners can navigate across their languages.

The Power of Dual Language Education

According to a robust body of research, dual language education is deemed the most effective instructional model for multilingual learners (e.g., Collier & Thomas, 2019; Lindholm-Leary, 2016), and, as of 2021, there were more than 3,600 identified dual language or immersion programs in U.S. public schools. Present in the majority of states, these programs use a partner language (e.g., Spanish, Arabic, Mandarin) for minimally 50% of the instructional day (American Councils for International Education & American Councils Research Center, 2021). The positive effectiveness of dual language immersion for all students, informed by Collier and Thomas's (2004) extensive studies, has remained steadfast over the years, and multilingual learners who participate in these programs generally outperform their monolingual peers academically.

Dual language education has a long history built on research and practice of bilingual, foreign language, and heritage language education while considering the global reality of multilingualism (Christian, 2011). Somerville and Faltis (2019) have gone further, coining the term *dual languaging* to describe translanguaging practices in mathematics and social studies classrooms that have grown directly from dual language instructional models. In part, dual languaging emphasizes the dynamic use of translanguaging pedagogies in these specialized programs and challenges the traditional structure of language separation with its dedicated independent time for each of two languages (Palmer et al., 2014).

With the growth of dual language programs has come the gradual acceptance of the multiple languages of our multilingual learners, as evidenced by the states' adoption of the Seal of Biliteracy (Figure 7.1; see https://sealofbiliteracy.org). As introduced in Chapter 3, the Seal of Biliteracy is "an award granted by a school, district, or state in recognition of students who have attained proficiency in two or more languages by high school graduation." The Seal of Biliteracy appears on the transcript or diploma of the graduating senior and is a statement of accomplishment for future employers and college admissions.

Stop and Think

Recognizing the Seal of Biliteracy

After over a decade of effort, presently all 50 states and Washington, DC, have approved a statewide Seal of Biliteracy. The Seal of Biliteracy is an important accomplishment for multilingual learners as it honors a student's bilingualism and biliteracy. More and more school districts are acknowledging the Seal of Biliteracy, and younger multilingual learners are pursuing the goals of dual language education. In joining in celebration, you might wish to investigate your state's Seal of Biliteracy to

Figure 7.1 Seal of Biliteracy

Source: iStock.com/PeterPencil

- Identify the criteria necessary for students to secure it
- Name the groups of students and their languages for which it applies
- Determine whether districts can award it and which ones have
- Campaign for the expansion of the Seal of Biliteracy to other student groups and languages
- Determine different student pathways to obtain the Seal of Biliteracy

Student Agency

The third trend in today's classrooms woven throughout the book is the importance of promoting student agency over their learning. With student voice and choice come agency; with agency comes empowerment; and with empowerment comes opportunities for eliciting academic languaging.

An essential ingredient of academic languaging is for teachers to acquiesce a portion of their locus of control to students. Student voice, choice, and ownership of their learning are essential precursors for establishing their agency. Given the continuum in Figure 7.2 that leads to student

Figure 7.2 Moving From Teacher-Directed to Student-Driven Teaching and Learning: The Students' Role in the Process

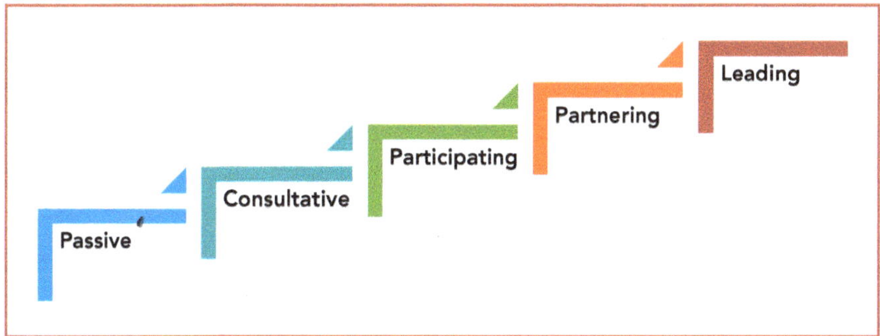

Adapted from Imamudeen, 2018 (https://judyimamudeen.com/the-only-thing-you-need-to-do-to-develop-student-agency/).

agency, you might want to ponder about where you and your multilingual learners are positioned on the scale and where you wish to go.

Developing student agency entails student participation in and analysis of teaching and learning so that multilingual learners' perspectives inform classroom practices. Innovative AI tools are rapidly creating more interactive learning experiences in schools and serve as stimuli for generating student motivation, increasing engagement, and thus, promoting agency (Holcombe & Wozniak, 2024). Ultimately, building and supporting student agency assist multilingual learners in facing and combating social, racial, and other injustices that minoritized students face today.

So, what does student agency have to do with academic languaging? Simply stated, if students do not have confidence in themselves, are not proud of their cultures and heritage, do not have positive language identities, and are not self-motivated, then they will be hesitant to take risks to defend themselves and their stances. One of the goals of social and emotional learning, closely associated with agency, is to allow students to make their own decisions. As a result, students can help determine their own learning pathways that lead to academic languaging. Table 7.3 gives some tips to determine the extent to which you facilitate student agency in your classroom.

Table 7.3 Exerting Student Agency in Teaching and Learning

You may wish to complete the rating scale as a needs assessment to determine how and to what extent your students exhibit agency. Once you have collected the information, discuss with colleagues how your students can play a greater role in initiating and engaging in academic languaging. The rating scale can readily be converted to one in which your older students can respond to evaluate their sense of agency.

AS AGENTS OF LEARNING, STUDENTS (YOU)	AT TIMES	MOST TIMES	ALL THE TIME
1. Have a voice in classroom decision making			
2. Display original work with pride all over the classroom and halls			
3. Choose partners to work with in a range of activities			
4. Help (re)arrange the classroom for different groupings			
5. Make suggestions for tasks and projects of personal interest			

AS AGENTS OF LEARNING, STUDENTS (YOU)	AT TIMES	MOST TIMES	ALL THE TIME
6. Select the modalities to show evidence for learning			
7. Have access to a range of technologies and resources of choice (e.g., podcasts, videos, games, websites)			
8. Are involved in outreach and social action through classroom projects			
9. Are liaisons to and advocates for families and their funds of knowledge			
10. Have time to reflect on learning in their language of choice and to help set next steps			
11. Feel secure in freely participating in class			
12. Exert independence in thoughts and actions			

Adapted from Gottlieb & Castro, 2017

This resource is available for download at https://companion.corwin.com/courses/Academic-Languaging.

Look Closer

Promoting Student Agency

All students have the capacity to be agentive—to be motivated to make decisions, act on them, and influence the world around them—engaging in academic languaging in the process. For multilingual learners, culturally sustaining instructional practices that capitalize on the richness of their languages and cultures in authentic ways facilitate agency. The following articles and books add to available resources.

Bruno, J. (2021). How to build student agency in your classroom. *Teach Learn Grow*. Northwest Evaluation Association.

Cavagnetto, A. R., Hand, B., & Premo, J. (2020). Supporting student agency in science. *Theory Into Practice*, *59*(2), 128–138. https://doi.org/10.1080/00405841.2019.1702392

Gutstein, E. (2007). "And that's just as it starts." Teaching mathematics and developing student agency. *Teachers College Record*, *10*(2), 420–448.

(Continued)

(Continued)

Marshall, T. R. (2022). The promise, power, and practice of student agency. *Educational Leadership, 80*(3), 33–38.

Vaughn, M. (2021). *Student agency in the classroom: Honoring student voice in the curriculum.* Teachers College Press.

Revisiting the Anchors for Academic Languaging

Before we close, let's revisit the 10 anchors of academic languaging that undergird multilingual education and offer some practical suggestions to jump-start conversations among educators—teachers, coaches, counselors, specialists, and administrators.

1. *Valuing and maintaining students' multiple languages and cultures*

   Admittedly, students' multiple languages and cultures bring invaluable wealth to be seamlessly incorporated into a warm and welcoming classroom to form a trusting community of learners. Equally valuable is tapping the linguistic and cultural "funds of knowledge" (González et al., 2005) of families and the community. Additionally, a myriad linguistic and cultural resources available through AI are at your and your students' fingertips.

2. *Learning from our students*

   Our students are wonderful sources of information and reservoirs of linguistic and cultural knowledge that can help enhance the richness of your classroom. You may not be conversant in multiple languages or familiar with multiple cultures, but that's where multilingual learners can assist you and become your teachers! Our students bring unique perspectives or traditions you may not be aware of that will give you insight into their identities and personalities.

3. *Connecting to students' lives and experiences*

   Learning involves relationship building, where teachers make ties to students' personal, social, cultural, and world experiences (Zacarian, 2013). A real-life example that connects to your students' interests should stimulate each lesson embedded in units of learning. Another effective strategy is to invite students to update their autobiographical portraits and goals for learning at the beginning of each quarter. Students might choose to add photos and reactions to events (through images, orally, or in writing) along with milestones they have reached.

4. *Becoming aware of the language we use*

   Teachers of mathematics, science, and social studies often concentrate on presenting the concepts of the subject matter without taking advantage of the language in which it is embedded. No matter the content area, however, language is a vehicle for learning, as language is often the medium to access the content of a lesson and communicate learning. Being cognizant of the language we use can spark collaboration between content and language specialists and facilitate interaction to build strong relationships.

5. *Making language visible to students*

   Just like the quote "fish cannot see water," we are often unaware of the language we use and its potential impact on others. As multilingual learners develop language, they must be made conscious of their linguistic surroundings. We also have to become more sensitive to the linguistic realities others face and be their advocates.

   We have illustrated throughout the book how modeling language enables students to see and show its meaning in a particular context. Supporting language development through academic languaging across modes and language domains reinforces multiple means of language use. It also fosters a language-rich classroom environment where students take risks and develop linguistic awareness.

6. *Using linguistically and culturally sustaining practices*

   Employing pedagogical practices that are linguistically and culturally sustaining is a commitment on the part of educators. In fact, it can be viewed as the final stage in a series of spirals that moves from (1) acknowledging the acceptance of multilingual learners' languages and heritage to (2) advocating for just curriculum and assessment to (3) embedding principles of linguistic and cultural consciousness into schooling to (4) seamlessly infusing linguistic and cultural sustainability into one's identity and life. Figure 7.3 depicts these four stages—starting with being respectful and supportive of others' languages and cultures to culminating in full-blown sustainability, where linguistic and cultural beliefs, practices, and traditions are safeguarded, preserved, and perpetuated (Gottlieb, 2024b).

Figure 7.3 Pathways Leading to Linguistic and Cultural Sustainability

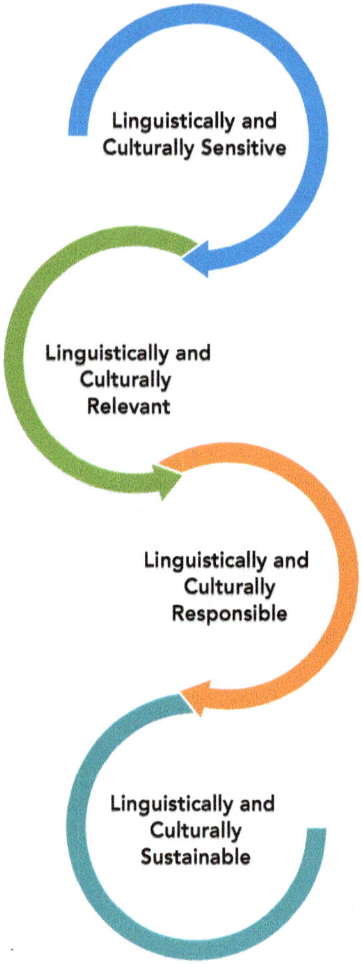

Linguistically and Culturally Sensitive

Linguistically and Culturally Relevant

Linguistically and Culturally Responsible

Linguistically and Culturally Sustainable

7. *Carving opportunities for translanguaging*

   Translanguaging assumes that language is an exclusive social practice and action of bi-/multilingual persons who choose to communicate in two or more languages. Translanguaging occurs within sociocultural contexts that give meaning to the interaction between languages. Teachers' acceptance of translanguaging enables multilingual learners, like Montserrat, to freely communicate and helps dispel the myth that English is the sole avenue to success for multilingual learners. Students' display of translanguaging reflects their full linguistic resources.

"Translanguaging, or engaging in bilingual or multilingual discourse practices, is an approach to bilingualism that is centered not on languages as has been often the case, but on the practices of bilinguals that are readily observable."

—Ofelia García (2009, p. 44)

In essence, translanguaging prompts academic languaging. With the explosion of translanguaging as a communication tool has come the recognition that multilinguals do not possess a single linguistic repertoire, but rather have multiple languages at their disposal. Said another way, multilingual learners have access to and can draw on their full linguistic resources to make sense of the world around them. Bi-/multilingual learners are advantaged when engaging in translanguaging practices as they have more opportunities to authentically express themselves in cross-linguistic and cross-cultural ways.

8. *Developing linguistic and cultural consciousness through metalinguistic and metacultural awareness*

   In many ways, this anchor works in tandem with academic languaging as it boosts multilingual learners' pride in their languages and cultures, giving them the confidence to experiment with language with others. It is related to translanguaging, as multilingual learners who are metalinguistically aware have a deeper understanding of how language works, including the similarities and differences between languages. In partnership with linguistic consciousness, cultural consciousness assumes an awareness of and respect for one's own cultures and those of others. Being mindful and accepting of multilingual learners' languages and cultures means that educators are incorporating these critical elements into curriculum, instruction, and assessment to optimize potential for student success.

9. *Strengthening language development within content learning*

   Content and language learning have a reciprocal relationship. Multilingual learners and their teachers must be able decipher between the two while simultaneously understand how content affects language and content. Through model texts, we have illustrated how the dimensions of language—discourse, sentences, words/phrases, and symbols—interact to form meaningful communication. Reinforcing language directly associated with students' conceptual development enables multilingual learners to gain a deeper understanding of the close ties and interactions between the two. It is the responsibility of both content and language teachers who share multilingual learners to collaborate in co-constructing integrated learning goals to reinforce the power of combining content and language.

10. *Applying academic languaging as a transformative priority*

    Taking these anchors together, academic languaging has the transformative potential of reshaping schooling through a linguistic and culturally sustainable lens that centers multilingual learners. In having a commitment to fairness and advocacy for our students and instilling agency and confidence within them, we enable them to take ownership and engage in academic languaging that makes sense for their unique identities and talents. Through our own actions, we come to understand community and the knowledge, traditions, and experiences our students bring and cherish. As a community of learners, we can instill a collective responsiveness to dismantle discriminatory practices through academic languaging while fostering inclusive environments that embed the diversity of perspectives of students, families, and community into curriculum, instruction, and classroom assessment.

Inspired by home and community life, we have described academic languaging as action taken by multilingual learners, in large part, throughout the school day (and beyond) to promote their agency and leadership. Table 7.4 offers you an opportunity to confer with colleagues to discuss your impression of each of the 10 anchors for academic languaging and its application to one or more content areas in your setting.

Table 7.4 Anchors for Academic Languaging in the Content Areas

ANCHOR FOR ACADEMIC LANGUAGING	A CLASSROOM OR SCHOOLWIDE EXAMPLE
1. Valuing and maintaining students' multiple languages and cultures	
2. Learning from our students	
3. Connecting to students' lives and experiences	

ANCHOR FOR ACADEMIC LANGUAGING	A CLASSROOM OR SCHOOLWIDE EXAMPLE
4. Becoming aware of the language we use	
5. Making language visible to students	
6. Using linguistically and culturally sustaining practices	
7. Carving opportunities for translanguaging	
8. Developing linguistic and cultural consciousness through metalinguistic and metacultural awareness	
9. Strengthening language development within content learning	
10. Applying academic languaging as a transformative priority	

This resource is available for download at https://companion.corwin.com/courses/Academic-Languaging.

We realize that there is a wide variety of often conflicting ideologies, theories, policies, and practices surrounding the education of multilingual learners (Wright et al., 2015). There may be instructional trends and seductive bandwagons to jump on. However, no matter which philosophy or pedagogical approach you may take, opportunities for academic languaging should be at the heart of teaching and learning.

Chapter Summary

Influenced by home, community, and school, we have argued for the adoption of academic languaging, offering a rationale for a dynamic action-oriented stance for students and educators that affords students a more prominent role in the learning process. Three main factors have influenced our reconceptualization of academic language to make it more actionable: (1) the increasing recognition of multiliteracies, including translanguaging, (2) the expansion of dual language education, and (3) the emphasis on student agency for fostering self-autonomy. We close the book with a recap of the 10 key anchors of academic languaging that both guide educators and establish a framework for supporting multilingual learners, their identities, and their contributions to language and content learning.

Extensions

For Reflection

1. Examining linguistic and cultural influences in instructional materials and teaching practices gives us a glimpse into a range of educational stances for multilingual learners. Figure 7.3 presents a continuum of pedagogical practices, from those that are linguistic and culturally sensitive to those considered linguistic and culturally sustainable. Where do you feel you fall on the scale? To what extent do content area teachers in your setting embrace this notion? Where are your school and district positioned?
2. Moving from teacher-directed to student-driven teaching and learning, as illustrated in Figure 7.2, is a long and often challenging journey as teachers foster agency by transferring their ownership over to students. To what extent do you feel that teachers should retain control, and how much flexibility should they offer students to make choices and other decisions? How might teachers gradually assume the role of facilitators?

For Action

1. Given the 10 anchors for academic languaging in Table 7.4, how might you rank them, and which ones do you consider your or your team's priorities? How might you enact the examples you gave, who would be involved, and how might you bring multilingual learners into the fold? Lastly, how might you create a plan for infusing academic languaging into curriculum that is linguistically and culturally sustainable?
2. We have attempted to justify the need to convert "academic language," which has become a rather controversial construct when speaking of multilingual learners, to "academic languag*ing*," one we believe is more actionable. By being more centered on what to do with language for specific purposes rather than arguing its legitimacy, we feel that academic languaging can be recognized within the language development process across the content areas. Do you agree or disagree with our rationale? Why or why not? What might you do to convince others of the value of academic languaging for multilingual learners?

References

Alim, H. S., & Paris, D. (2015). Whose language gap? Critical and culturally sustaining pedagogies as necessary challenges to racializing hegemony. *Journal of Linguistic Anthropology*, *25*(1), 79–81.

Altavilla, J. (2020). How technology affects instruction for English learners. *Kappan*, *102*(1), 18–23.

Alter, G. T. (2017). Discovery, engagement, and transformation: Learning about gender and sexual diversity in social education. *Social Education*, *81*(5), 279–285.

American Councils for International Education & American Councils Research Center. (2021). *2021 Canvass of dual language and immersion programs in US public schools*. https://www.americancouncils.org/sites/default/files/documents/pages/2021-10/Canvass%20DLI%20-%20October%202021-2_ac.pdf

Andrews, S. (2007). *Teacher language awareness*. Cambridge University Press.

The Art of Maths, Co-funded by the Erasmus+ Programme of the European Union. (2020). *Tool 2: Islamic art and geometry*. https://artofmaths.eu/wp-content/uploads/2020/02/TOOL_2.pdf

Ascenzi-Moreno, L. (2024). Toward a multilingual perspective on reading: Aligning emergent bilinguals' resources with theories of reading and implications for instruction. *The Reading Teacher*, *77*(6).

Au, K. H. (2011). *Literacy achievement and diversity: Keys to success for students, teachers, and schools*. Multicultural Education Series. Teachers College Press.

August, D., & Shanahan, T. (2017). *Developing literacy in second-language learners: Report of the National Literacy Panel on Language-Minority Children and Youth*. Routledge.

Bailey, A. L., & Butler, F. (2003). An evidentiary framework for operationalizing academic language for broad application to K–12 education: A design document. *CSE Report 611*. CRESST/University of California, Los Angeles.

Bailey, A. L., & Heritage, M. (2008). *Formative assessment for literacy grades K–6: Building reading and academic language skills across the curriculum*. Corwin.

Bailey, E. (2024). Reading beyond the page. *Language Magazine*, *23*(7), 34–35.

Bartolomé, L. (1998). *The misteaching of academic discourses*. Westview Press.

Barwell, R., Wessel, L., & Parra, A. (2019). Language diversity and mathematics education: New developments. *Research in Mathematics Education*, *21*(2), 113–118. https://doi.org/10.1080/14794802.2019.1638824

Becker, A. L. (1991). Language and languaging. *Language & Communication*, *11*(1–2), 33–35. http://www.sciencedirect.com/science/article/pii/027153099190013L

Bialystok, E. (2002). Acquisition of literacy in bilingual children: A framework for research. *Language Learning*, *52*, 159–199. https://doi.org/10.1111/1467-9922.00180

Bloome, D., Power-Carter, S., Baker, D. W., Castanheira, M. L., Kim, M., & Rowe, L. (2022). *Discourse analysis of languaging and literacy events in educational settings: A microethnographic perspective*. Routledge.

British Council Serbia. (2013, November 29). *David Crystal—The effect of new technologies on English* [Video]. YouTube. https://www.youtube.com/watch?v=qVqcoB798Is&ab_channel=BritishCouncilSerbia

Brown, J. C. (2017). A metasynthesis of the complementarity of culturally responsive and inquiry-based science education in K–12 settings: Implications for advancing equitable science teaching and learning. *Journal of Research in Science Teaching, 54*(9), 1143–1173. https://doi.org/10.1002/tea.21401

Brugar, K. A., & Dickman, A. H. (2013). Oh, say can you see? Visualizing American symbols in the fifth-grade classroom. *Social Studies and the Young Learner, 25*(4), 17–22.

Bruno, J. (2021). How to build student agency in your classroom. *Teach Learn Grow.* Northwest Evaluation Association.

Bunch, G. C. (2014). The language of ideas and the language of display: Reconceptualizing "academic language" in linguistically diverse classrooms. *International Multilingual Research Journal, 8*(1), 70–86.

Bunch, G. C., Kibler, A. K., & Pimentel, S. (2012, April 5). Realizing opportunities for English learners in the Common Core English language arts and disciplinary literacy standards. In K. Hakuta & M. Santos (Eds.), *Understanding language: Commissioned papers on language and literacy issues in the Common Core State Standards and Next Generation Science Standards* (pp. 1–16). Stanford University. https://ul.stanford.edu/sites/default/files/resource/2021-12/UL%20Stanford%20Final%205-9-12%20w%20cover.pdf#page=13

Bunch, G. C., & Martin, D. (2021). "From "academic language" to the "language of ideas": A disciplinary perspective on using language in K–12 settings. *Language and Education, 35*(1), 1–18. https://doi.org/10.1080/09500782.2020.1842443

Burns, K. (Director). (2023). *The American buffalo* [Film]. Florentine Films; WETA-TV.

Bussi, M. G. B., Baccaglini-Frank, A., & Ramploud, A. (2014). Intercultural dialogue and the geography and history of thought. *For the Learning of Mathematics, 34*(1), 31–33. http://www.jstor.org/stable/43894877

Calabrese Barton, A., & Tan, E. (2020). Beyond equity as inclusion: A framework of "rightful presence" for guiding justice-oriented studies in teaching and learning. *Educational Researcher, 49*(6), 433–440.

Calderón, M., Espino, G., & Slakk, S. (2019). *Integrando lenguaje, lectura, escritura y contenidos en español e inglés: Integrating language, reading, writing, and content in English and Spanish.* Velázquez Press.

Calderón, M., & Montenegro, H. (2022). *Empowering long-term ELs with social emotional learning, language, and literacy.* Velázquez Press.

Carleton, L., & Marzano, R. J. (2010). *Vocabulary games for the classroom.* Marzano Research Laboratory.

Carr, J., Sexton, U., & Lagunoff, R. (2006). *Making science accessible to English learners: A guide for teachers.* WestEd.

Carter, R. (2003). Language awareness. *ELT Journal, 57*(1), 64–65.

Castro, M. (2020, September). Translanguaging: Teaching at the intersection of language and social justice. *WIDA Focus Bulletin.* Board of Regents of the University of Wisconsin System. https://wida.wisc.edu/sites/default/files/resource/Focus-Bulletin-Translanguaging.pdf

Castro, M., & Gottlieb, M. (2021, October). Multiliteracies: A glimpse into bilingual language arts classrooms. *WIDA Focus Bulletin.* Board of Regents of the University of Wisconsin System. https://wida.wisc.edu/sites/default/files/resource/FocusBulletin-Multiliteracies-ENGLISH.pdf

Castro, M., & Henn-Reinke, K. (2024). Transliderando el cambio: Transforming pedagogical leadership in dual-language programs. In S. I. Johnson, M. A. Romero, & M. Jurado (Eds.), *Cultivating the pedagogy of translanguaging for K–12 transformative education: Approaches, activities, and strategies for students and teachers* (pp. 18–29). Velázquez Press.

Cavagnetto, A. R., Hand, B., & Premo, J. (2020). Supporting student agency in science. *Theory Into Practice*, *59*(2), 128–138. https://doi.org/10.1080/00405841.2019.1702392

Cazden, C. (1988). *Classroom discourse: The language of teaching and learning*. Heinemann.

Celedón-Pattichis, S., Lunney Borden, L., Pape, S. J, Clements D., Peters S. A., Males J., Chapman O., Leonard J. (2018). Asset-based approaches to equitable mathematics education research and practice. *Journal for Research in Mathematics Education*, *49*(4), 373–389.

Cenoz, J., & Gorter, D. (2011). Focus on multilingualism: A study of trilingual writing. *The Modern Language Journal*, *95*(3), 356–369.

Chan, C., Chia, A., & Choo, S. (2017). Understanding multiliteracies and assessing multimodal texts in the English curriculum. *The English Teacher*, *46*(2), 73–87.

Chao, T., Murray, E., & Gutiérrez, R. (2014). *What are classroom practices that support equity-based mathematics teaching?* (Research brief). National Council of Teachers of Mathematics.

Christian, D. (2011). Dual language education. In E. Hinkel (Ed.), *Handbook of research in second language teaching and learning* (Vol. II, pp. 3–20). Routledge.

Civil, M., & Crespo, S. (2017). *Access and equity: Promoting high quality mathematics, grades 6–8*. National Council of Teachers of Mathematics.

Clark, R., & Fairclough, N., Ivanič, R., & Martin-Jones, M. (1990). Critical language awareness: Part I. A critical review of three current approaches to language awareness. *Language and Education*, *4*(4), 249–260.

Cohan, A., Honigsfeld, A, & Dove, M. G. (2020). Partners in learning. *Educational Leadership*, *77*(4), 34–39.

Collier, V. P., & Thomas, W. P. (2004). The astounding effectiveness of dual language education for all. *NABE Journal of Research and Practice*, *2*(1), 1–20.

Collier, V. P., & Thomas, W. P. (2019). *The role of bilingualism in improving literacy achievement*. International Literacy Association. https://www.literacyworldwide.org/docs/default-source/where-we-stand/ila-role-bilingualism-improving-literacy-achievement.pdf

Colorín Colorado. (n.d.). *Discussing political violence with ELLs, immigrants, and refugees*. https://www.colorincolorado.org/discussing-political-violence-ells-immigrants-and-refugees

Contreras, E. S. L. (2023). Transforming language development for MLLs with UDL and Toontastic 3D. *WAESOL Educator*, *48*(2). https://educator.waesol.org/index.php/WE/article/view/22/10

Cook, M. (2009). William Paul Thurston. In *Mathematicians: An outer view of the inner world* (pp. 76–77). Princeton University Press. https://www.jstor.org/stable/j.ctt2jc8h2.37

Coppens, K. (2022). Equity in science: Starting the conversation with your class and yourself. *Science Scope*, *46*(1). https://www.nsta.org/science-scope/science-scope-septemberoctober-2022/equity-science

Council of Chief State School Officers. (2012). *California Common Core State Standards in Spanish language arts and literacy in history/social studies, science, and technical subjects*. Common Core en Español. https://www.sdcoe.net/common-core-espanol/ca-ccss-en-espanol

Council of the Great City Schools. (2023). *A framework for foundational literacy skills instruction for English Learners: Instructional practice and materials considerations*. https://www.cgcs.org/cms/lib/DC00001581/Centricity/domain/35/publication%20docs/CGCS_Foundational%20Literacy%20Skills_Pub_v11.pdf

Coxhead, A. (2000). A new academic word list. *TESOL Quarterly*, *34*(2), 213–238. https://doi.org/10.2307/3587951

Crespo, S., Celedón-Pattichis, S., & Civil, M. (2018). *Access and equity: Promoting high quality mathematics, grades 3–5*. National Council of Teachers of Mathematics.

Cruz, B. C., & Thornton, S. J. (2013). *Teaching social studies to English language learners: Teaching English language learners across the curriculum* (2nd ed.). Routledge.

Crystal, D. (2008). *Txtng: The gr8 db8* (E. McLachlan, Illustrator). Oxford University Press.

Cummins, J. (1981). Four misconceptions about language proficiency in bilingual education. *NABE Journal*, *5*(3), 31–45.

Cummins, J. (2008). BICS and CALP: Empirical and theoretical status of the distinction. In B. Street & N. H. Hornberger (Eds.), *Encyclopedia of language and education: Vol. 2. Literacy* (2nd ed., pp. 71–83). Springer Science + Business Media.

CUNY-NYS Initiative on Emergent Bilinguals. (2021). *Translanguaging guides*. https://www.cuny-nysieb.org/translanguaging-resources/translanguaging-guides/

Curry, C., Cohen, L., & Lightbody, N. (2006). Universal design in science learning. *The Science Teacher*, *73*(3), 32–37.

Dale, T. C., & Cuevas, G. J. (1992). Integrating mathematics and language learning. In P. Richard-Amato & A. Snow (Eds.), *The multicultural classroom: Readings for content area teachers* (pp. 330–348). Addison-Wesley.

Dalton, B. (2020). Bringing together multimodal composition and maker education in K–8 classrooms. *Language Arts*, *97*(3), 159–171.

de Araujo, Z., Orrill, C. H., & Jacobson, E. (2018). Designing communication-rich problem-centered mathematics professional development. *International Journal of Mathematical Education, Science, & Technology*, *49*, 323–340.

de Araujo, Z., Roberts, S.A., Willey, C., & Zahner W. (Eds.). (2020). Special issue on multilingual learners: Translanguaging. *Teaching for Excellence and Equity in Mathematics*, *11*(2). https://www.todos-math.org/assets/documents/TEEM/TEEM11-No2FINAL.pdf

de Oliveira, L.C. (2023). *Teaching social studies to multilingual learners*. Routledge.

Derewianka, B., & Jones, P. (2023). *Teaching language in context* (3rd ed.). Oxford University Press.

Deverel-Rico, C., & Furtak, E. M. (2024). *How do we get to culturally responsive and sustaining approaches to classroom assessment?* PowerPoint presentation at the 2024 National Council on Measurement in Education Classroom Assessment Conference, Chicago, September 19–20. https://drive.google.com/file/d/1RRfydGYjhfvlpDB1vHV76D5VWETClw6I/view

Duke, N. K., & Cartwright, K. B. (2021). The science of reading progresses: Communicating advances beyond the simple view of reading. *Reading Research Quarterly*, *56*(1), 525–544.

Egbert, J., & Ernst-Slavit, G. (2010). *Access to academics: Planning instruction for K–12 classrooms with ELLs*. Pearson.

Egbert, J., & Ernst-Slavit, G. (2017). *Views from inside: Languages, cultures, and schooling for K–12 educators*. Information Age.

Egbert, J., & Panday-Shukla, P. (2024). *Task engagement across disciplines: Research and practical strategies to increase student achievement*. Taylor & Francis.

English, L. D. (2023). Ways of thinking in STEM-based problem solving. *ZDM Mathematics Education*, *55*, 1219–1230. https://doi.org/10.1007/s11858-023-01474-7

English Learners Success Forum. (2024, October 31). *Guidelines for improving science and engineering materials for multilingual learners*. https://assets-global.website-files.com/5b43fc97fcf4773f14ee92f3/63583dfce1ea050576a1b335_ELSF_Science_Guidelines-02b.pdf

Erath, K., Ingram, J., Moschkovich, J. N., & Prediger, S. (2021, February). Designing and enacting instruction that enhances language for mathematics learning: A review of the state of development and research. *ZDM: The International Journal on Mathematics Education*, *53*, 245–262. https://doi.org/10.1007/s11858-020-01213-2

Ernst-Slavit, G., & Mason, M. R. (2011). "Words that hold us up:" Teacher talk and academic language in five upper elementary classrooms. *Linguistics and Education*, *22*(4), 430–440.

Ernst-Slavit, G., & Mason, M. R. (2012). *Making your first ELL home visit: A guide for classroom teachers*. ¡Colorín colorado! http://www.colorincolorado.org/article/59138/

Ernst-Slavit, G., & Morrison, S. J. (2019). "Unless you were Native American . . . everybody came from another country": Language and content learning in a Grade 4 diverse classroom. *The Social Studies*, *109*(6), 309–323. http://dx.doi.org/10.1080/00377996.2018.1539700

Ernst-Slavit, G., Newcomer, S. N., Morrison, S. J., Lightner, L. K., Morrison, J. A., Ardasheva, Y., & Carbonneau, K. J. (2022). Latina paraeducators' stories of resistance, resilience, and adaptation in an alternative route to teaching program. *Journal of Career Development*, *49*(5), 1021–1038. https://doi.org/10.1177/08948453211005000

Ernst-Slavit, G., & Pratt, K. L. (2017). Teacher questions: Learning the discourse of science in a linguistically diverse elementary classroom. *Linguistics and Education*, *40*, 1–10. https://doi.org/10.1016/j.linged.2017.05.005

Ernst-Slavit, G., & Slavit, D. (2013, March). Mathematically speaking. *Language Magazine*, 32–36. https://www.languagemagazine.com/mathematically-speaking/

Ernst-Slavit, G., & Wenger, K. J. (2016). Surrounded by water: Talking to learn in today's classrooms. *Kappa Delta Pi Record*, *52*(1), 28–34. https://doi.org/10.1080/00228958.2016.1123042

Esteban-Guitart, M., & Moll, L. C. (2014). Funds of identity: A new concept based on the funds of knowledge approach. *Culture & Psychology*, *20*(1), 31–48.

Evans, M. P. (2013). Educating preservice teachers for family, school, and community engagement. *Teaching Education*, *24*(2), 123–133.

Flores, N. (2020). From academic language to language architecture: Challenging raciolinguistic ideologies in research and practice. *Theory Into Practice*, *59*(1), 22–31.

Flores, N., & Rosa, J. (2015). Undoing appropriateness: Raciolinguistic ideologies and language diversity in education. *Harvard Educational Review*, *85* (2), 149–171.

Francis, D., & Stephens, A. (Eds.). (2018). *English learners in STEM subjects: Transforming classrooms, schools, and lives*. National Academies of Sciences, Engineering, and Medicine. https://nap.nationalacademies.org/read/25182/chapter/1

Franke, M. (2014). Foreword. In E. Kazemi & A. Hintz (Eds.), *Intentional talk: How to structure and lead productive mathematical discussions* (pp. vii–viii). Stenhouse.

Fuson, K. C. (2020). The best multidigit computation methods: A cross-cultural cognitive, mathematical, and empirical analysis. *Universal Journal of Educational Research*, *8*(4), 1299–1314. https://doi.org/10.13189/ujer.2020.080421

Fuson, K. C., & Leinwand, S. (2023). Building equitable Math Talk classrooms. *Mathematics Teacher Learning and Teaching*, *116*(3), 164–173. https://doi.org/10.5951/MTLT.2022.0285

Gabriel, R. (2021, May 1). The sciences of reading instruction. *Educational Leadership*, *78*(8), 58–64. https://ascd.org/el/articles/the-sciences-of-reading-instruction

Gándara, P. (2021). The gentrification of two-way dual language programs: A commentary. *Language Policy*, *20*, 525–530.

Gannon, M. J., & Pillai, R. (2015). *Understanding global cultures: Metaphorical journeys through 34 nations, clusters of nations, continents, and diversity*. Sage.

García, O. (2009). *Bilingual education in the 21st century: A global perspective*. Wiley/Blackwell.

García, O., Johnson, S. I., & Seltzer, K. (2017). *The translanguaging classroom: Leveraging student bilingualism for learning*. Brookes.

García, O., & Kleifgen, J. A. (2019). Translanguaging and literacies. *Reading Research Quarterly*, *55*(4), 553–571.

García, O., & Sylvan, C. E. (2011). Pedagogies and practices in multilingual classrooms. *The Modern Language Journal*, *95*(3), 385–400.

Gassalasca4. (2013, May 11). *David Crystal on texting (S1E2 of It's only a theory)* [Video]. YouTube. https://www.youtube.com/watch?v=h79V_qUp91M&ab_channel=Gassalasca4

Gay, G. (2010). *Culturally responsive teaching: Theory, research, and practice*. Teachers College Press.

Gay, G. (2023). *Educating for equity and excellence: Enacting culturally responsive teaching*. Teachers College Press.

Gee, J. P. (1990). *Social linguistics and literacies: Ideology in discourses*. Falmer Press.

Gee, J. P. (1992). *The social mind: Language, ideology, and social practice*. Bergin and Garvey.

Gee, J. P. (2004). *Situated language and learning: A critique of traditional schooling*. Routledge.

Gee, J. P. (2011). *An introduction to critical discourse analysis in education*. Taylor and Francis.

Gibbons, P. (2002) *Scaffolding language, scaffolding learning teaching second language learners in the mainstream classroom*. Heinemann.

Gibbons, P. (2009). *English learners, academic literacy, and thinking: Learning in the challenge zone*. Heinemann.

González, N., Moll, L. C., & Amanti, C. (Eds.). (2005). *Funds of knowledge: Theorizing practices in households, communities, and classrooms*. Erlbaum.

Gottlieb, M. (2016). *Assessing English language learners: Bridges to equity* (2nd ed.). Corwin.

Gottlieb, M. (2021a). *Classroom assessment in multiple languages: A handbook for teachers*. Corwin.

Gottlieb, M. (2021b, October 27). To translanguage or not translanguage? Where does translanguaging fit into assessment? *Multilingual Mysteries #4*. Center for Applied Linguistics blog series. https://www.cal.org/cal_blog/to-translanguage-or-not-to-translanguage/

Gottlieb, M. (2022). *How can multilingual learners and their teachers make a difference in classroom assessment?* Center for Applied Linguistics. https://www.cal.org/wp-content/uploads/2022/06/CAL-WP-Classroom_Assessment_Gottlieb_2022.pdf

Gottlieb, M. (2023). *Right from the start: Enriching learning experiences for multilingual learners through multiliteracies*. Center for Applied Linguistics. https://www.cal.org/publications/how-can-multilingual-learners-and-their-teachers-make-a-difference-in-classroom-assessment/

Gottlieb, M. (2024a). *Assessing multilingual learners: Bridges to empowerment* (3rd ed.). Corwin.

Gottlieb, M. (2024b). *The hibiscus framework: Infusing linguistic and cultural sustainability into preK–12 educational practices*. Comprehensive Center Network. https://region19cc.org/wp-content/uploads/2024/05/The-Hibiscus-Framework.pdf

Gottlieb, M. (2025, March). Rooted in the Science of Reading: Seeing multilingual learners come into full bloom through multiliteracies. *Language Magazine, 24*(7).

Gottlieb, M., & Castro, M. (2017). *Language power: Key uses for accessing content*. Corwin.

Gottlieb, M., & Ernst-Slavit, G. (2013a). (Eds.). *Academic language in diverse classrooms: Language Arts*. Corwin.

Gottlieb, M., & Ernst-Slavit, G. (2013b). (Eds.). *Academic language in diverse classrooms: Mathematics*. Corwin.

Gottlieb, M., & Ernst-Slavit, G. (2014). *Academic language in diverse classrooms: Definitions and contexts*. Corwin.

Gottlieb, M., & Honigsfeld, A. (2025). *Collaborative assessment for multilingual learners and teachers: Pathways to partnerships*. Corwin.

Gough, P. B., & Tunmer, W. E. (1986). Decoding, reading, and reading disability. *Remedial and Special Education, 7*(1), 6–10. https://doi.org/10.1177/074193258600700104

Grabe, W., & Yamashita, J. (2022). *Reading in a second language: Moving from theory to practice* (2nd ed.). Cambridge University Press.

Granger, E. M., Bevis, T. H., Saka, Y., Southerland, S. A., Sampson, V., & Tate, R. L. (2012). The efficacy of student-centered instruction in supporting science learning. *Science, 338*(6103), 105–108. https://doi.org/10.1126/science.1223709

Granville, S. (2003). Contests over meaning in a South African classroom: Introducing critical language awareness in a climate of social change and cultural diversity. *Language and Education, 17*(1), 1–20.

Grapin, S. E. (2019). Multimodality in the new content standards era: Implications for

English learners. *TESOL Quarterly*, *53*(1), 30–55. https://doi.org/10.1002/tesq.443

Grapin, S. E. (2023). The complex terrain of equity for multilingual learners in K–12 education. *Educational Researcher*, *53*(3). https://doi.org/10.3102/0013189X231215345

Graves, J. L., Jr., Kearney, M., Barabino, G., & Malcom, S. (2022). Inequality in science and the case for a new agenda. *Proceedings of the National Academy of Sciences*, *119*(10), Article e2117831119. https://doi.org/10.1073/pnas.2117831119

Grosjean, F. (1989). Neurolinguists, beware! The bilingual is not two monolinguals in one person. *Brain and Language*, *36*, 3–15.

Gruenwald, D. A., & Smith, G. A. (Eds.). (2014). *Place-based education in the global age: Local diversity*. Routledge.

Gutstein, E. (2007). "And that's just how it starts." Teaching mathematics and developing student agency. *Teachers College Record*, *109*(2), 420–448.

Halliday, M. A. K., & Martin, J. R. (1993). *Writing science: Literacy and discursive power*. Routledge.

Hargrave, M., Fisher, D., & Frey, N. (2024). *The artificial intelligence playbook: Time-saving tools for teachers that make learning more engaging*. Corwin.

Heafner, T. L., & Plaisance, M. (2016). Exploring how institutional structures and practices influence English learners' opportunities to learn social studies. *Teachers College Record*, *118*(8), 1–36. https://doi.org/10.1177/016146811611800804

Heath, S. B. (1983). *Ways with words: Language, life and work in communities and classrooms*. Cambridge University Press.

Hernández García, M., Schleppegrell, M. J., Sobh, H., & Monte-Sano, C. (2023). The translanguaging school. *Phi Delta Kappan*, *105*(2), 8–12. https://doi.org/10.1177/00317217231205934

Hira, A., & Hynes, M. M. (2018). People, means, and activities: A conceptual framework for realizing the educational potential of makerspaces. *Education Research International*, *2018*(1), Article 6923617. https://doi.org/10.1155/2018/6923617

Holcombe, A., & Wozniak, S. (2024, July 1). Using AI to fuel engagement and active learning. *Educational Leadership*. https://ascd.org/el/articles/using-ai-to-fuel-engagement-and-active-learning

Honey, M., Alberts, B., Bass, H., Castillo, C., Lee, O., Strutches, M. M., Vermillion, L., & Rodriguez, F. (2020). *STEM education for the future: A visioning report*. National Science Foundation. https://nsf-gov-resources.nsf.gov/files/STEM-Education-2020-Visioning-Report.pdf

Hornberger, N. (1990). Creating successful learning contexts for bilingual literacy. *Teachers College Record*, *92*(2), 212–229. https://journals.sagepub.com/doi/abs/10.1177/016146819009200202

Hornberger, N. H. (2003). *Continua of biliteracy: An ecological framework for educational policy, research, and practice in multilingual settings*. Multilingual Matters.

Howard, E. R., & Simpson, S. (2023). Navigating tensions between translanguaging and separation of languages in dual language programs. *Dual Language of New Mexico Monograph Series*, (7), 2–27. https://www.dlenm.org/wp-content/uploads/2023/11/Navigating-Tensions-Between-Translanguaging-and-Separation-of-Languages-in-Dual-Language-Programs.pdf

Huinker, D., & Bill, V. (2017). *Taking action: Implementing effective mathematics teaching practices in K–grade 5*. National Council of Teachers of Mathematics.

Hull, G. A., & Moje, E. B. (2012). What is the development of literacy the development of? In K. Hakuta & M. Santos (Eds.), *Understanding language: Commissioned papers on language and literacy issues in the Common Core State Standards and Next Generation Science Standards* (pp. 52–63). Stanford University. https://ul.stanford.edu/sites/default/files/resource/2021-12/UL%20Stanford%20Final%205-9-12%20w%20cover.pdf#page=64

Imamudeen, J. (2018, November 24). The only thing you need to do to develop student agency. *The Joy of Learning*. https://judyimamudeen.com/the-only-thing-you-need-to-do-to-develop-student-agency/

IMPACT Social Studies. (2020). *Our place in the world, Grade 1, research companion.* McGraw-Hill K–12.

InDifferentLanguages.com. (2025). *Once upon a time in different languages: Learn how to say and translate.* https://www.indifferentlanguages.com/words/once_upon_a_time

International Dyslexia Association. (2019). *Structured Literacy™: An introductory guide.* https://app.box.com/s/mvuvhel6qaj8tghvu1nl75iondnlpoyz

International Society for Technology in Education. (2016). *Estándares ISTE: Estudiantes.* https://cdn.iste.org/www-root/Libraries/Documents%20%26%20Files/Standards-Resources/ISTE%20Standards_One-Sheets-Students_Bilingual.pdf?

International Society for Technology in Education. (2017). *ISTE standards for students, educators, education leaders, and coaches.* https://iste.org/standards

International Society for Technology in Education (ISTE). (2024). *ISTE standards: Students.* https://iste.org/standards/students?

Jackovino, D. (2024, March 31). Students learn science hands on at Makers Day. *Essex News Daily.* https://essexnewsdaily.com/headlne-news/students-learn-science-hands-on-at-makers-day

Jaffee, A. T. (2016). Community, voice, and inquiry: Teaching global history for English language learners. *The Social Studies, 107*(3), 1–13. https://doi.org/10.1080/00377996.2016.1140626

Jaffee, A. T. (2018). Developing culturally and linguistically relevant historical thinking skills: Lesson from U.S. history teachers for newcomer English language learners. In L. C. de Oliveira & K. M. Obenchain (Eds.), *Teaching history and social studies to English language learners: Preparing pre-service and in-service teachers* (pp. 7–37). Palgrave Macmillan.

Jaffee, A. T., & Yoder, P. J. (2019). Teaching social studies to English language learners: Current research, theories, and pedagogical practices. In L. C. de Oliveira (Ed.), *The handbook of TESOL in K–12* (pp. 307–321). Wiley.

Janks, H. (2000). Domination, access, diversity and design: A synthesis for critical literacy education. *Educational Review, 52*(2), 175–186.

Jensen, B., Valdés, G., & Gallimore, R. (2021). Teachers learning to implement equitable classroom talk. *Educational Researcher, 50*(8), 546–556. https://doi.org/10.3102/0013189X211014859

Johnson, E. J. (2014). From the classroom to the living room: Eroding academic inequities through home visits. *Journal of School Leadership, 24*(2), 357–385.

Johnson, E., & Johnson, A. (2016). Enhancing academic investment through home-school connections and building on ELL students' scholastic funds of knowledge. *Journal of Language and Literacy Education, 12*(1), 103–121.

Joshi, A. (2023, March 21). *5 ways to make your science classroom more culturally responsive.* Edutopia. https://www.edutopia.org/article/5-tips-creating-culturally-responsive-science-curriculum/

Kazemi, E., & Hintz, A. (2014). *Intentional talk: How to structure and lead productive mathematical discussions.* Stenhouse.

Kelly, L. B., Ogden, M. K., & Moses, L. (2019). Collaborative conversations: Speaking and listening in the primary grades. *Young Children, 74*(1), 30–36.

Kids Count Data Center. (2022). *Children who speak a language other than English at home.* https://datacenter.aecf.org/data/tables/81-children-who-speak-a-language-other-than-english-at-home#detailed/1/any/false/2048,1729,37,871,870,573,869,36,868,867/

Ladson-Billings, G. (1995). But that's just good teaching! The case for culturally relevant pedagogy. *Theory Into Practice, 34*(3), 159–165. https://doi.org/10.1080/00405849509543675

Lake [Medicine Grizzlybear], R. (1990). An Indian father's plea. *Teacher Magazine, 2,* 48–53.

Larsen-Freeman, D. (2003). *Teaching language: From grammar to grammaring.* Thomson-Heinle.

Lattimer, H. (2014). *Real-world literacies: Disciplinary teaching in the high school classroom*. National Council of Teachers of English.

Lee, O. (2021). Asset-oriented framing of science and language learning with multilingual learners. *National Association for Research in Science Teaching, 58*(7), 1073–1079. https://www.okheelee.com/wp-content/uploads/2021/08/Lee-2021.pdf

Lee, O., & Buxton, C. A. (2013). Guiding principles for fostering productive disciplinary engagement: Explaining an emergent argument in a fifth-grade classroom. *The Journal of the Learning Sciences, 22*(2), 180–217.

Lee, O., & Grapin, S. E. (2024). Transforming STEM by focusing on justice. *Educational Leadership, 81*(7), 64–68.

Lee, O., Quinn, H., & Valdés, G. (2013). Science and language for English language learners in relation to Next Generation Science Standards and with implications for Common Core State Standards for English language arts and mathematics. *Educational Researcher, 42*(4). https://doi.org/10.3102/0013189X13480524

Leinwand, S., Brahier, D. J., Huinker, D., Berry, R. Q., Dillon, F. L., Larson, M. R., Leiva, M. A., Martin, W. G., & Smith, M. S. (2014). *Principles to actions: Ensuring mathematical success for all.* National Council of Teachers of Mathematics.

Lent, R. (2016). *This is disciplinary literacy: Reading, writing, thinking, and doing content area by content area.* Corwin.

Lesseig, K., Slavit, D., & Simpson, A. (2023). Transdisciplinary STEM: Examples of student thinking within nonformal learning experiences. *Education Sciences, 13*, Article 435. https://doi.org/10.3390/educsci13050435

Leung, C., & Valdés, G. (2019). Translanguaging and the transdisciplinary framework for language teaching and learning in a multilingual world. *Modern Language Journal, 103*(2), 348–370. https:///doi.org/10.1111/modl.12568

Lindholm-Leary, K. (2016). Bilingualism and academic achievement in children in dual language programs. In E. Nicoladis & S. Montanari (Eds.), *Bilingualism across the lifespan: Factors moderating language proficiency* (pp. 203–223). American Psychological Association. https://doi.org/10.1037/14939-012

LópezLeiva, C. A., & Argüello de Jesús, J. T. (2024). Juntos animating mathematical concepts through wonder and translanguaging. In S. I. Johnson, M. A. Romero, & M. Jurado (Eds.), *Cultivating the pedagogy of translanguaging for K–12 transformative education: Approaches, activities, and strategies for students and teachers* (pp. 104–116). Velázquez Press.

Lowell, B. R., & Lowenhaupt, R. (2024). Leading for a new vision of science teaching. *Educational Leadership, 81*(7), 48–53.

Lowell, B. R., & McNeill, K. L. (2019). Keeping critical thinking afloat: Shifting from activity-based to phenomenon-based planning. *Science Scope, 43*(1), 64–69.

MacDonald, R., Crowther, D., Braaten, M., Binder, W., Chien, J., Dassler, T., Shelton, T., & Wilfrid, J. (2020). *Design principles for engaging multilingual learners in three-dimensional science* (WCER Working Paper No. 2020-1). University of Wisconsin–Madison, Wisconsin Center for Education Research. https://wida.wisc.edu/resources/design-principles-engaging-multilingual-learners-three-dimensional-science

MacSwan, J. (2020). Academic English as standard language ideology: A renewed research agenda for asset-based language education. *Language Teaching Research, 24*(1), 28–36. https://doi.org/10.1177/1362168818777540

Malone, S., Altmeyer, K., Vogel, M., & Brunken, R. (2020). Homogeneous and heterogeneous multiple representations in equation-solving problems: An eye-tracking study. *Journal of Computer Assisted Learning, 36*(6), 781–798. https://doi.org/10.1111/jcal.12426

Mancenido, Z., & Pello, R. (2020). What do we know about how to effectively prepare teachers to engage with families? *School Community Journal, 30*(2), 9–38.

Marshall, T. R. (2022). The promise, power, and practice of student agency. *Educational Leadership, 80*(3), 33–38.

Martell, M. A. N., & Yangua-Peña, J. (2024). Supporting multilingual learners' sense making in science through translanguaging. In S. I. Johnson, M. A. Romero, & M. Jurado (Eds.), *Cultivating the pedagogy of translanguaging for K–12 transformative education: Approaches, activities, and strategies for students and teachers* (pp. 82–91). Velázquez Press.

Martínez, R. B. (2023). *La trascendencia de los materiales de calidad en la educación bilingüe y de inmersión dual* [*Materials matter: Parity and quality for Spanish language arts*]. English Learners Success Forum. https://cdn.prod.website-files.com/5b43fc97fcf4773f14ee92f3/660bebb975579398c3a849ff_ELSF-Final-Dual-Language-Report_240228.pdf

Mason, M. R., & Ernst-Slavit, G. (2010). Representations of Native Americans in elementary school social studies: A critical look at instructional language. *Multicultural Education, 18*, 10–17. https://www.proquest.com/openview/f42c1d99636f272c3a09fca4fba5fdde/1?pq-origsite=gscholar&cbl=33246

McDonald, A. (2018, February 11). *How to use funds of knowledge in your classroom and create better connections.* No Time for Flash Cards. https://www.notimeforflashcards.com/2018/02/funds-of-knowledge.html

McSweeney, M. A. (2017). I text English to everyone: Links between second-language texting and academic proficiency. *Languages, 2*(3), 7. https://doi.org/10.3390/languages2030007

Metropolitan Museum of Art. (2004). *Islamic art and geometric design: Activities for learning.* https://www.metmuseum.org/-/media/files/learn/for-educators/publications-for-educators/islamic_art_and_geometric_design.pdf

Michaels, S., & O'Connor, C. (2012). *Talk science primer.* TERC.

Milan Urban Food Policy Pact. (2015). *How it works.* https://www.milanurbanfoodpolicypact.org/the-milan-pact/#

Mizell, J. D. (2020). *Culturally sustaining systemic functional linguistics (CS SFL): A critical examination of languaging and literacies for/with/by youth* [Doctoral dissertation]. University of Georgia. https://esploro.libs.uga.edu/esploro/outputs/doctoral/CULTURALLY-SUSTAINING-SYSTEMIC-FUNCTIONAL-LINGUISTICS-CS/9949365550702959

Moll, L. C., Amanti, C., Neff, D., & Gonzalez, N. (1992). Funds of knowledge for teaching: Using a qualitative approach to connect homes and classrooms. *Theory Into Practice, 31*(2), 132–141. http://www.jstor.org/stable/1476399

Morris, A. (with Heyman, K., illustrator). (1989). *Bread, bread, bread.* Lothrop, Lee & Shepard Books.

Morrison, S. J. (2022). *"A sense of where we are in the world": First-year bilingual, bicultural teachers from an alternative route to teaching program.* PhD dissertation, Washington State University.

Moschkovich, J. N. (2008, December). *Beyond words: Language(s) and learning in mathematics.* [Workshop presentation]. Silicon Valley Mathematics Initiative, Fremont, CA.

Moschkovich, J. N. (2013). Preface. In M. Gottlieb & G. Ernst-Slavit (Series Eds.), *Academic language in diverse classrooms: Mathematics series* (pp. vii–xi). Corwin.

Moschkovich, J. N. (2024). Language and learning mathematics: A sociocultural approach to academic literacy in mathematics. In J. Wang (Ed.), *Proceedings of the 14th International Congress on Mathematical Education: Vol. II: Invited lectures* (pp. 459–472). World Scientific.

NASA. (2012, November 19). *Departing space station commander provides tour of orbital laboratory* [Video]. YouTube. https://www.youtube.com/watch?v=doN4t5NKW-k&ab_channel=NASA

National Academies of Sciences, Engineering, and Medicine. (2017). *Promoting the educational successes of children and youth learning English: Promising futures. Consensus Study Report.* National Academies Press. https://nap.nationalacademies.org/read/24677/chapter/2

National Council for the Social Studies. (n.d.). *About National Council for the Social Studies*. http://www.socialstudies.org/about

National Council for the Social Studies. (2013). The College, Career, and Civic Life (C3) Framework for social studies state standards: Guidance for enhancing the rigor of K–12 civics, economics, geography, and history. https://www.socialstudies.org/c3

National Council for the Social Studies. (2016, May/June). A vision of powerful teaching and learning in the social studies. *Social Education, 80*(3), 180–182. https://www.socialstudies.org/social-education/80/03/vision-powerful-teaching-and-learning-social-studies

National Council of Teachers of English. (2011). *Literacies of disciplines: A policy research brief produced by the National Council of Teachers of English*. https://literacysummit.wordpress.com/wp-content/uploads/2013/05/literaciesofdisciplines.pdf

National Council of Teachers of English. (2018). *Expanding opportunities: Academic success for culturally and linguistically diverse students*. https://ncte.org/statement/expandingopportun/?

National Council of Teachers of English. (2019). *Position statement: Definition of literacy in a digital age*. https://ncte.org/statement/nctes-definition-literacy-digital-age/

National Governors Association Center for Best Practices & Council of Chief State School Officers. (2010). *Common Core State Standards for English language arts and literacy in history/social studies, science, and technical subjects*. https://www.thecorestandards.org/ELA-Literacy/

National Governors Association Center for Best Practices & Council of Chief State School Officers. (2010). *Standards for Mathematical Practice*. https://www.thecorestandards.org/Math/Practice/

National Research Council. (2012). *A framework for K–12 science education: Practices, crosscutting concepts, and core ideas*. National Academies Press.

National Research Council. (2013). *Next Generation Science Standards: For states, by states*. National Academies Press.

The New London Group. (1996). A pedagogy of multiliteracies: Designing social futures. *Harvard Educational Review, 66*(1), 60–92. https://www.sfu.ca/~decaste/newlondon.htm

Newcomer, S. N. (2017). Investigating the power of authentically caring teacher-student relationships for Latinx students. *Journal of Latinos and Education, 17*(2), 179–193. https://doi.org/10.1080/15348431.2017.1310104

Newcomer, S. N., & Ernst-Slavit, G. (in press). ¡Juntos logramos más!: Apoyando a futuros docentes a promover la participación familiar y comunitaria. In E. J. Johnson & L. A. Murillo (Eds.), *Alianzas familiares en la educación multilingüe/Family alliances in multilingual education*. Information Age.

Newcomer, S. N., Ernst-Slavit, G., Morrison, S. J, Morrison, J. A., Lightner, L. K., Ardasheva, Y., & Carbonneau, K. J. (in press). "An important piece of the puzzle": Preparing future teachers for family and community engagement. *Teaching Education*.

Norton, B. (2013). Identity, literacy and the multilingual classroom. In S. May (Ed.), *The multilingual turn: Implications for SLA, TESOL, and bilingual education* (pp. 103–122). Routledge.

Once upon a time. (2025, February 12). In *Wikipedia*. https://en.wikipedia.org/w/index.php?title=Once_upon_a_time&oldid=1275320678

Osborne, J., & Quinn, H. (2017). The *Framework*, the NGSS, and the practices of science. In C. V. Schwarz, C. Passmore, & B. J. Reiser (Eds.), *Helping students make sense of the world using next generation science and engineering practices* (pp. 23–31). NSTA Press.

Oxford University Press. (2025). Have. In *Oxford English Dictionary*. https://www.oed.com/search/advanced/Entries?q=have&sortOption=Frequency?

Palmer, D. K., & Martínez, R. A. (2016). Developing biliteracy: What do teachers *really* need to know about language? *Language Arts, 93*(5), 379–385.

Palmer, D. K., Martínez, R., Mateus, S. G., & Henderson, K. (2014). Reframing the debate on language separation: Toward a vision for translanguaging pedagogoies in the dual language classroom. *The Modern Language Journal*, *98*(3), 757–772.

Paris, D. (2012). Culturally sustaining pedagogy: A needed change in stance, terminology, and practice. *Educational Researcher*, *41*(3), 93–97.

Paris, D., & Alim, H. S. (2014). What are we seeking to sustain through culturally sustaining pedagogy? A loving critique forward. *Harvard Educational Review*, *84*(1), 85–100. https://doi.org/10.17763/haer.84.1.982l873k2ht16m77

Paris, D., & Alim, H. S. (2017). *Culturally sustaining pedagogies: Teaching and learning for justice in a changing world.* Teachers College Press.

Pearson, P. D., Palincsar, A. S., Biancarosa, G., & Berman, A. I. (Eds.). (2020). *Reaping the rewards of the Reading for Understanding Initiative.* National Academy of Education.

Penuel, B. (2022). To promote equity, prepare students for what science could be. *Science Scope*, *46*(1). https://www.nsta.org/science-scope/science-scope-septemberoctober-2022/equity-science

Pratt, K. L., & Ernst-Slavit, G. (2019). Equity perspectives and restrictionist policies: Tensions in dual language bilingual education. *Bilingual Research Journal*, *42*(3), 356–374. https://doi.org/10.1080/15235882.2019.1647900

Prediger, S. (2019). Investigating and promoting teachers' expertise for language-responsive mathematics teaching. *Mathematics Education Research Journal*, *31*(4), 367–392. https://doi.org/10.1007/s13394-019-00258-1

Prediger, S., & Buró, R. (2024). Fifty ways to work with students' diverse abilities? A video study on inclusive teaching practices in secondary mathematics classrooms. *International Journal of Inclusive Education*, *28*(2), 124–143. https://doi.org/10.1080/13603116.2021.1925361

Prediger, S., & Neugebauer, P. (2023). Can students with different language backgrounds equally profit from a language-responsive instructional approach for percentages? Differential effectiveness in a field trial. *Mathematical Thinking and Learning*, *25*(1), 2–22. https://doi.org/10.1080/10986065.2021.1919817

Proctor, C. P. (2020, January 13). *Academic languaging and translanguaging.* https://www.cpatrickproctor.com/blog/academic-languaging-translanguaging

Proctor, C. P., Silverman, R. D., Harring, J. R., Jones, R. L., & Hartranft, A. M. (2020). Teaching bilingual learners: Effects of a language-based reading intervention on academic language and reading comprehension in grades 4 and 5. *Reading Research Quarterly*, *55*, 95–122. https://doi.org/10.1002/rrq.258

Quinn, H., Lee, O., & Valdés, G. (2012). Language demands and opportunities in relation to Next Generation Science Standards for English language learners: What teachers need to know. *Commissioned papers on language and literacy issues in the Common Core State Standards and Next Generation Science Standards*, *94*(2012), 32–32. https://ul.stanford.edu/sites/default/files/resource/2021-12/UL%20Stanford%20Final%205-9-12%20w%20cover.pdf#page=44

Reading League & National Committee for Effective Literacy. (2023). *Understanding the difference: The Science of Reading and implementation for English learners/emergent bilinguals (Els/EBs).* https://www.thereadingleague.org/wp-content/uploads/2023/09/TRLC-ELEB-Understanding-the-Difference-The-Science-of-Reading-and-Implementation.pdf

Regional Educational Laboratory Pacific. (2025). *Āina-based education, place-based education, and project-based learning.* Institute of Education Sciences, U.S. Department of Education. https://ies.ed.gov/rel-pacific/2025/01/aina-based-education-place-based-education-and-project-based-learning-infographic

Reigh, E., Miller, E. A., Simani, M. C., & Severson, A. (2023). Toward equity for multilingual learners: The standards offer a new opportunity to engage multilingual learners in science. *Science and Children, 60*(4), 26–29. https://doi.org/10.1080/00368148.2023.12291867

Remy, R. C., Patrick, J. J., & Clayton, G. E. (2008). *Civics today: Citizenship, economics, and you*. McGraw-Hill.

Resor, C. W. (2017). *Investigating family, food, and housing themes in social studies*. Rowman & Littlefield.

Roberts, S. A., de Araujo, Z., Willey, C., & Zahner, W. (2022). Three ways to enhance tasks for multilingual learners. *Mathematics Teacher: Learning and Teaching PK–12, 115*(7), 458–467.

Roehr-Brackin, K. (2018). *Metalinguistic awareness and second language acquisition*. Routledge.

Ruiz, R. (1984). Orientations in language planning. *NABE Journal, 8*(2), 15–34. https://doi.org/10.1080/08855072.1984.10668464

Said, S. (n.d.). *Supporting students' ability to process conflict in our world*. Confianza. https://ellstudents.com/blogs/the-confianza-way/supporting-students-ability-to-process-conflict-in-our-world

Sang, Y. (2017). Expanded territories of "literacy": New literacies and multiliteracies. *Journal of Education and Practice, 8*(8), 16 19.

Scarborough, H. S. (2001). Connecting early language and literacy to later reading (dis)abilities: Evidence, theory, and practice. In S. Neuman & D. Dickinson (Eds.), *Handbook for research in early literacy* (pp. 97–110). Guilford Press.

Scarcella, R. (2003). Academic language: A conceptual framework. *Technical Report 2003-1*. University of California Linguistic Minority Research Institute.

Schell, E. M. (2020–2021). Cultivating global citizenship. *Social Studies Review*, 2–6. bit.ly/3mnC5du

Schleppegrell, M. J. (2004). *The language of schooling: A functional linguistics perspective*. Lawrence Erlbaum.

Schwinge, D. (2016). Biliteracy and multiliteracy in bilingual education. In O. García, A. Lin, & S. May (Eds.), *Bilingual and multilingual education* (pp. 1–13). Springer.

Seltzer, K., & de los Ríos, C. V. (2021). *Understanding translanguaging in US literacy classrooms*. National Council of Teachers of English. https://ncte.org/wp-content/uploads/2021/04/SquireOfficePolicyBrief_Translanguaging_April2021.pdf

Sembiante, S. F., & Tian, Z. (2021). Culturally sustaining approaches to academic languaging through systemic functional linguistics. *Language and Education, 35*(2), 101–105.

Simpson, A., Slavit, D., & Lesseig, K. (2025). STEM ways of thinking: Elementary grade learners' possibility and adaptive thinking in STEM-rich contexts. In L. D. English & T. H. Lehmann (Eds.), *Ways of thinking in STEM-based problem solving: Learning in a new era* (pp. 47–61). Taylor & Francis.

Simpson, J. A., & Weiner, E. S. C. (1989). *The Oxford English dictionary* (2nd ed.). Oxford University Press.

Slavit, D., Lesseig, K., & Grace, E. (2021). Student ways of thinking in STEM contexts: A focus on claim making and reasoning. *School Science and Mathematics, 121*(8), 466–480.

Slavit, D., Lesseig, K., & Simpson, A. (2022). An analytic framework for understanding student thinking in STEM contexts. *Journal of Pedagogical Research, 6*(2), 132–148. https://doi.org/10.33902/JPR.202213536

Smithsonian National Air and Space Museum. (n.d.). *Ice cream in a bag*. https://docs.google.com/document/d/1qdz83vda-COB_H1myFoH6-RkY8Y-v1e1r9lRf8mBloc/edit?tab=t.0#heading=h.wogmczi4t5ho

Smithsonian National Air and Space Museum. (2015, July 19). *We all scream—even in space—for ice cream*. https://airandspace.si.edu/stories/editorial/we-all-scream-even-space-ice-cream

Snow, C. E. (2017). The role of vocabulary versus knowledge in children's language learning: A fifty-year perspective / El papel del vocabulario frente al conocimiento en el aprendizaje lingüístico de los niños: Una perspectiva de cincuenta años. *Infancia y Aprendizaje, 40*, (1), 1–18. https://doi.org/10.1080/02103702.2016.12634

Snow, C. E., & Uccelli, P. (2009). The challenge of academic language. In D. R. Olson & N. Torrance (Eds.), *The Cambridge handbook of literacy* (pp. 112–133). Cambridge University Press.

Solórzano, D. (1997). Images and words that wound: Critical race theory, racial stereotyping and teacher education. *Teacher Education Quarterly, 24*(3), 5–19.

Somerville, J., & Faltis, C. (2019). Dual languaging as strategy and translanguaging as tactic in two-way dual language programs. *Theory Into Practice, 58*(2), 164–75. https://doi.org/10.1080/00405841.2019.1569380

Soto, I., Sagun, T. R., & Beiersdorf, M. (2023). *Equity moves to support multilingual learners in mathematics and science, grades K–8*. Corwin.

Stewart, L. (2019). *The Science of Reading: Evidence for a new era of reading instruction*. Zaner-Bloser.

Stinton, D. (2012, July 25). *How would you define spatial literacy?* Diana Maps. https://dianamaps.com/2012/07/25/how-would-you-define-spatial-literacy/

Stoll, L. (2022, May 25). *Language IS essential for science: The need to improve materials for multilingual learners*. English Learner Success Forum. https://www.elsuccessforum.org

Suárez, E. (2020). "Estoy explorando science": Emergent bilingual students problematizing electrical phenomena through translanguaging. *Science Education, 104*(5), 791–826.

Subtirelu, N. C., Borowczyk, M., Hernández, R. T., & Venezia, F. (2019). Recognizing *whose* bilingualism? A critical policy analysis of the Seal of Biliteracy. *The Modern Language Journal, 103*(2), 371–390.

Swain, M. (2006). Languaging, agency and translanguaging in advanced second language proficiency. In H. Byrnes (Ed.), *Advanced language learning: The contribution of Halliday and Vygotsky* (pp. 95–108). Continuum.

Teachers of English to Speakers of Other Languages. (2010). *Position paper on language and literacy development for young English language learners (ages 3–8)*. https://www.tesol.org/media/brtdsnng/literacyyoungell2010.pdf

Vaish, V. (2020). *Translanguaging in multilingual English classrooms: An Asian perspective and contexts*. Springer.

Valdés, G. (2023). Social justice challenges of "teaching" languages. *Daedalus, the Journal of the American Academy of Arts & Sciences, 152*(3), 52–68.

Valdez, V. E., Freire, J. A., & Delavan, M. G. (2016). The gentrification of dual language education. *The Urban Review, 48*, 601–627.

van Leeuwen, T., & Jewitt, C. (2001). (Eds.) *A handbook of visual analysis*. Sage.

van Lier, L. (2007). Action-based teaching, autonomy, and identity. *Innovation in Language Learning and Teaching, 1*(1), 46–65.

Vaughn, M. (2021). *Student agency in the classroom: Honoring student voice in the curriculum*. Teachers College Press.

Vélez-Ibáñez, C. G., & Greenberg, J. B. (1992). Formation and transformation of funds of knowledge among U.S.-Mexican households. *Anthropology and Education Quarterly, 23*(4), 313–335.

Waldrip, B., Prain, V., & Carolan, J. (2006). Learning junior secondary science through multi-modal representations. *Electronic Journal of Science Education, 11*(1), 87–107.

Wallace, L. (2024, July 9). Why so many stories begin with "Once upon a time." *Mental Floss*. https://www.mentalfloss.com/posts/once-upon-a-time-history

Walqui, A., & Heritage, M. (2018). Meaningful classroom talk: Supporting English learners' oral language development. *The American Educator, 42*, 18. https://www.aft.org/ae/fall2018/walqui_heritage

Walqui, A., & van Lier, L. (2010). *Scaffolding the academic success of adolescent English language learners: A pedagogy of promise*. WestEd.

Walter, H. A. (2018). Beyond turn and talk: Creating discourse. *Teaching Children Mathematics, 25*(3), 180–185.

Weiss, J. C., & Sandstead, M. G. (2020). *English learners and English language arts*. English

Learners Success Forum. https://www.elsuccessforum.org/resources/english-learners-and-english-language-arts-education

Westerlund, R., & Miller, E. A. (2023). *Multilingual learners as scientists: The synergy of NGSS and WIDA. Wisconsin CESA 2.* https://www.cesa2.org/whitepapers/Multilingual-Learners-as-Scientists.pdf

WIDA. (2004). *English language proficiency standards: Kindergarten through Grade 12.* State of Wisconsin.

WIDA. (2012). *Amplification of the English language development standards, Kindergarten–Grade 12.* Board of Regents of the University of Wisconsin System, on behalf of the WIDA Consortium.

WIDA (2019). *Guiding principles of language development.* Board of Regents of the University of Wisconsin System, on behalf of WIDA. https://wida.wisc.edu/sites/default/files/resource/Guiding-Principles-of-Language-Development.pdf

WIDA. (2020). *WIDA English language development standards framework, 2020 edition: Kindergarten–grade 12.* Board of Regents of the University of Wisconsin System.

WIDA. (2021). *Marco de referencia de las artes del lenguaje del español de WIDA: Aplicación para la actualización y desarrollo de estándares.* Board of Regents of the University of Wisconsin System. https://wida.wisc.edu/sites/default/files/resource/Marco-ALE-Estandares.pdf

WIDA. (2023). *Marco de los estándares del desarrollo auténtico del lenguaje español de WIDA: Kinder al 12º grado.* Board of Regents of the University of Wisconsin System.

WIDA. (2024). *Research-based guideposts for equitable literacy instruction.* Board of Regents of the University of Wisconsin System. https://wida.wisc.edu/sites/default/files/resource/Reading-Guideposts-Development-Multilingual-Learners.pdf

Wilkinson, L. C. (2018). Learning language and mathematics: A perspective from *Linguistics and Education. Linguistics and Education, 49,* 86–95. https://doi.org/10.1016/j.linged.2018.03.005

Wright, W. E., Boun, S., & García, O. (Eds.). (2015). *Handbook of bilingual and multilingual education.* Wiley.

YERME MathEd. (2021, February 4). *YERME interview series: Interview with former ERME President Susanne Prediger* [Video]. YouTube. https://www.youtube.com/watch?v=q5RAHh7lvf0

Yoder, P. J., Kibler, A., & van Hover, S. (2016). Instruction for English language learners in the social studies classroom: A meta-synthesis. *Social Studies Research and Practice, 11*(1), 20–39.

Yoon, B., & Pratt, K. L. (2023). *Primary language impact on second language and literacy learning: Linguistically responsive strategies for classroom teachers.* Lexington Books.

Yosso, T. J. (2005). Whose culture has capital? A critical race theory discussion of community cultural wealth. *Race Ethnicity and Education, 8,* 69–91. http://dx.doi.org/10.1080/1361332052000341006

Zacarian, D. (2013). *Mastering academic language: A framework for supporting student achievement.* Corwin.

Zwiers, J. (2008). *Building academic language: Essential practices for content classrooms.* Jossey-Bass.

Zwiers, J., & Hamerla, S. (2018). *The K–3 guide to academic conversations: Practices, scaffolds, and activities.* Corwin.

Index

CORWIN

To help every educator
help every student

We believe that every single student deserves a great education

We believe that knowing our impact is both a privilege and a responsibility

We believe that a fair, stable, and thriving society is built on education